AFRICAN AMERICAN BIOGRAPHY

AFRICAN AMERICAN REFERENCE LIBRARY

AFRICAN AMERICAN BIOGRAPHY

VOLUME 3
K–R

An Imprint of Gale Research Inc.

AFRICAN AMERICAN BIOGRAPHY

STAFF

Carol DeKane Nagel, *U·X·L Developmental Editor*
Thomas L. Romig, *U·X·L Publisher*

Amy Marcaccio, *Acquisitions Editor*

Shanna P. Heilveil, *Production Assistant*
Evi Seoud, *Assistant Production Manager*
Mary Beth Trimper, *Production Director*

Cynthia Baldwin, *Art Director*
Arthur Chartow, *Technical Design Services Manager*

Weigl Educational Publishers Limited, *Page and Cover Design and Typesetting*

This book is printed on acid-free paper that meets the minimum requirements of American National Standard for Information Sciences—Permanence Paper for Printed Library Materials, ANSI Z39.48-1984. ♾™

ISBN 0-8103-9234-8 (Set)
ISBN 0-8103-9235-6 (Volume 1)
ISBN 0-8103-9236-4 (Volume 2)
ISBN 0-8103-9237-2 (Volume 3)
ISBN 0-8103-9238-0 (Volume 4)

Printed in the United States of America

Published simultaneously in the United Kingdom
by Gale Research International Limited
(An affiliated company of Gale Research Inc.)

AFRICAN AMERICAN REFERENCE LIBRARY

AFRICAN AMERICAN REFERENCE LIBRARY

The **African American Reference Library** fills the need for a comprehensive, curriculum-related reference covering all aspects of African American life and culture. Aimed primarily at middle school and junior high school students, this nine-volume set combines appropriate reading level and fascinating subject matter with quality biographies, statistics, essays, chronologies, document and speech excerpts, and more.

The **African American Reference Library** consists of three separate components:

African American Biography (four volumes) profiles three hundred African Americans, both living and deceased, prominent in their fields, from civil rights to athletics, politics to literature, entertainment to science, religion to the military. A black-and-white portrait accompanies each entry, and a cumulative subject index lists all individuals by field of endeavor.

African American Almanac (three volumes) provides a comprehensive range of historical and current information on African American life and culture. Organized by subject, the volumes contain 270 black-and-white illustrations, a selected bibliography, and a cumulative subject index.

African American Chronology (two volumes) explores significant social, political, economic, cultural, and educational milestones in black history. Arranged by year and then by month and day, the volumes span from 1492 until June 30, 1993, and contain 106 illustrations and maps, extensive cross references, and a cumulative subject index.

Comments and suggestions

We welcome your comments on *African American Biography* as well as your suggestions for topics to be featured in future **African American Reference Library** series. Please write:

Editors, **African American Reference Library**, U·X·L, 835 Penobscot Bldg., Detroit, Michigan 48226-4094; call toll-free: 1-800-877-4253; or fax: 313-961-6348.

CONTENTS

AFRICAN AMERICAN BIOGRAPHY

Volume 1: A-E

Hank Aaron

Kareem Abdul-Jabbar

Ralph David Abernathy

Alvin Ailey

Muhammad Ali

Marian Anderson

Maya Angelou

Louis Armstrong

Molefi Kete Asante

Arthur Ashe

Pearl Bailey

Augusta Baker

Josephine Baker

James Baldwin

Amiri Baraka

Ida B. Wells Barnett

Marguerite Ross Barnett

Marion Barry

Count Basie

Daisy Bates

Kathleen Battle

Harry Belafonte

Chuck Berry

Halle Berry

Mary McLeod Bethune

Dave Bing

Julian Bond

Bobby Bonilla

Arna Bontemps

Riddick Bowe

Ed Bradley

Carol Moseley Braun

Edward W. Brooke III

Gwendolyn Brooks

Claude Brown

H. Rap Brown

James Brown

Ron Brown

Ed Bullins

Grace Bumbry

Ralph Bunche

Yvonne Brathwaite Burke

Octavia E. Butler

Cab Calloway

Roy Campanella

Naomi Campbell

Stokely Carmichael

Benjamin Carson

George Washington Carver

Wilt Chamberlain

Ray Charles

Charles Waddell Chesnutt

Alice Childress

Shirley Chisholm

Joe Clark

Eldridge Cleaver

George Clements

Jewel Plummer Cobb

Johnnetta Betsch Cole

Natalie Cole

Nat "King" Cole

Bessie Coleman

Marva Collins

John Coltrane

Anna J. Cooper

Don Cornelius

Bill Cosby

Clementine Hunter
Zora Neale Hurston
Ice-T
Roy Innis
Janet Jackson
Jesse Jackson
Mahalia Jackson
Michael Jackson
Shirley Ann Jackson
John Jacob
Daniel James, Jr.
Mae C. Jemison
Beverly Johnson
Earvin "Magic" Johnson
James Weldon Johnson
John H. Johnson
Robert Johnson
Bill T. Jones
James Earl Jones
Jones, LeRoi
    See Amiri Baraka
Quincy Jones
Sissieretta Jones
Scott Joplin
Barbara Jordan
Michael Jordan
Vernon E. Jordan, Jr.
Jackie Joyner-Kersee

Volume 3: K-R

Elizabeth Keckley
Patrick Kelly
Sharon Pratt Kelly
Flo Kennedy
Kersee, Jackie Joyner
    See Jackie Joyner-Kersee
B.B. King
Coretta Scott King

Martin Luther King, Jr.
Yolanda King
Jewel Stradford Lafontant
Jacob Lawrence
Spike Lee
Carl Lewis
Elma Lewis
Little Richard
Louverture, Toussaint
    See Toussaint-Louverture
Joe Louis
Joseph E. Lowery
Naomi Long Madgett
Malcolm X
Annie Turnbo Malone
Eugene A. Marino
Branford Marsalis
Wynton Marsalis
Paule Marshall
Thurgood Marshall
Biddy Mason
Willie Mays
George Marion McClellan
Hattie McDaniel
Claude McKay
Floyd B. McKissick
Terry McMillan
Thelma "Butterfly" McQueen
James Meredith
Ron Milner
Thelonious Monk
Audley Moore
Garrett Morgan
Toni Morrison
Constance Baker Motley
Willard Motley
Elijah Muhammad
Eddie Murphy

Pauli Murray
Gloria Naylor
Huey Newton
Jessye Norman
Hazel O'Leary
Shaquille O'Neal
Jesse Owens
Satchel Paige
Gordon Parks
Rosa Parks
Sidney Poitier
Adam Clayton Powell, Jr.
Colin Powell
Leontyne Price
Charley Pride
Barbara Gardner Proctor
Richard Pryor
Public Enemy
Lloyd Albert Quarterman
Queen Latifah
Dudley Randall
A. Philip Randolph
William Raspberry
Ishmael Reed
Eslanda Goode Robeson
Paul Robeson
Jackie Robinson
Charlemae Hill Rollins
Diana Ross
Carl T. Rowan
Wilma Rudolph
Bill Russell
Bayard Rustin

Volume 4: S-Z

Edith Sampson
Sonia Sanchez
Dred Scott

Gloria Scott
Bobby Seale
Attalah Shabazz
Ntozake Shange
Al Sharpton
Althea T.L. Simmons
Carole Simpson
Naomi Sims
John Singleton
Bessie Smith
Wesley Snipes
George Stallings, Jr.
Shelby Steele
William Grant Still
Juanita Kidd Stout
Niara Sudarkasa
Henry Ossawa Tanner
Mildred Taylor
Susan Taylor
Susie Baker King Taylor
Mary Church Terrell
Clarence Thomas
Jean Toomer
Jackie Torrence
Toussaint-Louverture
Robert Townsend
William Monroe Trotter
Sojourner Truth
Harriet Tubman
Nat Turner
Mario Van Peebles
Sarah Vaughan
Denmark Vesey
Charleszetta Waddles
Alice Walker
Madame C.J. Walker
Maggie L. Walker
Sippie Wallace

PHOTO CREDITS

The photographs and illustrations appearing in *African American Biography* were received from the following sources:

On the covers: **Schomburg Center for Research in Black Culture, The New York Public Library, Astor, Lenox and Tilden Foundations:** Althea Gibson; **AP/Wide World Photos:** Josephine Baker; **Archive Photos:** Elijah Muhammad.

AP/Wide World Photos: pages 1, 4, 6, 9, 12, 18, 22, 26, 33, 36, 44, 47, 49, 51, 54, 62, 76, 80, 84, 94, 98, 113, 115, 117, 122, 124, 127, 141, 185, 231, 236, 238, 241, 257, 259, 270, 275, 277, 282, 287, 290, 295, 303, 305, 313, 336, 340, 343, 344, 350, 352, 356, 377, 380, 386, 388, 390, 393, 399, 415, 418, 431, 444, 447, 450, 463, 471, 475, 477, 483, 497, 499, 506, 521, 528, 534, 539, 553, 561, 566, 569, 574, 577, 584, 588, 590, 593, 612, 622, 625, 631, 633, 642, 658, 666, 668, 671, 681, 683, 692, 703, 712, 724, 737, 740, 745, 762, 765, 770, 774, 790, 794, 797, 799, 805; **Courtesy of Molefi Kete Asante:** page 24; **Schomburg Center for Research in Black Culture, The New York Public Library, Astor, Lenox and Tilden Foundations:** pages 29, 30, 41, 103, 174, 179, 208, 216, 244, 246, 267, 308, 359, 383, 420, 492, 515, 635, 679, 706, 732, 772; **Courtesy of Belafonte Enterprises:** page 56; **UPI/Bettmann Newsphotos:** pages 59, 199, 360, 434, 459, 468, 578, 637, 756, 777; **U.S. Office of War Information, Prints and Photographs Division, Library of Congress:** page 63; **Ed Haun/Detroit Free Press:** page 66; **UPI/Bettmann:** pages 68, 144, 147, 494, 526, 689, 767; **Reuters/Bettmann:** pages 72, 82, 157, 676; **Harper Brothers:** page 87; **Photograph by Larry McLucas:** page 90; **Courtesy of the United Nations (31216):** page 105; **Raymond W. Smock, Historian:** page 108; **National Education Television:** page 120; **Jazz Institute of Rutgers University:** pages 131, 229; **Photograph by Willard Moore:** page 136; **Courtesy of Shirley Chisholm:** page 139; **Courtesy of Jewel Plummer Cobb:** page 149; **Rick Diamond Photography:** page 151; **The Bettmann Archive:** pages 159, 422; **Courtesy of Marva Collins:** page 162; **Downbeat:** page 164; **Moorland-Spingarn Research Center, Howard University:** pages 167, 328, 543, 647, 708; **Photograph by Marco Sacchi:** page 169; **Photograph by Howard Bingham, Copyright © 1990 Universal City Studios Inc.:** page 172; **American Broadcasting Company:** pages 181, 316, 453; **Photograph by Anthony Barbaoza, © 1988 CBS Records Inc.:** page 187; **Universal

AFRICAN AMERICAN BIOGRAPHY

Elizabeth Keckley

White House dressmaker
Born around 1818, Dinwiddie, Virginia
Died May 26, 1907, Washington, D.C.

"I had a great desire to work for the ladies of the White House, and to accomplish this end I was ready to make almost any sacrifice consistent with propriety."

When Abraham Lincoln was president, a former slave, Elizabeth Keckley, was the close friend and confidante of his wife, Mary Todd Lincoln. Officially, Keckley was employed simply as a dressmaker, but the two women got on so well that Keckley soon acquired many more roles and became the First Lady's personal maid, fashion designer, traveling companion, and trusted friend. Their friendship undoubtedly increased Lincoln's concern for African Americans.

Keckley had so much influence in the Lincoln household that there was considerable gossip about her in Washington. She was a tall, strong-willed woman, dignified and self-reliant, with a driving sense of purpose. It was entirely through her own efforts that she managed to get where she did. Like so many people born into slavery, she learned very young that she had to fend for herself.

The years in slavery

One of Keckley's earliest memories was of being whipped for not minding a baby properly. She and her mother Agnes were slaves of the Burwell family, and Mrs. Burwell had placed four-year-old Elizabeth in charge of her baby, telling her to rock the cradle and keep the flies off. So eager was Elizabeth to perform this task well that she rocked the cradle too hard—and pitched the baby onto the floor. She was frantically trying to scoop it up with a fire shovel when a furious Mrs. Burwell arrived, attracted by the screaming.

Like most slave children, Keckley was punished for the slightest mistake. And like many, she lived in a family that was broken up. She hardly ever saw her father George Pleasant Hobbs, who was owned by another master and allowed to visit only twice a year. Later, he disappeared from Keckley's life altogether, because his master moved west, taking his slaves with him.

During her teenage years, Keckley had to face an additional burden. She was pestered by a white man, Alexander Kirkland, who eventually made her pregnant with a child she named George. Soon after the baby's birth, the Burwells' married daughter, Anne Burwell Garland, moved to St. Louis, Missouri, whereupon Keckley, her son, and her mother were moved to St. Louis too.

In St. Louis, the Garlands decided to hire out Keckley's elderly mother in order to pay for their needs. Determined to spare her mother such hard labor, Keckley did the earning instead, working as a seamstress and dressmaker. Through her efforts, she virtually supported the Garlands and their five children, as well as the slaves of their household. She later wrote that she "kept bread in the mouths of seventeen persons for two years and five months."

While in St. Louis, she married James Keckley, believing him to be a free man. It

Elizabeth Keckley

turned out that not only was he a slave like herself, but he was "dissipated, and a burden instead of a helpmate." After eight unpleasant years, she escaped from the marriage—though, of course, what she most wanted to escape from was slavery. The easiest way out was to buy her freedom, but when she asked Garland how much this would cost, he set the sum at $1,200 for herself and her son George.

How could a slave like Keckley possibly come up with such a sum? All the money she earned went straight to the Garlands. She had no savings, but she did have some very appreciative clients whose dresses she had made over the years, and they clubbed together to lend her the money. As a result, Elizabeth Keckley and her son became free citizens in 1855.

Dressmaker and White House modiste

Since Keckley could now keep her earnings, she was soon able to repay the loan. She then moved to Baltimore before settling in Washington in 1860. There she quickly built up a good business, and before long she was employing twenty young women, who were made to sit up straight and behave like ladies even when they were stitching seams. This was the key to Keckley's own success because, as well as being an excellent dressmaker, she had a dignified and elegant manner, which impressed her clients and made them feel she was a cut above other dressmakers. As a result, some of Washington's top society women came to have their clothes made by her.

Her reputation led to her position as Mary Lincoln's dressmaker almost as soon as the Lincolns arrived in Washington in 1861. She was called in when Mrs. Lincoln spilled coffee on the dress she had intended to wear at her husband's inauguration. Not only did Keckley make a replacement in record time, but she helped the First Lady dress for the ceremony. And so began the friendship between the former slave and the president's wife.

Until 1868, Madame Keckley—as she was now called—remained the dressmaking friend and confidante of Mrs. Lincoln. They were drawn together partly by shared grief. In 1861, Madame Keckley's son was killed in the Civil War, and the following year Mrs. Lincoln's eleven-year-old son William died. The women comforted each other in their loss, and when President Lincoln was assassinated in 1865, Madame Keckley was one of the few people Mrs. Lincoln wanted to see.

The friendship might have continued throughout their lives had not Madame Keckley decided to write a book about her experiences. Whether she wrote it herself or had the help of a ghostwriter has been a matter of much discussion, but she certainly provided the information for it, including some personal letters from Mrs. Lincoln. As Keckley was to explain repeatedly, her aim was to help Mrs. Lincoln by setting the record straight and making some money for her. But Mrs. Lincoln was not pleased. Published in 1868, the book was called *Behind the Scenes, Or, Thirty Years a Slave and Four Years in the White House,* and it did indeed take the reader behind the scenes, even to the extent of repeating Mrs. Lincoln's private views about a number of important people.

No longer was Keckley the most sought-after dressmaker in Washington. So many of her clients deserted her that she had to close down her business. In 1892–93, she briefly had a job teaching domestic science at Wilberforce University, but in her last years she lived mostly on the pension paid her as the mother of a Union soldier who had died in the war. She eventually became so poor that she moved into a "home for the destitute" in Washington, yet she never lost her elegance and dignity. Each Sunday, as the stately old lady moved up the aisle toward her pew in the Fifteenth Street Presbyterian Church, the other churchgoers would watch her in admiration and whisper, "Here comes Madame Keckley."

Patrick Kelly

Fashion designer
Born September 24, 1954, Vicksburg,
    Mississippi
Died January 1, 1990

"My message is, 'You're beautiful just the way you are.'"

P atrick Kelly made history in June 1988 by becoming the first American to be elected to the Chambre Syndicale du Prêt-à-Porter, the French designer's association. This award reflected the great enthusiasm and appreciation that members of the fashion world, particularly in France, had for Kelly's designs. His trademarks were buttons, bows, and black doll pins. He told *People* that he designed them "for fat women, skinny women, all kinds of women. My message is 'You're beautiful just the way you are.'"

Designed gowns for neighborhood girls

By the time Kelly was six years old, he was looking at his grandmother's fashion magazines and wondering why there were no black models. In an *Ebony* interview, Kelly said, "Even at that young age, I knew that wasn't right and wanted to do something about it." A few years later he lived up to his word by designing gowns for girls in his neighborhood to wear to dances and proms. He also designed department store windows and did sketches for newspaper ads.

After graduating from Vicksburg Senior High School, he studied art history and African American history at the all-black Jackson State University. He was a rebel at the university, and a teacher, Michael Thomas, told him he would never amount to anything, so he dropped out of college. Kelly headed to Atlanta, where he spent six months with a pimp he'd met on the streets. He also decorated

Patrick Kelly

Yves Saint Laurent windows for free. "He was my hero. I tried to do them just the way Mr. Saint Laurent would have wanted them," he told *Time*. To gain a few extra dollars, Kelly sold stained glass taken from homes that were to be torn down, and he taught at the local Barbizon School of Modeling. Kelly received a job sorting clothes for Amvets (a veterans' organization), which gave him access to discarded Chanel suits and old beaded gowns. He used these clothes to set up his own used clothing store and adapted some of them to his own style. Of course, as a young man who used to sew for a living, his friends made him the butt of a few jokes. In a *People* interview, he said, "[where I grew up] you had to be a *boy*.... A boy sewing a dress? Oooo-EEEE!"

Kelly met several fashion models, and one of them, Pat Cleveland, told him to go to New York, the fashion capital of the United States. While in New York, he took classes at the elite Parsons School of Design and continued making dresses on his own. He sold them to models and used the money to pay tuition, but he still could not break into the fashion industry. Kelly ran into Cleveland again, and she suggested he try his luck in Paris. He was interested, but could not afford the airfare. The next day an anonymous person sent Kelly a one-way ticket to Paris.

Buttons and bows

During a party on his first evening in Paris, he was interviewed and hired as a costume designer for dancers in a discotheque. He continued to create his own fashions and sell them on the street and in flea markets. When he ran short of money he sold fried chicken. After several years of selling his designs on the street, Kelly became a recognizable figure. In 1984, the buyers for Victorie, an exclusive Paris boutique, purchased his dresses and provided him with a workshop and showroom. At about the same time, Kelly formed a partnership called Patrick Kelly Paris with his longtime friend, Bjorn Amelan, a photographer's agent. These changes provided him with a larger audience and more free-lance contracts, but he continued to lack financial security.

Kelly's big break occurred in June 1987, when Gloria Steinem, who came to interview Kelly for NBC's *Today Show*, introduced him to Linda Wachner, the chief executive officer of Warnaco. Eventually the two worked out a multimillion dollar deal, with Kelly developing a special line for Warnaco, a clothing manufacturer with international connections. A few weeks later, Kelly became the first American to show a couture collection in Paris.

With the exposure provided by Warnaco, Kelly was able to realize his childhood dream of being a fashion designer and employing several black models for his shows. His designs became noted for their references to African American history and culture. Most of his inspiration came from his grandmother, who used to replace buttons on his shirts in different colors, adding extra buttons for decoration. Big, colorful buttons became a Kelly trademark. He also used watermelon slices and blackfaced images. Some of his signature pieces featured three thousand buttons or tiny satin bows. "I design differently because I am Patrick Kelly, and Patrick Kelly is black, is from Mississippi," he said in a *Washington Post* interview.

Kelly also used doll faces, many that were likenesses of the character Aunt Jemima, making him a target for accusations of racism in the United States. A collector of six thousand black dolls, Kelly told *Vogue*, "Blacks and whites both think it's racist. But look, my grandmother was a maid and one of the chicest women I know. If you don't know where you've been in your history, then you don't know where to go." Tiny black doll pins became a trademark as he gave them away as souvenirs to all of his visitors, reportedly at a rate of eight hundred a month.

Inducted into Chambre Syndicale

Kelly was the first American to be inducted into the forty-four member French designer's organization called Chambre Syndicale du Prêt-à-Porter in June 1988. This achievement placed him within the exclusive ranks of the profession that had previously rejected him.

Membership in this group allowed Kelly to show his collections at the elegant Louvre Palace. It also offered him a coveted position in the fashion world. In less than a year and a half, Kelly's ride to the top of the fashion world was over. Just when he was licensing contracts for his buttons and future designs, as well as discussing an autobiographical movie, Kelly died on New Year's Day 1990 of a bone marrow disease; some say his death was AIDS related. His style was successfully exported and he is still widely imitated.

Sharon Pratt Kelly

Mayor of Washington, D.C.
Born January 30, 1944, Washington, D.C.

"I've always been fascinated by people who shape public policy, such as Franklin Delano Roosevelt and Martin Luther King. Mr. King had excellent communications skills. He took complex issues and made them simple for everyone else."

Even as a university student, Sharon Pratt Kelly realized she wanted a career in politics. She became actively involved in that area in 1977 when she was elected the Democratic National Committeewoman for the District of Columbia. She followed that by serving as the Democratic National Committee Eastern Regional Chairwoman and was the first female Democratic National Committee Treasurer. Her biggest political victory occurred in 1990 when she was elected mayor of Washington, D.C. Kelly now hopes to set new standards for public service, responsibility, and leadership.

Father shaped her philosophies

Kelly was born on January 30, 1944, in Washington, D.C., to Carlisle and Mildred Pratt. Her mother died when Kelly was four, and her grandmother, Hazel Pratt, and aunt, Aimee Elizabeth Pratt, became her mother figures. Her father, a former Washington, D.C., superior court judge, held her and his other daughters in high regard. "He is the person who shaped my philosophies of life," Kelly once said. "My father stressed developing the mind, hard work, and a commitment to public service."

Kelly attended public schools in the city and enjoyed team sports, especially baseball. An all-boys baseball team once offered her a position, but she declined. "I was at that adolescent stage when you worry about looking good, so I turned them down," she recalled. Kelly was an average student at first, but she devoted more time to her studies after enrolling at Roosevelt High School. She studied five hours every night and graduated in 1961 with honors.

Kelly enrolled at Howard University in Washington. She was originally interested in acting, but decided to study political science. "I always wanted to be an actress," she said in an interview. "But my commitment to the public service steered me in a direction in which I could initiate change." Since childhood she had been interested in people who shaped public policy, such as Franklin Delano Roosevelt and Martin Luther King. She also admired Malcolm X for his willingness to share knowledge with others; Patricia Harris, who served in the Carter administration; and Flaxie Pinkard, an astute businesswoman.

As an undergraduate, Kelly became the first woman to run for student council president. She was honored as a member of the Pi Sigma Alpha national political science honor society and was named a Falk Fellow in political science. She graduated with a B.A. in political science in 1965 and then continued her studies at Howard University's School of Law, earning her law degree three years later. While in law school in 1966, Kelly married Arrington Dixon, who would go on to become Washington, D.C., council chairman. She gave birth to daughter Aimee Arrington Dixon the same year she received her law degree. In 1970 the Dixons had another daughter, Sharon Pratt Dixon, before divorcing in 1982. Kelly married banker-turned-businessman James Kelly III in 1991.

Family and consumer law

From 1970 to 1971 Kelly was house counsel for the Joint Center for Political Studies in Washington, D.C. She then became an associate with the law firm Pratt and Queen, where she stayed until 1976. She fought for the rights of children involved in custody battles, provided juveniles with strong and competent legal representation, and protected the rights of families.

Kelly also joined the faculty at the Antioch School of Law in 1972. During her four-year stay, Thomas "Tip" O'Neill, former Speaker of the House of Representatives, appointed her to the District of Columbia Law Revision Commission. According to the *Washington*

Times, this commission "transferred the city's criminal code from Congress to the District."

In 1976 Kelly took a position in the general counsel's office at Potomac Electric Power Company (PEPCO). She was eventually appointed vice-president for public policy—the first African American and later the first woman vice-president of consumer affairs. She initiated and implemented new programs for assisting low-income residents in Washington, D.C., and for senior citizens. She also created jobs with new satellite branches of PEPCO. "I wanted PEPCO to adopt new policies and a general approach of how to deal with changing methods," she said. "Ideas, concepts and policies drive me!"

Her interest in politics caused her to seek election as the Democratic National Committeewoman for the District of Columbia. She was elected to four terms, from 1977 to 1980. From 1980 to 1984, Kelly was the Democratic National Committee Eastern Regional Chairwoman. She was the first woman to serve as the Democratic National Committee Treasurer, from 1985 to 1989. She has also been a member of the American Bar Association, Unified Bar of the District of Columbia, and the District of Columbia Women's Bar Association. Organizations that recognized Kelly for her work include the Washington, D.C., chapter of the NAACP; the United Negro College Fund; and the Association of Black Women Attorneys.

Concerned with D.C.'s fiscal problems, soaring crime rates, record homicide rates, and drug addiction, Kelly decided to run for the mayor's office. "I set the goal to win the nomination, then I set the goal to serve. The key is to put yourself in a position to effect the changes you want to take place," she said. On November 6, 1990, she became the first woman to win the mayoral race in the District of Columbia.

Goals as mayor

Since assuming office, Kelly stated she wants new standards for public service, responsibility, and leadership. Her main goal is to facilitate black and Hispanic ownership of business and community properties. She also plans to implement programs that will assist both the city's seniors and youths. Hoping to end the city's drug problems, Kelly told the *Georgetowner* she intends to "implement a Fresh Start drug treatment program to be administered by local church and community groups; target seized drug capital for drug fighting units and treatment programs and establish a Neighborhood Oriented Policing program

Sharon Pratt Kelly

where churches, community groups, businesses and the police work together."

Kelly is also concerned that women have not tried to place themselves in positions of authority. She told the *Washington Post*: "We need a political genesis, a renaissance in which masculine politics and the 'dog eat dog' mentality that earmarked it, is replaced by a feminine kind of politics in which you do what is right, not what is expedient." She also told the newspaper that the mayor's position was "a means to an end, not the end."

Flo Kennedy

Civil and women's rights activist, lawyer
Born February 11, 1916, Kansas City,
   Missouri

"I'm just a loud-mouthed middle-aged colored lady with a fused spine and three feet of intestines missing and a lot of people think I'm crazy. Maybe you do too, but I never stop to wonder why I'm not like other people. The mystery to me is why more people aren't like me."

During the turbulent 1960s and 1970s, there were many issues that people wanted to sweep under the rug, among them civil rights, homosexuality, prostitution, women's rights, minority values, and the poor. Florynce Rae Kennedy—known as Flo to her friends and enemies—provided a voice for these issues. Educated as a lawyer, Kennedy spoke on these subjects not only on the courtroom floor, but also at the lecture theaters of more than two hundred colleges and at rallies. Patricia Burstein in *People Weekly* once referred to her as "the rudest mouth on the battleground where feminist-activists and radical politics join in mostly common cause."

"I knew I was something"

Kennedy was born in Kansas City, Missouri, the second of five daughters, and spent her early years in Missouri and California. Her father, Wiley, worked at various times as a Pullman porter and waiter, and ran his own taxi company. Her mother, Zelda, was educated in the normal school when very few black people went to school. For the most part Zelda stayed at home, but during the Great Depression she worked as a domestic.

"Our parents had us convinced we were precious that by the time I found out I was nothing, it was already too late—I knew I was something," Kennedy said in her 1976 autobiography, *Color Me Flo: My Hard Life and Good Times*. Neither parent used excessive discipline, but rather encouraged their children in their endeavors. Kennedy graduated from Lincoln High School in Kansas City at the top of her class. She then worked at a variety of jobs including selling hats and operating an elevator. In 1942 she went to live with her sister Grayce in New York City. Two years later she enrolled at Columbia University and graduated in 1948 with a bachelor's degree in pre-law. Kennedy applied to the Columbia Law School, but was rejected despite an "A" average. She decided her rejection was based on race and threatened to fight the university if it didn't reverse its decision. The university changed its mind and in 1951, she received her law degree. She passed the New York Bar Exam the following year. Kennedy clerked at a New York law firm for about three years and then struck out on her own.

In 1957 Kennedy married Charles "Charlie" Dudley Dye. She was thirty-one at the time and he was ten years older. She later described him as a "Welsh science-fiction writer and a drunk." The marriage dissolved after a short period of time, and Dye died an alcoholic. This union did not produce any children, and Kennedy never remarried.

Don Wilkes joined Kennedy's law practice for a short time, during which they represented Eleanora McKay (better known as Billie Holiday) when she faced indictment under a federal statute requiring people convicted on charges of narcotics possession to register each time they left the country. Holiday's agent, Associate Booking Corporation, had neglected to tell her of this statute when it sent her on a European tour. A long legal battle took place, but in the end, Wilkes was able to convince the U.S. attorney not to indict Holiday. A few days after the win, Holiday died.

Kennedy continued to represent Holiday's estate and later added jazzman Charlie Parker's estate to her files. Both cases involved a fight to recoup money owed to them in royalties and sales denied to them because they were black. Another big name client of Kennedy was activist H. Rap Brown. Her experience with these cases led her to consider being an activist in the civil rights movement.

"Handling the Holiday and Parker estates taught me more than I was really ready for about government and business delinquency and the hostility and helplessness of the courts in rectifying the imbalance between the talented performers and the millionaire parasites who suck their blood. These experiences, together with Wilkes' takeoff, marked the beginning of a serious disenchantment, if indeed I ever was enchanted with the practice of law," Kennedy said in her autobiography.

A spokesperson on unspoken issues

Kennedy felt she was not making a decent living from the legal profession. She also thought she couldn't accomplish social change through her actions. She decided to fight four types of oppression: personal, private, public, and political. She began to speak out on a variety of civil rights issues and served as a spokesperson for homosexuals, prostitutes, minorities, women, and the poor. She spoke out publicly on many unspoken issues that affected the lives of many.

In 1966 Kennedy founded the Media Workshop, an organization she said was designed to deal with racism in media and advertising. She was an original member of the National Organization of Women, but eventually decided their goals did not coincide with her own. Kennedy encouraged black women to join the women's liberation movement, and she later helped form the Feminist Party. Well-known feminist Gloria Steinem told *Ebony* that, "for those who had been part of the black movement when it was still known as the civil rights movement or in the consumers movement that predated Ralph Nader, or in the women's movement when it was still supposed to be a few malcontents in sneakers, or in the peace movement when there was more

Flo Kennedy

worry about nuclear fallout than about Vietnam, Flo was a political touchstone—a catalyst."

In 1967 Kennedy was invited to speak at an anti-war convention in Montreal, Quebec. When she discovered that Bobby Seale, the co-founder of the controversial Black Panthers Party, was not going to be allowed to speak, she went to the platform and began yelling and screaming. The event garnered many headlines, and Kennedy was invited to speak in Washington for a fee of $250, plus expenses. It was the beginning of a major speaking career. By the mid-seventies, Kennedy had lectured at more than two hundred colleges and universities and at rallies dealing with a host of issues.

Kennedy attended all four Black Power Conferences, including the planning stage of the First National Conference on Black Power. She also attended black political caucuses in 1968 and 1972, both in Gary, Indiana.

Challenges the Catholic church

In 1972 Kennedy moved her residence from New York to California. That same year she filed a complaint against the Catholic Church with the Internal Revenue Service. She alleged that the church violated the tax-exempt requirements in that it spent money to influence political decisions, particularly those that dealt with the abortion issue. Kennedy, who filed the complaint on behalf of the Feminist Party, felt that the church's activities were unconstitutional. Nothing more is known about the outcome of the lawsuit.

Kennedy and Diane Schulter co-authored one of the first books on abortion, *Abortion Rap*. The book documents the class-action suit filed to test New York's abortion laws. Kennedy was a part of the legal team that challenged the constitutionality of the New York law, collaborating on briefs and cross-examining witnesses in pretrial hearings.

Friends and colleagues paid tribute to Kennedy in 1985 with a roast in her honor at the Playboy's Empire Club in New York City. The celebration marked her seventieth birthday and the guests included comic-activist Dick Gregory, civil rights lawyer William Kunstler, and television talk show host Phil Donahue. Kennedy was recognized for her outstanding achievements as a civil rights activist, attorney, writer, and organizer.

Civil court judge Leonard Cohen wrote a tribute to Kennedy's career in the poem, "She is Everywhere," which was published in her autobiography in 1976. Kennedy is still on the speaking circuit and can be found wherever there is a cause she believes must be brought to the public's attention.

Jackie Joyner Kersee

See **Joyner-Kersee, Jackie**

B. B. King

Blues singer and guitar player
Born September 16, 1925, near Indianola,
  Mississippi

"Blues is what I do best. If Frank Sinatra can be tops in his field, Nat Cole in his, Bach and Beethoven in theirs, why can't I be great, and known for it, in blues?"

B. King has been hailed as the world's most accomplished blues guitarist. With more than fifty albums to his credit, he has a huge following of enthusiastic fans. "There is hardly a rock, pop, or blues player anywhere who doesn't owe him something," wrote *Guitar Player* magazine.

Blues evolved on the Southern plantations during the years of slavery, and the music has a sad, haunting quality in keeping with its subject matter. The songs have traditionally described misfortunes, though they usually contain a touch of humor. Most of Kings's songs are about hard times or unsatisfactory relationships with women. He writes many of this own songs, and others have been composed by his contemporaries, including the hits "How Blue Can You Get," "Rock Me Mama," and "Sweet Sixteen."

King plays on an electric guitar named Lucille. He has called all his guitars Lucille ever since the 1950s, when two men fighting over a woman named Lucille accidentally started a fire in the hall where King was performing. It was a memorable occasion for King, since he almost lost his life when he went back into the blazing building to rescue his guitar.

Learned guitar from his preacher uncle

King's childhood was full of toil and sorrow. Named Riley B. King, he was born on a cotton plantation near Indianola in the Mississippi Delta, the son of Albert and Nora (Pully) King. When King was four years old, his parents separated and his mother took him to the Mississippi hill country near Kilmichael. But she died when King was nine, and the boy was left to fend for himself. He survived by working for a local farmer until he was about thirteen, when his father found him and took him back to Indianola.

The change of location did not make life much easier for the teenager. During the rainy months he had to walk ten miles each day to attend a small one-teacher school, and the rest of the year he worked on the cotton plantation. It was in the cotton fields that King became familiar with blues music. "I guess the earliest sound of blues that I can remember was in the fields while people would be pickin' cotton or choppin' something," he told *Living Blues* magazine. In Indianola King had his first lessons on the guitar. He was taught by an uncle, who was a guitarist and preacher belonging to a strict religious sect. When King bought his own guitar, he was not allowed to play blues—which was viewed as "devil's music"—but he formed a quartet to sing spirituals. He first began to play blues during his time in the army during World War II.

King stayed in the army only a short while, because the draft board decided he could be more use in the cotton fields than in the trenches. This suited King just fine. On Saturday nights, after the week's work was done, he would play the blues on street corners in the neighboring towns. These street performances brought in only a few pennies at first, but by the end of the war they were earning King more than he made in an entire week picking cotton.

Developed a loyal following

In 1947 King hitchhiked to Memphis, Tennessee, to stay with his cousin, Bukka White, a famous slide guitarist. In his efforts to make the same sounds on his own guitar, King developed the trilling vibrato that has become his specialty. King had not been long in Memphis when he landed a job singing commercials on WDIA radio. The radio then took him on staff as a disc jockey, and it was during this period that he became known as B. B. King. When King first took the job he was billed as "Riley King, the Blues Boy from Beale Street." This was later shortened to "The Blues Boy" and then simply to "B. B."

King was already making a name for himself as a blues musician. Being a disc jockey left him plenty of time to perform, and in the evenings he could usually be found playing in one of the many Memphis clubs and bars. King made his first records in 1949, when he recorded four sides for the Bullet record company. The following year he had his first hit with Lowell Fulson's "Three O'Clock Blues," which was at the top of the rhythm and blues charts for four months.

However, topping the charts did not mean that King had a huge audience. Blues music was not very popular during this period. It was considered low class by black music lovers, and it had not yet been taken up by whites. Blues musicians had a hard time finding work. Throughout the 1950s and into the 1960s King followed an exhausting schedule as a touring musician, playing in tawdry black bars and dance halls, some of which did not even pay him. Sometimes he played in 300 different towns in a single year. In 1956 he had 342 one-night stands. Only occasionally was he able to get a booking at a major theater. One of these occasions was in 1964, when King's classic *Live at the Regal* was recorded.

By the mid-1960s King had made quite a number of records, most of which had sold well and some of which had been hits. But even such memorable numbers as "Woke Up This Morning" and "Everyday I Have the Blues" did not bring in much money. Cheaply made and quickly produced, the albums sold for ninety-nine cents on drugstore racks. Nevertheless they gathered King a small but loyal following of fans who liked his style and recognized his genius.

Recognized as the world's best blues guitarist

King's small group of fans blossomed into hundreds of thousands in the 1960s, when blues music made a comeback in the wake of

B. B. King

rock and roll. For the first time, blues had a huge following among whites as well as blacks.

King was introduced to white rock audiences largely through the efforts of guitarist Mike Bloomfield, who had long been one of his fans. King's first concert to a mainly white audience was held in 1966 at the Fillmore Auditorium in San Francisco. A few months later jazz critic Ralph Gleason announced that King was "one of the greatest guitarists of his time." Many others thought so too. In 1968 King made his first European tour and had his first engagement at a prestigious New York nighclub. In 1969 he had a Top 20 pop hit with "The Thrill Is Gone." In 1970 he was named the world's top blues guitarist by *Guitar Player* magazine.

Since then King has gone from success to success, gathering an ever larger number of fans. Twice married and divorced, with eight children and several grandchildren, he contin-

ues to tour for much of each year. But he no longer plays in seedy bars. Today King entertains in smart Las Vegas nightclubs and at such world-famous locations as Carnegie Hall. He lives in a very different world from the days when he felt embarrassed to admit to being a blues singer: "People kind of looked down on you a lot of times when you mentioned the word blues. But I thank God today I can stick out my chest and say, yeah, I'm a blues singer!"

Since the world's rediscovery of blues—and of B. B. King—the great blues guitarist has won many awards. These range from the Académie du Jazz award, which King received from the French in 1969, to an honorary doctorate of music presented by Yale University in 1977. King won a Grammy Award as best male rhythm and blues vocalist in 1970 for "The Thrill is Gone," and another Grammy for best traditional blues recording in 1986 for *My Guitar Sings the Blues*. In 1987 he was presented with a Lifetime Achievement Award by the National Academy of Recording Arts and Sciences.

Coretta Scott King

Civil rights activist, singer
Born April 27, 1927, Heiberger, Alabama

*"Those of you who believe in what Martin Luther King, Jr., stood for, I would challenge you today to see that his spirit never dies....
We are going to continue his work to make all people truly free and to make every person feel that he is a human being."*

When Martin Luther King, Jr., was assassinated in 1968, his widow understandably could have retired from public life and devoted herself to bringing up her children. Instead, Coretta Scott King carried on her husband's work, trying to fulfill his dream of an America in which all people had equal rights.

Since that time, King has become a forceful public figure and an important leader in the civil rights movement. She has given hundreds of speeches, abroad as well as at home, and been active in such organizations as the National Council of Negro women and the Women's Strike for Peace. She has also taken on the role of writer, publishing a collection of her husband's quotations, *The Words of Martin Luther King, Jr.* (1983), and her autobiography, *My Life with Martin Luther King, Jr.* (1969).

Childhood in Heiberger

King spent her childhood on her parents' farm in Heiberger, near Marion, Alabama. The farm had been in the family since the Civil War, but the Scotts were not at all rich. They were so hard hit during the Depression that the children picked cotton to help earn money. There were three children—Edythe, Coretta, and Obie. Obie was named after his father, Obediah Scott, a resourceful man who was the first black person in the district to own a truck and who eventually opened a country store. Their mother, Bernice (McMurray) Scott, was also a strong character.

As a young child, King walked five miles each day to attend the one-room Crossroads School. When she was older, she studied at Lincoln High School in Marion, nine miles away. Since this was too far to walk, her mother hired a bus and drove all the black students in the area to and from school—a most unusual course of action for a black woman in the 1930s. The alternative would have been for the children to stay in Marion all week, returning home only at weekends, but Mrs. Scott did not want her children to be away from home so much.

King inherited a love of music from her mother, and at Lincoln High School she learned to play the trumpet and piano, and sang as a soloist at school recitals. An intelligent and hard-working student, she did well in her schoolwork too and was at the top of her class when she graduated in 1945. She then enrolled at Antioch College, Ohio, where her sister Edythe had been the first full-time black student to live on campus.

Student in the North

At Antioch College, King majored in music and education. She also took part in the college's work-study program, acting as a camp counsellor, library assistant, and nursery school attendant. The fact that she was African American was not a barrier in any of these roles, but when she began to teach as part of her education course, she suddenly found her way blocked. Ordinarily, the education students did their practice teaching in the local public schools, but these schools had no black teachers and would not accept her. Her protests fell on deaf ears, even when she appealed to the college president, and in the end she had to do her teaching at the Antioch Demonstration School.

Coretta Scott King

During this time, King was also a music student, learning the violin as well as studying singing and piano. She sang in the choir at the Second Baptist Church in Springfield, Ohio, and gave her first solo concert there in 1948. By the time she graduated in 1951, she had decided to become a professional singer rather than a schoolteacher and had been accepted by the New England Conservatory of Music in Boston.

Although King had a scholarship to cover her tuition at the conservatory, it did not pay for anything else, and she barely scraped by during her first year in Boston. To pay for her bed and breakfast, she cleaned the stairwells of the house she lived in, and for supper she usually made do with peanut butter and crackers. The following year was easier, because she received state aid from Alabama, but she still had to watch every penny.

While studying at the conservatory she met Martin Luther King, Jr., who was also a student in Boston at the time, and they were married in 1953. The following year, after Coretta Scott King had graduated from the conservatory, they moved to Montgomery, Alabama, where Martin Luther King, Jr. began his work as a minister.

Mrs. King

In marrying a man committed to civil rights, King knew that she would not live the life of a quiet minister's wife. Their first child, Yolanda ("Yoki"), was born in 1955, just two weeks before the beginning of the Montgomery bus boycott. With the boycott came danger—the King house was bombed in 1956—and from then on King had to be constantly alert on behalf of her children as well as her husband. The Kings were to have three more children: Martin Luther III, Dexter, and Bernice.

The next few years saw Coretta King sharing as full partner in her husband's work, walking beside him in marches, travelling abroad with him, and giving speeches when he was unable to do so. She also made her own personal contribution. On behalf of the Women's Strike for Peace, she was a delegate at the Disarmament Conference in Geneva in 1962, and she often gave concerts on behalf of the civil rights movement, for she was still keeping up with her music.

When her husband was assassinated in Memphis, Tennessee, in 1968, Coretta King took it for granted that she would continue his work. Just four days after his death she led a march of fifty thousand people through the streets of Memphis, and later that year she took his place in the Poor People's March to Washington.

The following year, King traveled to India to accept an award that had been granted to her husband the previous year, and on the way there she visited Italy, where she was given a special audience by the Pope. She also stopped off in Britain, where she preached at St. Paul's Cathedral—probably the first woman ever to do so. However, King's main concern in 1969 was the Martin Luther King, Jr., Center for Nonviolent Social Change, which she planned to create in Atlanta, Georgia.

Over the years, King has worked hard to raise funds for the center, which now covers three full blocks and houses a library and archives of the civil rights movement. King oversees the center, which succeeded in achieving her other major goal—to get her husband's birthday honored as a national holiday. She has a third goal too, and this is a continuing one, for she continues to speak out against injustice, especially racial injustice, doing what she can to make her husband's "dream" of fairness and equality come true.

Martin Luther King, Jr.

Civil rights leader, minister
Born January 15, 1929, Atlanta, Georgia
Died April 4, 1968, Memphis, Tennessee

"I've been to the mountaintop ... and I've seen the promised land. I may not get there with you. But I want you to know tonight that we as a people will get to the promised land."

It was the aim of Martin Luther King, Jr., to gain social, political, and economic equality for blacks by peaceful means. For this cause, he was denounced by racists and violently attacked. For this cause, he died—gunned down by an assassin's bullet in Memphis, Tennessee, at the age of thirty-nine.

In the ten years before his death, King had been the dominant force in the civil rights movement, raising the consciousness of people throughout the nation. In 1964, he was awarded the Nobel Peace Prize for attempting to achieve his aims without the use of violence. In the years since his death he has been honored in many ways. Schools and colleges have been named after him, monuments have been dedicated to him, and his birthday has been made a federal holiday. King is the only twentieth-century American whose birth has been honored in this way.

A religious upbringing

King was originally called Michael, after his father Michael Luther King, but when he was six his father changed their names to Martin Luther King. King's father was pastor of Ebenezer Baptist Church, and his mother, Alberta (Williams) King, also came from a family of ministers. She had been a teacher before her marriage, and she made sure that her children were well instructed in the Bible. There were three children in the family: Christine, Martin Luther, and Albert Daniel.

Since King attended all-black schools and lived in a comfortable middle-class home, he did not suffer the harsher effects of racism as he was growing up. A good student, he did well in class and graduated from Booker T. Washington High School at the age of fifteen. He then enrolled at Atlanta's Morehouse College. He intended to become a lawyer or doctor, but he changed his mind while at Morehouse, and by the time he graduated with a B.A. in 1948, he had decided to become a minister.

King spent the next three years at Crozer Theological Seminary in Chester, Pennsylvania, where he was one of only six black students among almost a hundred whites. After graduating with a bachelor of divinity degree in 1951, he went on to Boston University to study for a Ph.D. During these years, King also attended lectures on philosophy and ethics at the University of Pennsylvania and at Harvard University, and he became a great admirer of Mohandas Gandhi, a religious leader who had led nonviolent protests in India. King later said that he gained his "operational technique" from Gandhi and his "ideals" from his Christian background.

While he was in Boston King met Coretta Scott, whom he married in 1953, the year he completed his studies. The following year the newlyweds moved to Montgomery, Alabama, where King began his ministry as pastor of the Dexter Avenue Baptist Church. While settling in there and completing the dissertation for his Ph.D., he became good friends with a fellow Montgomery minister, Ralph Abernathy. Great things were to come of this friendship.

Montgomery bus boycott

King and Abernathy often discussed the need to improve conditions for their people, and when a seamstress named Rosa Parks was arrested in December 1955, they seized the opportunity to take action. Parks was arrested for refusing to give up her seat on a bus when a white man demanded it. The buses in Montgomery were segregated—whites at the front, blacks at the back, with an area in between where black passengers had to give up their seats if the white section was full. This was where Parks had been sitting, and she had refused to move.

The local Women's Political Council and other groups decided to protest Parks's arrest by refusing to ride on the buses, and King joined forces with them, forming the Montgomery Improvement Association to organize the boycott. He printed leaflets explaining how people could take part, and he persuaded black taxi drivers to take passengers at reduced rates. When the city blocked this measure, he laid on carpools.

The boycott lasted for 382 days and ended in triumph when the U.S. Supreme Court ruled against segregation on Montgomery buses. But it had been a tense time. King suffered harrassment and arrest, and his house was bombed—an act that nearly caused a riot. Only his pleas for nonviolence prevented the angry crowd from taking revenge on his behalf.

Southern Christian Leadership Conference

The bus boycott focused national attention on King and encouraged Southerners in other cities to make similar efforts. In 1957 King met with a group of ministers in Atlanta, Georgia, and formed the Southern Christian Leadership

Conference (SCLC), of which he was chosen president. Their aim was to end segregation throughout the South.

King traveled back and forth across the South, giving more than two hundred speeches in 1957 alone. The following year he visited the new African country of Ghana, having been invited to the independence celebrations there, and the year after that he fulfilled his long-standing ambition to visit India. Meanwhile, he continued to press for civil rights at home, and he also found time to write a book about the Montgomery boycott. He was later to write other books, as well as papers and monographs.

In 1960, King moved to Atlanta, accepting his father's offer to become co-pastor at the Ebenezer Baptist Church so that he would have more time for his civil rights activities. King was immensely busy because, besides running his own campaigns, he was working with groups such as the Student Nonviolent Coordinating Committee (SNCC), which organized sit-ins to protest segregated lunch counters and other discriminatory practices. Many of the protests were successful and achieved their aims without violence, though in 1961 the SCLC failed to get segregation removed in Albany, Georgia, and then was unable to prevent angry members of the black community from turning to violence.

Letter from Birmingham City Jail

King's activities often led to his arrest, the most notable occasion being in Birmingham, Alabama, where in 1963 he led a march to demand desegregation in the department stores and fairer hiring practices in the city. The march turned into a mass rally, with college students and schoolchildren joining in. When the marchers refused to disperse, the police went into action with clubs and firehoses.

The protests continued for more than a month, during which time thousands of people were arrested, including King and Abernathy. While King was in prison, he wrote his famous "Letter from Birmingham City Jail" in answer to white clergy who had criticized his actions. This letter, together with the media coverage of young black people being brutally attacked by police, caused outrage across the nation and drew many whites into the civil rights movement. Meanwhile, President John F. Kennedy sent a representative to Birmingham, who helped draw up an agreement that met most of King's demands. But there was further violence from both whites and blacks before calm was restored.

Civil rights

The publicity over the Birmingham protests led to similar efforts in towns and cities throughout the country, often with strong white support. In August 1963, some 60,000 whites were among the 250,000 people who marched to Washington in support of the civil rights bill that was then before Congress. When they gathered at the Lincoln Memorial, King delivered a speech that has echoed down the years. "I have a dream," he declared, "that one day this nation will rise up, live out the true meaning of its creed."

King was chosen as *Time* magazine's Man of the Year in 1963, and the following year he received the Nobel Peace Prize. He had come a long way in the previous few years, yet he

Martin Luther King, Jr.

was well aware that full civil rights had not yet been won, despite the Civil Rights Act of 1964. In the South, it was still very difficult for black people to register as voters, so King launched a voting-registration drive in Selma, Alabama, in 1965. Later that year the Voting Rights Act was passed, which made it far easier for black citizens to register. Poverty was another target, because blacks could never attain equality with whites until both groups had equal economic advantages. In 1966 King tried to get something done about the Chicago slums, but he did not have much success.

Around this time, King was having difficulties within his own organization. The more strident young activists were critical of his policy of nonviolence and were promoting black power. They wanted a more aggressive leader. Meanwhile, King offended other supporters by speaking out against the Vietnam War. This caused a major rift within the civil rights movement, for many felt that he should stick to civil rights and not weaken his support by crusading for peace.

In fact, King was turning more and more to human rights—the rights of all people—and this was at the heart of the Poor People's Campaign he was planning. The idea was to organize a march to Washington by thousands of poor people of all races to draw attention to their plight. While touring the country in 1968 to raise support for this campaign, King agreed to speak to striking garbage workers in Memphis, Tennessee, and it was there that his life was brought to a sudden end. While standing on the balcony of the Lorraine Motel, he was shot in the neck.

King's assassination set off a wave of violence in the major cities—the anger being all the more tragic because of his commitment to nonviolence. Meanwhile, millions of people throughout the nation mourned more peaceably, quietly sharing in the grief of his wife and four children. King is buried near the Ebenezer Baptist Church in Atlanta, in an area named the Martin Luther King, Jr., National Historic Site.

Yolanda King

Civil rights activist
Born November 17, 1955, Montgomery, Alabama

"It was hours before Daddy came on. I couldn't have sat still that long! All I knew was kids in school the next day were going crazy, saying, 'Your daddy talked about you in his speech."

While millions of Americans know the public Dr. Martin Luther King, Jr., very few know the private side of the legendary civil rights leader. One of those few was his oldest daughter, Yolanda King. She would sometimes accompany him on his campaigns for racial justice and saw first-hand how her father's eloquence and dedication to nonviolence changed the country. After her father was assassinated, she supported her mother, Coretta, as she assumed a more prominent role in the black movement.

After graduating from college, King has struck out on her own to support civil rights. She formed a theater company whose work addresses many of her father's concerns, and she works at the Martin Luther King, Jr., Center for Nonviolent Social Change. In her spare time, King gives school lectures on her father's vision.

Yolanda King

Thought "everybody went to jail, right?"

King was born on November 17, 1955, in Montgomery, Alabama, and she was just three weeks old, when her father, the minister of the Dexter Avenue Baptist Church, led a black boycott to protest the city's segregated bus policy. For the next thirteen years, Dr. King risked imprisonment and death to lead sit-in demonstrations and freedom marches. His message of racial justice was heard by millions, and eventually reached the corridors of power where civil rights became a matter of legislation.

Despite her father's enormous popularity, King did not realize he was anyone special until she was eight or nine. She told *Rolling Stone:* "I had no awareness he was anybody special. Since all our friends were in the movement, I thought what Daddy did was natural. Everybody went to jail right? Then one day some kids at school called my daddy a jailbird and it upset me. That was the beginning of my awareness."

Dr. King felt someone would try to attack him through his family, so he rarely had his children accompany him. Occasionally King would attend some of the smaller rallies. Dr. King and his followers would go from county to county, head into the nearest town, say a few words at the local church, and then move on to the next town.

King grew up in a modest part of the community. They lived in a house in one of the worst ghettos in Atlanta, Georgia. Her father felt it was important to stay close to the people he represented.

When Dr. King made his famous "I have a dream" speech in Washington, D.C., in 1963, King was at home, watching the event on television. Although it was one of the most historic events of the civil rights movement, King was too young to understand its significance. "I didn't know why I had to just watch it on TV. Not that I really even watched. Are you kidding? It was hours before Daddy came on. I couldn't have sat still that long! All I knew was kids in school the next day were going crazy, saying, 'Your daddy talked about you in his speech!' (... King said he prayed that 'my four little children will one day live in a nation where they will not be judged for the color of their skin but the content of their character.) So when Mother got back, first thing I said to her was, 'What is this content of character stuff?'"

Her father is assassinated

On April 4, 1968, Dr. King was showing his support of striking sanitation workers in Memphis, Tennessee, when he was assassinated by a sniper. King was at home in Atlanta when it happened. With her mother on the telephone, a television announcer said there would be a special announcement. For several minutes no one said anything until the TV announcer said Dr. King had been shot. King went to another room and prayed that her father would not die. She then went to help her mother pack a suitcase and watched her leave for Memphis to be with Dr. King. A few minutes later a family friend telephoned, and while King was talking with her, she heard over the radio that her father was dead.

Four days after Dr. King's death, Coretta led her four children to a mammoth demonstration in Memphis, where she called for a peaceful society. She went on to become an instrumental leader in the civil rights movement, picking up where her husband left off.

With her mother active in the movement, King attended Grady High School in Atlanta. She was interested in English because it reflected her interest in speech and drama. She was also captain of the pep squad, played basketball, and ran track for school.

King was also interested in music. She told *Seventeen:* "I can sing. I don't have a voice like my mother's but I can sing pretty well, I guess. I used to be in the choir at church. I used to play the clarinet and I still play the piano. The clarinet I sort of put down and I pick it up every now and then."

After graduating from high school, she considered attending Antioch College in Yellow Springs, Ohio, where her mother graduated. One of her main reasons for going to college was to try to get a liberal arts background. "Take my mother, for instance—she wanted to be a singer. If she had gone to school just to become an opera singer—that's what she wanted to be—and had not gone to college, right now she wouldn't be prepared or able to do what she has to do," she told *Seventeen.*

In 1979 King graduated from New York University with a master's degree in fine arts. She performed in, wrote, produced, and directed plays while she attended college and appeared in several showcase and Off-Broadway productions. Some of her acting roles were considered controversial. She once portrayed a prostitute in the play *The Owl and the Pussycat,* and many critics said it was not an appropriate role for her. King responded to this criticism in *Seventeen* by saying: "If people could really get to understand it, that prostitutes are people and in most cases they're not prostituting because they want to, even this could help to see them a little bit better instead of just saying, 'Oh, she's a prostitute and she's too low for me.' This could help solve the problem."

Portrayed Rosa Park in *King*

In 1977 she made an appearance of public and private significance: In the television film *King,* she portrayed Rosa Parks, the woman who had inspired Dr. King's involvement in the Montgomery bus boycott twenty-two years before. That same year she created a six-week program called the Atlanta Inter-Art Explosion with two acting and two dance students at NYU. They offered dance, acting, and voice classes, and over one hundred people, ranging in age from six to sixty, attended.

While in her early twenties, King met Attallah Shabazz, daughter of slain activist Malcolm X, through a mutual acquaintance. The two became fast friends, and they decided to collaborate on a theatrical work. They created *Stepping into Tomorrow,* a play that focused on the ten-year reunion of six high school friends. The play warned against dropping out of school, doing drugs, and teenage pregnancy. It led to the formation of Nucleus, a theater company based in New York and Los Angeles, whose work addresses many of the issues Malcolm X and Martin Luther King, Jr., used to raise in their speeches. The company was soon in demand and now performs in about fifty cities a year.

In a *Rolling Stone* interview, Shabazz described her relationship with King: "The concept of the two of us together may seem strange. But look at us standing here, both of us clearly the products of our individual households. And yet we still have reason for union."

A decade after the two formed Nucleus, they still find time to act together, as well as give school lectures. Most of King's time is spent at the Martin Luther King, Jr., Center for Nonviolent Social Change.

Jewel Stradford Lafontant

Lawyer, ambassador
Born April 22, 1928, Chicago, Illinois

"I hate those self-fulfilling prophecies, those 'I gave you a chance and you couldn't make (it)' kind of generalizations. So I see recruitment efforts as part of my role and I am not doing nearly enough."

As the daughter of Francis Stradford, famous Chicago lawyer, Jewel Stradford Lafontant had large shoes to fill. She followed in his footsteps, assisting him on some of his best-known cases, and then found her own place with a distinguished law firm. As her reputation grew, she was asked to sit on numerous boards and committees. In August 1989, Lafontant received her highest honor; she was named an ambassador at large and the United States coordinator for refugee affairs.

Her father's apprentice

Lafontant was born in Chicago, Illinois, on April 22, 1928, to Francis and Aida Stradford.

Jewel Stradford Lafontant

She received a bachelor of arts degree from Oberlin College and a doctor of laws degree from the University of Chicago. In 1947 she became a trial attorney with the Legal Aid Bureau, and eight years later she became an assistant United States district attorney in Chicago. The *Washington Star News* reported that "Lafontant is very conscientious in following her father's footsteps to the Supreme Court." The newspaper also noted that it was because of her father that she attended Oberlin.

As a young practicing attorney, Lafontant worked with her father. He had taken several high profile cases, including the Hansberry case, which he won before the U.S. Supreme Court in the mid-1940s. The decision allowed blacks to live in a Chicago area that had previously been off-limits to them. The case involved Carl and Nannie Hansberry, a couple who moved with their family to an all-white neighborhood on Chicago's South Side. The Hansberrys and the Stradfords were close

friends. Lafontant remembers sitting in the Hansberry's living room as bricks came crashing through their windows.

Lafontant's own career as a lawyer included a senior partnership with Vedder, Price, Kaufman and Kammholz. She was also the executive vice-president and director of Ariel Capital Management Company. She took a leave of absence from these positions after receiving an offer to become the first female deputy solicitor general of the United States during the Nixon administration. In this position she argued cases before the United Nations Supreme Court and also served as United States representative to the United Nations.

Lafontant has served on numerous boards and committees. She has served on the board of directors for Equitable Life, Revlon, Mobil Oil, Midway Airlines, the Hanes Corporation, Trans World Airlines, Pantry Pride, and TBG Broadcasting. She was also chairperson of the Illinois Advisory Committee to the United States Civil Rights Commission, commissioner of the Blue Ribbon Commission on the Administration of Justice in Cook County, commissioner of the Martin Luther King, Jr. Federal Holiday Commission, and commissioner of the Chicago Tourism Council. She was a member of the Labor Relations Committee of the United States Chamber of Commerce, the President's Commission on Executive Exchange, the visiting committee of the University of Chicago Law School, the board of overseers for the Hoover Institution, and director of the Capital Development Board of the State of Illinois.

Her other positions include director of Project HOPE, director of the Council on Foreign Relations, director of the Illinois Humane Society—Serving Vulnerable Children, a trustee of Howard University, a member of the Chicago Committee, the Citizen's Committee on the Juvenile Court, the national advisory board of the Salvation Army, and honorary member of Rotary International.

Named ambassador at large

In August 1989, she received her highest honor. President George Bush appointed her an ambassador at large and the U.S. coordinator for refugee affairs. She reported directly to the president in this position.

Due to her prowess, acumen, and experience, Lafontant is well respected in the corporate and black communities. She frequently encourages blacks to build skills and pursue their goals. In a *Dollars and Sense* interview, she stated that black entrepreneurs should encourage blacks to be producers as well as consumers: "They say that blacks don't measure up. Then you ask them where are they recruiting and they begin reciting all the black schools. I don't want to be treading on anyone's toes but I am partial to Oberlin College because I finished Oberlin and my father and his father, since it was the first college to admit blacks.... Some of the companies exclude schools like Oberlin and recruit from the all-black colleges in the deep South, where they have both good and bad schools. You also have some very poor ones that are barely accredited. So if you recruit at those you might have a legitimate reason for not hiring.... I asked them not to exclude black colleges, but include schools such as Oberlin. I hate those self-fulfilling prophecies, those 'I gave you a chance and you couldn't make (it)' kind of generalizations. So I see recruitment efforts as part of my role and I am not doing nearly enough."

In order for blacks to overcome certain biases in the corporate boardroom and the racist attitudes in some levels of middle-management, Lafontant says, individuals must be educated so that they do not place people in stereotypical roles. Corporations must recognize that even though people may look different, they can achieve as well as other groups. As she told *Dollars and Sense,* "incompetence is not distinguishable by color."

Lafontant was married to Ernest Lafontant, an attorney who died in October of 1976. They had one son, John W. Rogers, Jr., who has a degree in economics from Princeton. He is now president and chief executive of Ariel Capital Management. Lafontant is now married to Naguib S. Mankarious, an international business consultant.

Jacob Lawrence

Artist
Born September 7, 1917, Atlantic City, New Jersey

"I would describe my work as expressionist. The expressionist point of view is stressing your own feelings about something."

J acob Lawrence is widely regarded as the greatest living African American painter. He burst onto the international art scene nearly six decades ago with exhibitions on Toussaint L'Ouverture, Frederick Douglass, and Harriet Tubman. Lawrence has been commissioned to paint many historic works that capture the joy and pain of everyday life among African Americans. He has had a major influence on the next generation of artists through his teaching at prestigious art schools and universities.

Studies art at Utopia Children's Center

Lawrence was born on September 7, 1917, in Atlantic City, New Jersey, to Jacob and Rosalee Lawrence. Two years later the family moved to Easton, Pennsylvania. In 1924 the father abandoned the family, so Lawrence's mother moved them to Philadelphia. Six years later they moved to Harlem, New York, where Lawrence became interested in art. Since his mother wanted to keep him off the streets, she enrolled him in the Utopia Children's Center, an arts and crafts house. At Utopia, Lawrence met Charles Alston, a black painter, sculptor, and teacher, who became Lawrence's first mentor.

At age sixteen, Lawrence dropped out of school and supported his mother, brother, and sister by working in a laundry and at a printing plant. He also went to classes that Alston taught at the Harlem Art Workshop. In his spare time he would admire the early Italian Renaissance paintings at the Metropolitan Museum of Art, whose influence can be seen in some of his later works.

Lawrence rented studio space for a few dollars a week at Alston's Harlem studio. It was a gathering place for many prominent African American artists. "I came in contact with so many older people in other fields of art, ... dancers, ... musicians.... It was like a school," Lawrence said in an interview.

In 1936 Lawrence began producing his first significant works, mainly studies of everyday street life in Harlem. Some of these better known works were *Street Scene—Restaurant* (1936–38), *Interior Scene* (1937), and *Street Orator* (1937). During the last years of the Great Depression, Lawrence worked with the Civilian Conservation Corps on the construction of a dam in Middletown, New York. In 1937 he won a two-year scholarship to the American Artists School, where he studied with Sol Wilson and Philip Reisman. Later that year, Lawrence's paintings were exhibited for the first time at the Harlem Artists Guild.

By the end of 1938, he had held his first solo exhibit at the Harlem YWCA and was accepted into the Works Project Administration's Federal Arts Project. "It was my education," he told *Who's Who in America*. "I met people like [William] Saroyan before he got famous. They all used to talk about what was going on in the world. Oh, not only about art, but everything."

The next year Lawrence unveiled forty-one paintings, called the "Toussaint L'Ouverture Series" at the Baltimore Museum of Art. In 1940 the series took second place at the American Negro Exposition. He followed this with series on Frederick Douglass and Harriet Tubman. These two series marked the first time Lawrence used casein tempera, a water-based medium applied to gesso, which resulted in greater vividness and color.

"Migration of the Negro" brings national recognition

Lawrence received a Julius Rosenwald Fund Fellowship in 1940 that enabled him to move to his own studio. He began work on "The Migration of the Negro," a series of sixty paintings that commemorated the mass migration of southern blacks to the north in search of jobs after World War I. This series brought Lawrence national recognition. The exhibition opened at the prestigious Downtown Gallery in Manhattan on December 7, 1941, and *Fortune* magazine reproduced twenty-six of the paintings to commemorate the event. The show received rave reviews and was so popular with the public that the Museum of Modern Art in New York and the Phillips Memorial Gallery (now the Phillips Collection) in Washington, D.C., bid for it. They eventually decided to split the collection. The exhibition's success led the Downtown Gallery to represent Lawrence on a regular basis.

In 1943 Lawrence entered the United States Coast Guard and served as a steward's mate at a station in St. Augustine, Florida. The following year he was reassigned to a weather ship and later to a troop carrier. With the captain's help, he was able to receive a public relations rating of petty officer that enabled him to continue painting. He made a series of forty-eight works that documented life on a Coast Guard ship. When some of the paintings were exhibited at the Museum of Modern Art in 1944, *Magazine of Art* proclaimed, "Lawrence's latest phase as an artist is encouraging. His ... Coast Guard paintings [mark] a great advance over the ... promises of his youth."

Lawrence was released from the Coast Guard in December 1945, and the next summer he taught at Black Mountain College in North Carolina. It was here that he met the famous German-born painter and teacher Josef Albers, who greatly influenced his later works. After receiving a Guggenheim Foundation fellowship, Lawrence produced a compilation of fourteen reflective paintings about World War II. In 1947 *Fortune* commissioned him to do series on opportunities for African Americans in the postwar South. The resulting group of ten paintings, called "In the Heart of the Black Belt," was reproduced in *Fortune* in August 1948.

Nine-month hospital stay

Suffering from stress, Lawrence admitted himself to Hillside Hospital in the borough of Queens in New York City in October 1949. He has called the nine-month stay "one of the

Jacob Lawrence

most important" periods of his life. While undergoing treatment, Lawrence created a series of eleven paintings of his fellow patients entitled "Sanitarium." The series was exhibited at the Downtown Gallery in October 1950, a few months after his release from the hospital.

Lawrence released several highly acclaimed exhibitions in the early 1950s. He also continued teaching by taking positions at the Pratt Institute in Brooklyn, New York, the Art Students League in New York, and Brandeis University in Waltham, Massachusetts. In 1960–61, a Ford Foundation grant funded a touring retrospective of fifty-eight of Lawrence's paintings. In 1962 he visited Nigeria, West Africa, for the opening of an exhibition of his "Migration" series. He returned two years later for an eight-month period that resulted in several paintings of outdoor markets. In 1969 Lawrence became artist-in-residence at California State University at Hayward and at the University of Washington in Seattle the next year.

The civil rights movement became the focus of Lawrence's paintings during the mid- and late 1960s. He changed his style to include more gray tones, sharply-angled perspectives (often extreme closeups), and a strong graphic element usually found in illustrative work. In the late 1960s, racial harmony became the central theme of his work, and his paintings usually portrayed blacks and whites working together.

Lawrence accepted a full-time position at the University of Washington in 1971 and resigned in 1983. He and his wife, fellow painter, Gwendolyn Knight, now live full time in Seattle. During the 1970s and 1980s, Law-rence worked on a series of commissioned works including a poster for the Summer Olympic Games in Munich (1972); a print of the inauguration of President Jimmy Carter (1977); a mural for Howard University, entitled *Exploration* (1980); and a poster for the seventy-fifth anniversary of the National Urban League (1984).

In 1978 Lawrence was appointed to a six-year term on the National Council of the Arts, and in 1983, he was elected to the American Academy of Arts and Letters. He has been the subject of major retrospectives by New York's Whitney Museum of American Art and by the Seattle Art Museum.

Lawrence summed up his work in an interview with *Modern Maturity:* "My pictures express my life and experience. I paint the things I have experienced. The things I have experienced extend into my national, racial and class group. So I paint the American scene."

Spike Lee

Filmmaker, actor
Born March 20, 1957, Atlanta, Georgia

"You can take an unknown, all-black cast and put them in a story that comes from a black experience, and all kinds of people will come to see it if it's a good film. I wish Hollywood would get that message."

He has been called "one of the most original young filmmakers in the world," and each movie he makes proves the point more thoroughly. Since Shelton Jackson

"Spike" Lee burst on the scene in the mid-1980s, he has made a series of witty, hard-scoring films that have aroused their fair share of controversy while being enormously successful in the theaters.

Lee is one of the first directors to make films on specifically African American subjects, and he maintains that blacks, not whites, should be making such films. In the first place, he believes whites cannot portray black life as accurately as blacks. Secondly, a film can be just as popular with the public whether it is made by blacks or whites. "An all-black film directed by a black person can still be universal," says Lee. "I mean, nobody stopped coming to see Duke Ellington's music because he had an all-black band."

The young rebel

Spike Lee comes from a family of achievers. His father, Bill Lee, was a prominent jazz bass player in the 1960s and also a composer. His mother, Jacquelyn (Shelton) Lee, taught art and black literature at St. Anne's High School in Brooklyn. Lee's father and grandfather were both graduates of Morehouse College in Atlanta, and his mother and grandmother were graduates of Spelman College. A great-grandfather was a graduate of Tuskegee Institute and an author and educator.

With such a background, it not surprising that Lee was given a thorough grounding in the arts. During his childhood in the predominantly black district of Fort Greene in Brooklyn, going to the movies was just one of many cultural activities. Like his sister and three brothers, Lee was taken to museums and art galleries, taught the piano, taken to plays,

Spike Lee

and generally given a broad cultural base on which to build his life.

On graduating from John Dewey High School in Brooklyn, Lee followed the family tradition and enrolled at Morehouse College. It was there, while majoring in mass communications, that he decided on a career in film. After gaining his B.A. in 1979, he joined the graduate film school at New York University—which he very nearly had to leave because of the storm he stirred up over his first film. Called *The Answer,* it was Lee's answer to the racism in D. W. Griffith's classic film *Birth of a Nation* (1915), and it was about a black screenwriter who was hired to rewrite the script of Griffith's film. This irreverent treatment of "the father of cinema" offended the faculty, but Lee weathered the storm and the following year was made a teaching assistant.

For his master's thesis in his final year, Lee wrote and directed *Joe's Bed-Stuy Bar-*

bershop: We Cut Heads, which was filmed by fellow final-year student Ernest Dickerson. A wry comedy about a Brooklyn barbershop that fronts as a gambling joint, this was Lee's first prize-winning movie. It won the Student Academy Award and was picked for the New Directors/New Films series at New York's Lincoln Center in 1983, the first student film to be chosen for this series. It then went on to be shown at international film festivals.

Lee could hardly have graduated more auspiciously, and two talent agencies sought him out. But they could find nothing to offer him. Lee realized that if he was going to make his way in the film business, he would have to do it on his own.

Provocative filmmaker

To support himself, Lee took a job shipping film for a distribution company while he set about organizing his first commercial film. He wanted to make a movie about a black bicycle messenger in New York, and he obtained two grants as funding. But he soon ran into organizational problems and had to cancel the project, with the result that the largest of the grants was withdrawn. This left him only $18,000 with which to start work on another movie.

With so little money to spend, there could be no expensive location shooting and there had to be as few actors as possible. The result was *She's Gotta Have It,* which Lee wrote and produced in the summer of 1985. It was shot almost entirely in black and white and was filmed in twelve days, mainly in an attic apartment above a restaurant. The all-black cast included Lee's sister, some of his college friends, and Lee himself; the theme music was

written by his father. Lee did the editing in his apartment, working in the evenings on a rented machine.

She's Gotta Have It is a witty film about a young Brooklyn woman who has three lovers and is comfortably in charge of her life. One of Lee's aims was to portray black characters in a more realistic manner than is usually done in comedies—though he also had fun placing his heroine in the type of controlling situation normally held by men. The film was a phenomenal success from the moment it was first shown at the San Francisco Film Festival in 1986. It went on to win the Prix de Jeunesse at the Cannes Film Festival in France and eventually earned more than $7 million.

With this success behind him, Lee soon found backing for his next film, *School Daze,* a musical comedy about rival factions in a black college. Here, too, he ran into difficulties, in part because some of the language was considered offensive and also because of the controversial nature of the film. Its main theme was color prejudice within the black community—the friction between dark-skinned students and lighter-skinned students. Lee had arranged to shoot the film at Morehouse College, but the college officials soon became uneasy. "They said the film was a negative portrayal of black colleges and black people," Lee later explained. After only three weeks of shooting, he and his crew were turned off the campus.

Lee completed the movie at Atlanta University, but it continued to stir up trouble. The United Negro College Fund cancelled plans for a benefit premiere, and other groups found it offensive too. When the film was released in

1988, some black reviewers criticized Lee for exposing the faults of black campus life to white society. Lee maintained that these things ought to be aired in public. Many members of the black community agreed with him, and most simply enjoyed the film for what it was—a lively and amusing show. As before, Lee himself had a part in the movie, posing as one of the funniest characters. *School Daze* proved to be a fantastic success and was one of the top ten money-making films in 1988.

Lee stirred up another storm with his next film, *Do the Right Thing* (1989). This time he focused on the tension between African Americans and Italian Americans, placing the story in New York City in the heat of summer. The film ends with an angry black crowd burning down a pizzeria after a young black man has been killed by the police. This so appalled Paramount Pictures, which was funding the film, that it refused to release the film unless Lee changed the ending. Lee's reaction was typical: he kept the ending and changed film companies, taking the movie to Universal Pictures.

Inevitably, Lee was accused of inciting racial violence by including such a scene in the movie. He defended himself by saying that he was not promoting violence; he was promoting discussion about racial hatred. There was certainly plenty of discussion, and as usual the movie was a hit with the public. As the *New York Times* commented, "In all of the earnest, solemn, humorless discussion about the social and political implications ... an essential fact tends to be overlooked: it is one terrific movie."

Malcolm X

Lee began the 1990s with two more box-office hits, *Mo' Better Blues* (1990) and *Jungle Fever* (1991). He then launched his most ambitious film, *Malcolm X* (1992). Lee made the film with Warner Brothers, who put up $35 million—and then threatened to stop production when he went $6 million over budget. He raised the extra money from friends, but his quarrel with the studio continued. Warner Brothers wanted the movie to be no more than two and a half hours long; Lee insisted it should be just as long as Oliver Stone's film *JFK*. Lee also wanted South Africa's Nelson Mandela for the epilogue; Warner Brothers did not. Lee went public with his battle, accusing Warner Brothers of racism, and he won both points. But he had more battles to fight after the film was released. Some white reviewers accused him of using the film as propaganda, and some black reviewers said he was too bourgeois to be able to do justice to activist Malcolm X. However, most reviewers were impressed, and they said so.

A very powerful movie, *Malcolm X* confirmed the talent and resourcefulness that Lee had shown in his previous films. Clearly, here is a filmmaker who ranks among the top in the world. Without compromising his ideals, he has made a series of blockbuster films—on his own terms and in his own way—and has achieved his aim of giving African American themes universal appeal. As he says, "You can take an unknown, all-black cast and put them in a story that comes from a black experience, and all kinds of people will come to see it if it's a good film."

Carl Lewis

Olympic athlete
Born July 1, 1961, Birmingham, Alabama

"I always had an idea of where I wanted to go, and I felt that there had to be people with the same idea. I was lucky to find them."

For most of the 1980s, no one could outrun or outjump Carl Lewis. He was the number one ranked 100- and 200-meter sprinter and long jumper in the world. Arguably his greatest moment occurred during the 1984 Olympic Games in Los Angeles, California, when he won four gold medals. His success on the track has enhanced his financial success. Numerous commercial endorsements, personal appearances, and prizes from meets have made him a millionaire.

Parents form track club

Lewis is the son of Bill and Evelyn Lewis. Athletics were in his genes since his father ran track and starred in football at Tuskegee Institute and his mother represented the United States as a hurdler in the 1951 Pan-American Games. The Lewises moved to the middle-class Philadelphia suburb of Willingboro, New Jersey, where they became teachers and eventually established the Willingboro Track Club. Carl Lewis started running for his parents' track club when he was eight, but was not a standout. "I didn't mature until high school," he told *Inside Sports*. "While others began maturing in the seventh, eighth grade. There

Carl Lewis

was talent there all the time, but it was only when I got older that I really blossomed."

At age twelve Lewis won the long jump at a Jesse Owens Youth Program meet in Philadelphia with a leap of 17 feet 6 inches. Owens, a former Olympic hero, told the other participants to "take a lesson" from "this spunky little guy." Shortly before his junior year at Willingboro High School, Lewis had a growth spurt and his skills greatly improved. While at the 1978 national junior championships in Memphis, Tennessee, he ran the 100 yard in 9.3 seconds and set a national high-school record with a long jump of 25 feet 9 inches. As a high school senior, he was an All-American in the 200 meter and the long jump. By the time he finished high school he was the number-one-ranked high school track athlete in the country.

In 1979 Lewis accepted an athletic scholarship from the University of Houston and there met Tom Tellez, an expert in applying the laws of physics and kinesiology to track and field. He immediately noticed several flaws in Lewis's long-jump style—Lewis was inconsistent in his approach, causing his last four strides to be too long. Besides minimizing his distance, it placed undue stress on his knee, causing it to swell. Tellez told him to increase his approach run from under 150 feet, the conventional distance, to more than 170, a distance he covers in precisely twenty-three strides, building to a momentum of twenty-seven miles per hour.

Americans boycott Olympics

Lewis was set to participate in the 1980 Olympics when the U.S. led a boycott against the games in response to the Soviet Union's invasion of Afghanistan. The following year Lewis participated in the National Collegiate Athletic Association indoor championships, finishing first in the 100 meter with a time of 9.99 seconds (just .04 seconds behind Jim Hines's world record) and first in the long jump with a leap of 27 feet $^3/_4$ inches. This was the first time in the seventeen-year history of the meet that someone had ever won two track and field events. Lewis repeated his performance at the U.S. outdoor track and field championships in Sacramento, California. Later that year he was presented with the Sullivan Award from the Amateur Athletic Union as the best amateur athlete.

In 1982 Lewis achieved his third major double at the national outdoor championships in Knoxville, Tennessee. In the 100 meter he made his typical, calculated slow start, trailing the field for the first fifty meters before accelerating for the win. "The reason I'm so powerful the last forty or fifty meters," he told a reporter, "is because I can relax very well and when you relax you don't decelerate as much. Everybody decelerates from about sixty meters to the finish line—everybody! But the one who decelerates the least has the strongest finish."

Lewis was disqualified from collegiate competition for academic reasons during the 1981–82 season and competed under the auspices of the Santa Monica (California) Track Club. In 1983 he made his most memorable performance to date at the Athletics Congress (TAC) outdoor championships in Indianapolis. Besides registering 28 feet $10^1/_4$ inches, the world's best mark at low altitude in the long jump, he won the 100 meter in 10.27 seconds and the 200 in 19.75.

In August 1983, Lewis won three gold medals (100 meter, long jump, and 400-meter relay) at the world championships in Helsinki, Finland. In anticipation of the 1984 Olympics, Lewis wrote, in collaboration with composer Narada Michael Walden, the song "Going for the Gold," which he sang on a recording released shortly before the games. He lived up to this advance billing by winning gold in the 100 meter, long jump, and 200 meter, and anchored the U.S. 4 x 100 meter relay team. His accomplishments were tarnished since the Soviet Union and several of its allies withdrew from the games in retaliation for the U.S. boycott in 1980.

Gold in South Korea

After the Olympics, Lewis continued to compete in events across Europe and North

America. The Dallas Cowboys drafted him in the twelfth round of the 1984 National Football League draft and the Chicago Bulls hold the National Basketball Association's rights to him, but he was not interested in either sport. He set his sites on the 1988 Olympics in Seoul, South Korea, and went home with two golds and a silver. He won the 100 meter in a U.S. record time of 9.92 and the long jump with a jump of 28 feet and $7^1/_2$ inches. He lost the 200 meter to his training partner, Joe DeLoach, and the U.S. 4 x 100 meter relay team failed to qualify since Lewis sat out on the first round of heats and the American team bobbled the last exchange.

Lewis decided to continue training for the 1992 Olympics in Barcelona, Spain, but his performances began to deteriorate. During the U.S. track and field trials in New Orleans in 1992, Lewis failed to qualify for the Olympic team, both in the 100- and 200-meter sprints. Although he was the world record holder in the 100 meter, he only managed a sixth place finish and was named to the 4 x 100 meter relay team only as an alternate. He qualified for the long-jump competition after finishing second to Mike Powell. Few predicted him to do well, but he proved his detractors wrong. He reached 28 feet $5^1/_2$ inches to win the long jump, and when Mark Witherspoon went down with a ruptured Achilles tendon, Lewis anchored the relay team to a gold medal.

As Lewis's athletic career winds down, he is casting his sights toward a political career. He has even gone so far as to meet with local political consultants and fund raisers to explore a run for office. He has expressed an interest in seeking the mayor's chair in Houston. "I am extremely interested in the political scene of today and what's going on," Lewis told the *New York Times Magazine*. "I've been through a lot of the things that politicians have to go through in a political life, and I've weathered those storms."

Elma Lewis

Educator
Born September 15, 1921, Boston, Massachusetts

"Our goal is to develop good human beings, human beings who can hold their heads up high and be proud of being black; if in the process we develop good artists, that's all right too."

As a dancer, actress, choreographer, and teacher, Elma Lewis has been a lifelong promoter of Afro-American culture, and especially Afro-American artists. "I believe in Black artists rather than Black art," she says. In 1968 Lewis founded the National Center of Afro-American Artists, which the *New York Times* called "the nearest thing there is to a national center for Black culture in the United States." Eighteen years earlier she had founded the Elma Lewis School of Fine Arts.

Over the years Lewis has trained thousands of young people in dance, drama, and singing. She has also been a major force in cultural affairs—active on various arts councils and boards, a member of the American Academy of Arts and Sciences, and a consultant to the National Educational Association and other influential organizations. In 1977 she was invited to be a member of the board for the second World Festival of Black Arts, held in Nigeria.

Acquired solid professional background

Elma Ina Lewis was the only child of Edwardine (Jordan) Lewis and Clairmont Lewis, both of whom had come to the United States from Barbados. She grew up with two half brothers from her mother's first marriage, one of whom taught her to read when she was only three. That same year her father taught her a poem, which she recited at a meeting of Marcus Garvey's Universal Negro Improvement Association.

Lewis's parents were devoted followers of Marcus Garvey, the black nationalist from Jamaica who gained reknown in the early years of this century. All members of the family regularly attended the Garvey meetings in Boston, and both of Lewis's brothers were newsboys for the Garvey paper. "I really believe that being in the Garvey Movement gave me a sense of self," Lewis has said.

While attending public school in Boston, Lewis studied dance, voice, and piano and began to appear on the stage as a child actress and dancer. By the age of eleven she was earning $50 a week—a large sum in those days. When Lewis was fourteen she began to give dancing lessons at the Doris W. Jones School of Dance in Boston, and she later also gave elocution lessons. Since she was still a high school student, the teaching had to be fitted in after school and on weekends. Nevertheless, Lewis's schoolwork did not suffer,

and on graduating in 1939 she won a place at Emerson College, Boston.

Lewis paid her own way through college, for she continued to teach and perform. She would have liked to train as an actress, but black actresses were seldom given starring roles, and she had no desire to spend her life performing the part of a maid or slave. She therefore decided to concentrate on teaching, and after earning her bachelor's degree in 1943 she enrolled at Boston University School of Education. She graduated with a master's degree in 1944. During the next few years Lewis had a variety of teaching positions which ranged from speech therapist at the Massachusetts Mental Health Clinic to fine arts instructor at Harriet Tubman House, a social service agency in Boston's South End. From 1946 to 1948 she worked at the Robert Gould Shaw House, another social service agency, where she served as the director and choreographer for the twenty-one operas that were performed during her tenure.

Founded schools, prison programs, museums

In 1950 Lewis gathered together her savings, borrowed $300 from her father, rented a six-room apartment and a second-hand piano, and opened the Elma Lewis School of Fine Arts in the Roxbury district of Boston. The school offered "quality education in the arts to children in the neighborhood" and gave instruction in dancing and drama.

When the school started it had 4 teachers and 25 students. Over the years, as Lewis moved to new and larger quarters, the number of students increased, and by 1969 there were

250. By the early 1990s the number had risen to 350 and the curriculum had been greatly expanded. Today students can study ballet, primitive dance, African drumming, jazz, classical music, art, and a wide selection of drama (ranging from the plays of William Shakespeare to those of the African American playwright Langston Hughes). There are also social events and a Christmas pageant, *Black Nativity,* which is staged each year.

From the first, Lewis charged very small fees, and even these were reduced for students who could not afford them. The school was run partly on Lewis's own fundraising efforts and partly through the efforts of the parents, who organized bake sales and other activities to help support the enterprise. Classes were scheduled in the afternoons and evenings so that children could attend after their regular schooling. Although little advertising was done, there was always a long waiting list for places.

Since 1968 the Elma Lewis School of Fine Arts has been part of the National Center of Afro-American Artists, which Lewis founded that year. Along with the school, the center contains a museum and archives, and a theater that stages ballets, jazz performances, classical concerts, experimental plays, and numerous other shows. A reporter for the *Boston Globe* described the center as a major landmark: "In terms of developing tangible Black art, exposing a community to the arts, and stimulating involvement, I can't think of any other institution like this."

Lewis regarded the center in even broader terms: "We expose the srtudents to all of the art disciplines, and if they want to specialize they can do this and become professionals. But I like to think that the Center, most importantly, is a process during which the child, that most marvelous of human beings, not only learns cultural pride, but learns too how to deal with the world."

It was not only children whom Lewis helped "deal with the world." As an offshoot of her cultural activities she organized the Technical Theater Training Program for inmates at the Massachusetts Correctional Institution. Begun in 1970, the program trained inmates for careers as stage managers, sound men, and electricians, and it gave drama courses that involved staging shows in the prison. Lewis also provided programs that offered the inmates courses in writing, art, music, and African drumming.

Lewis has received many honors over the years, including twenty-six honorary degrees, but her greatest pride is the National Center of

Elma Lewis

Afro-American Artists—a living monument to black achievement in the arts. The center has been supported by generous grants from such bodies as the Ford Foundation and the National Endowment for the Arts, but the most important element has been Lewis herself, who conceived the idea in the first place and then energetically brought it into being. She sees the center as a place where "the creative energies of the nation's Black population will be nurtured and preserved for posterity," a place that is "worthy to be called a world institute."

Little Richard

Singer, songwriter
Born December 5, 1932, Macon, Georgia

"We decided that my image should be crazy and way-out so that the adults would think I was harmless. I'd appear in one show dressed as the Queen of England and in the next as the Pope."

After years of trying to reach music stardom, Little Richard almost stumbled upon it with his 1956 hit, "Tutti Frutti." He quickly followed it with a string of hits including "Long Tall Sally," "Rip It Up," "Keep A Knockin'," and "Good Golly Miss Molly." Then suddenly, during a tour of Australia in 1957, Richard turned his back on rock and roll to become a minister. Over the years he mounted several comebacks and now spends him time preaching against drugs and sex.

Showman and prankster

Richard was born Richard Wayne Penniman in Macon, Georgia, on December 5, 1932. His father, Bud Penniman, was a stonemason and a moonshine liquor dealer, and his mother was Leva Mae Penniman. Richard was born with a disproportionately shaped head, one eye larger than the other, and his left limbs were longer than his right. His disabilities made him walk with a twist, giving him a feminine quality. At times, he was called faggot, sissy, and freak. The name-calling eventually drove him down the path to homosexuality. Richard's mother described him in *The Life and Times of Little Richard* as "the most trouble of any" of her thirteen children. Others described him as a showman, a prankster, and having a strong mind and will.

Richard regularly attended the New Hope Baptist Church in Macon with his mother, but he preferred going to the Pentecostal Church because of the music. He also enjoyed the Holiness Church, where he mimicked the talking in tongues. By the age of ten, Richard considered himself a healer, and he would sing sacred songs while laying hands on the sick.

His interest in religion made him consider a church career. That changed when he became a freshman at Hudson High School in Macon and learned to play the alto saxophone with the school band. At home Richard gradually learned to play the piano, but it was his singing that most people noticed. He first sang in public as a member of the Tiny Tots, a juvenile gospel group at the New Hope Baptist Church. Richard and his siblings formed a group called the Penniman Singers. They traveled to other churches and revival meetings. His first performance before a large audience was at the Macon City Auditorium.

At fourteen, Richard left home and traveled across Georgia with a number of bands including Dr. Hudson's Medicine Show; B. Brown and His Orchestra, which billed him for the first time as Little Richard; and Sugarfoot Sam from Alabam. He learned many tricks of the trade along the way and developed his own trademarks, including his famous towering, processed pompadour, mascaraed eyes, and pancake makeup. Richard also met and was influenced by musicians such as B.B. King, Jimmy Witherspoon, and Billy Wright.

Records with RCA

It was Wright who put Richard in touch with Zenas Sears, a young disc jockey at WGST-Radio in Atlanta, which specialized in rhythm and blues. WGST was among the local stations that RCA Records were using as recording stations. Sears was vital in getting Richard a recording contract with RCA. Backed by Wright's session men, he recorded "Every Hour," which became a minor regional hit, and three other songs.

Richard returned home to perform one-night stands with Percy Welch and his orchestra. In January 1952, he had his second recording session for RCA and produced four songs that were poorly received.

A few weeks later, his father was shot dead, and Richard was forced to provide for the family. With RCA no longer interested, Richard took a dish-washing job. Clint Branley, a Macon talent promoter, decided to

Little Richard

back Richard. He formed a gospel-oriented band, the Tempo Toppers, which sang throughout the South and recorded under the Peacock label. This album was also poorly received.

Richard eventually left the group and went solo for a few months. He recruited drummer Charles Connors and pianist-saxophone player Wilbert Smith to form the rhythm-and-blues combination that finally sent him over the top. Richard added two more musicians and called the group, the Upsetters. In 1954 Richard met Lloyd Price, a singer who had signed with Specialty Records, a small, independent black label in Los Angeles. At Price's suggestion, Richard sent a recording to Bumps Blackwell, who was in charge of musical policy and production. Blackwell persuaded Art Rupe, the owner of Specialty, to call Richard for a recording session in their Atlanta studio.

Richard recorded several songs, but it was not quite the sound Blackwell was looking for. "I heard that Richard's stage act was really wild, but in the studio that day he was really inhibited," Blackwell once said. At lunch, they headed to a nearby club, where Richard went over to the piano and started playing "Tutti Frutti." Blackwell knew then he had a hit on his hands. "Tutti Frutti" sold more than 200,000 copies within a month. It soared to number two on Billboard's R&B chart and to twenty-one on its Hot 100 chart. Richard followed this success with "Long Tall Sally," a song that hit number one on the R&B charts and, along with its flip side, "Slippin' and Slidin'," made the national top twenty charts.

When his records went gold, Richard moved to Hollywood and bought all the trappings of success—expensive sequined and silk clothing in loud colors, a mansion, and a Fleetwood Cadillac. In 1956 his song, "Rip It Up," and its flip side, "Ready Teddy," were number one across the charts. Later that year "Heebie-Jeebies" and "She's Got It" were number fifteen on the Billboard's R&B chart. His songs were also featured on several movies including *Mr. Rock and Roll* and *The Girl Can't Help It.*

Abruptly quits rock and roll

Richard was at the height of his popularity in 1957, when he abruptly renounced rock and roll in the middle of an Australian tour. He returned to the United States to become a minister in the Seventh Day Adventist Church. He also recorded sacred music on the Mercury, End, and Goldisc labels.

In 1962 he was approached by Don Arden to tour Great Britain, singing gospel songs. After Richard accepted, Arden placed ads stating Richard would perform his old hits. His first gospel performance disappointed and puzzled his audience. In his second performance, Arden pleaded with him to sing his old hits. After watching Sam Cooke ignite the audience before his performance, Richard tore into "Long Tall Sally," and the concert was a smash. He followed it with two more British tours.

After returning to the U.S. in 1964, Richard recorded "Bama Lama Bama Loo," which barely made the charts, but recaptured his old energy. He worked his way out of small clubs and into better venues in Las Vegas and Los Angeles. He made a steady stream of recordings during the 1970s that made the charts. "The kids brought me back," he told an interviewer. "They heard the Beatles talk about me, the Stones talk about me, Tom Jones talk about me. They wanted to hear for themselves."

In the mid-1970s, Richard became addicted to drugs and alcohol. After his brother Tony died, Richard retreated from show business and lived with his mother in Riverside, California. He eventually kicked his drug and alcohol problems, and in 1977 he went to work for a Bible company, singing and promoting the annotated *Black Heritage Bible* at churches and religious conventions.

Today Richard is a devout member of the Universal Remnant Church of God, which teaches strict adherence to the Ten Commandments. "I have rejected homosexuality. I have rejected sex. Now I get my thrills from the ministry," he once said. "When I meet people who have changed through my presentation of God's words, that makes me feel good."

Joe Louis

World heavyweight boxing champion
Born May 13, 1914, Lafayette, Alabama
Died April 12, 1981

"He can run but he can't hide."

W hile he may have been slow of foot, Joe Louis's exceedingly fast hands more than compensated. His left jab was an awesome weapon, but it was his straight right that most opponents feared. Louis won the world heavyweight boxing crown in 1937 and successfully defended it for twelve years. He faced all challengers and fought the best the world had to offer, defending his title a record twenty-five times. Throughout his reign, people cheered him as their champion, and radios echoed his victories throughout the streets of America. When Louis passed away in 1981, he was mourned and eulogized as few sports heroes before him.

Hauling ice builds muscles

Joseph Louis Barrow was born in Lafayette, Alabama, to Munn Barrow, a sharecropper, and Lilly Reese. They lived in a one-room hut in the cotton fields, and Reese would frequently take in laundry to make ends meet. When Louis was four his father died, and three years later his mother remarried to Patrick Brooks. Looking for a brighter future, the family moved to Detroit, Michigan, but jobs were scarce. Louis sold papers, shined shoes, and ran errands to help pay the bills. Eventually he became an assistant to an ice-wagon driver, and toting the huge blocks of ice helped him develop big shoulder muscles.

At age sixteen, Louis decided to become a sparring partner in a gymnasium. He picked up a few pointers and decided to try his luck in the ring. In his first match he was floored six times in three rounds. His next three matches were a different story—he won each by a knockout and became popular with the public. Louis appeared at a tournament in Boston, where he was thoroughly beaten by ex-football star Max Marek and outpointed by Bob Evans. Shortly afterwards he accepted a full-time job at the Ford automotive plant, but continued boxing until in 1934, he won the National A.A.U. light-heavyweight title in St. Louis.

Three months later he took the plunge into the professional ring, changing his name to Joseph Louis. His trainer, Jack Blackburn, felt he had potential, and after eight victories, Louis became known as the Brown Bomber of Detroit. He received national attention after knocking out Stanley Poreda and Lee Ramage. After James Johnson of Madison Square Gardens turned down the opportunity to promote the Brown Bomber, Louis turned to Mike Jacobs, a little-known promoter from the Bronx.

On June 25, 1935, Louis appeared for the first time before New York fans and was an immediate success, knocking out Primo Carnera. Fans were so impressed that they clamored for a match between him and Max Baer, who had lost the heavyweight championship only a few weeks before. The Baer-Louis bout took place later that year on September 24, and Louis never looked better. He pounded Baer for four rounds before the

Joe Louis

former champion was finally knocked out. By the end of the year Louis had appeared in fourteen bouts and earned an incredible $368,000.

First professional loss

Louis suffered his first professional defeat against Max Schmeling on June 19, 1936. Schmeling told reporters after the fight that he noticed Louis had a habit of lowering his left shoulder and arm, leaving his chin open for a right-hand counter punch. Although Schmeling was promised a title bout with heavyweight champion James Braddock, promoter Jacobs wanted Louis to get the chance. While Jacobs was stalling Schmeling, Louis was on the comeback trail, knocking out Jack Sharkey, Eddie Sims and Bobby Pastor. Braddock agreed to meet Louis on June 22, 1937, in Chicago, Illinois. By the eighth round, Braddock was lying on the ground, and Louis was the new champion.

The rematch between Schmeling and Louis was slated for June 22, 1938, in New York. This was the time when Adolf Hitler ruled Germany, and Hitler proudly proclaimed that Schmeling was one of his master race of supermen. Schmeling was a follower of Hitler and made disparaging remarks about Americans, and blacks in particular. When the fight was finally staged, Louis was in a rage. He hammered Schmeling with terrific head and body punches. After two minutes and four seconds, Schmeling was rushed to a local hospital, and eventually left for Germany. The bout set a record for turning back a challenger in a heavyweight title bout. It was also the first million-dollar gate Louis attracted in his career.

Louis ruled the boxing world for the next decade. Tony Galento knocked him down briefly before losing in 1939; Arturo Godoy's crouching nose-to-the-floor technique took Louis to the full fifteen rounds in 1940; and Buddy Baer (Max's brother) knocked Louis out of the ring for a nine-count in 1941 before succumbing.

Beginning in December 1940, Louis began what became known as the "bum of the month" campaign. He met challengers at a rate of one a month, a performance that no other heavyweight champion ever attempted. The closest he came to losing his title was on June 18, 1941, to Billy Conn of Pittsburg, Pennsylvania. Many analysts thought Conn would be able to outbox Louis and would be too speedy for him. The champion responded with his famous line: "He can run but he can't hide."

Conn held the upper hand during the first twelve rounds, but he changed his tactics in the thirteenth and tried to slug it out with

Louis. The move cost him—Louis knocked him down with two seconds left in the round. In the next few months Louis defeated Lou Nova, Buddy Baer, and Abe Simon. Shortly after defeating Simon, Louis joined the army; he traveled more than twenty-one thousand miles and staged ninety-six boxing exhibitions before two million soldiers.

Louis was discharged from the army on October 1, 1945, and soon agreed to defend his title against Conn. He knocked Conn out in the eighth round at Yankee Stadium on June 19, 1946. Louis successfully defended his title three more times—against Tami Mauriello and twice against Jersey Joe Walcott. On March 1, 1949, Louis offically retired.

Comeback bid fails

Louis later tried a comeback, but failed to regain his championship form. Ezzard Charles outpointed him in fifteen rounds at Yankee Stadium on Sept. 27, 1950. The end came on Oct. 26, 1951, when Rocky Marciano knocked him out in the eighth round. Although he had received a lot of money during his boxing days, Louis had little left when he retired. The government fined him $1.25 million in delinquent income taxes. Louis found the amount staggering. "I liked the good life," he once said. "I just don't know where the money went. I wish I did. I get 50 per cent of each purse and all kinds of expenses came out of my cut." By the mid-1960s the government and Louis managed to work out an agreement for him to pay his back taxes. In 1965, Dana Latham, the commissioner of the Internal Revenue Service, informed the U.S. Congress: "We have gotten all we could possibly get from Mr. Louis, leaving him with some hope that he can live. His earning days are over."

Louis turned to a variety of careers, including wrestling and commercial promotions. In 1969 he and Billy Conn set up the Joe Louis Food Franchise Corporation in the hopes of operating an inter-racial chain of food stores. Later that year he collapsed on a lower Manhattan Street and was rushed to the hospital for what was termed "a physical breakdown." In 1970 he spent five months at the Colorado Psychiatric Hospital and the Veterans Administration Hospital in Denver. His wife, Martha, and son, Joe Louis, Jr., said he suffered from paranoia. While institutionalized he missed a tribute to him in Detroit, which more than eight thousand people attended.

Louis held a job as a "greeter" at Caesar's Palace in Las Vegas, Nevada, but took time off in 1974 to referee the heavyweight fight between Joe Frazier and Jerry Quarry. He proclaimed Frazier the winner after the fifth round because of heavy cuts on Quarry's face. Louis was confined to a wheelchair in 1977 following surgery to correct an aortic aneurysm. In 1980 he received an electronic pacemaker. He passed away on April 12, 1981.

Louis was more than a boxing champion. He played a strong role in the black movement by providing inspiration to a generation of youngsters and to the later generations to whom he had become a legend. In 1993, fifty-five years after Louis's smashing defeat of Schmeling, a U.S. postage stamp was issued commemorating the event and the boxer. *Ebony* paid tribute to him in a 1970 article: "When Joe Louis fought, blacks in ghettos across the land were indoors glued to their radios, and when Louis won, as he nearly always did, they hit the streets whooping and hollering in celebration. For Joe's victory was their victory, a means of striking back at an oppressive and hateful environment. Louis was the black Atlas on whose broad shoulders blacks were lifted, for in those days, there were few authentic black heroes."

Louverture, Toussaint

See **Toussaint-Louverture**

Joseph E. Lowery

Clergyman and civil rights leader
Born October 6, 1924, Huntsville, Alabama

"We are still engaged in the struggle to replace violence and poverty with a system that will assure the dignity of every person."

Clergyman and president of the Southern Christian Leadership Conference, Joseph E. Lowery continues the work started by legendary civil rights leader Martin Luther King, Jr. King was the SCLC's first president, Lowery his vice-president. King frequently turned to Lowery for guidance and assistance.

Since becoming SCLC president in 1977, Lowery has fought for economic justice and human rights. The group has broadened its activities to keep pace with the new problems being faced by black Americans and to pre-vent erosion of the civil rights already attained. Also committed to the pulpit, Lowery has pastored the 2,500 member Cascade Church in Atlanta, Georgia, since 1986.

Active in Montgomery bus boycott

Lowery was born on October 6, 1924, in Huntsville, Alabama. The son of a mortician, he attended Knoxville College, Alabama A&M College, Paine College and Paine Theological Seminary, Garrett Theological Seminary, and Chicago Ecumenical Institute, and was ordained to the ministry of United Methodist (UM) church in 1952. He served as pastor to the Warren Street Church in Mobile, Alabama, then worked as administrative assistant to UM Bishop Golden for three years. From his pulpit he campaigned vigorously against racial injustice.

In 1955 he took an interest in the attention over Rosa Parks, a black woman who refused to yield her seat on a segregated bus. Lowery joined other blacks who decided to boycott the buses and helped Parks as she took her case to the U.S. Supreme Court. Lowery was a member of the boycott group, which was initially called the Southern Negro Leaders Conference. They underwent several name changes, including the Southern Leadership Conference, before they settled on the Southern Christian Leadership Conference. The SCLC was founded in 1957, with Dr. Martin Luther King elected president and Lowery vice-president. The SCLC wanted to work as a regional organization that would work for civil rights through the black churches in the South.

The success of the boycott created celebrities of some of the SCLC leaders, most notably King. There was some jealousy about how the press seemed to focus exclusively on King and none of the other leaders. Lowery was in his twenties at the time and was known for being soft-spoken.

In 1959 Lowery and three other staffers were sued for libel by the commissioners of Montgomery, Alabama, because their names appeared on an ad run in the *New York Times* that was trying to raise money for a King defense fund. King had been arrested on charges of perjury for swearing falsely to the accuracy of his 1956 and 1958 Alabama tax returns. King held Lowery in high regard and often sought his advice. Besides assisting with the SCLC, Lowery continued his work in the pulpit.

From 1964 to 1968 Lowery was pastor of St. Paul's Church in Birmingham, Alabama. He then moved to Atlanta, Georgia, where he served for eighteen years as pastor of Central Church, the city's oldest and largest predominantly black UM church. Under his leadership, 2,000 people joined the church, and he managed to implement his vision of economic justice by building Central Methodist Gardens, a 240-unit housing complex for low-income earners. Since 1986 Lowery had been pastor of Cascade Church in Atlanta.

Became SCLC president

Lowery succeeded Reverend Ralph David Abernathy in 1977 as SCLC president. He received international coverage when he led a ten-member delegation from SCLC on a fact-finding mission to the Middle East in 1979. His delegation was sent over after a meeting was held between U.S. Ambassador Andrew Young

Joseph E. Lowery

and a member of the Palestine Liberation Organization (PLO). A meeting of this type was against U.S. policy, and Young was forced to resign. This began a fight between black and Jewish leaders. On his trip Lowery met with PLO leaders, and in retaliation Israeli leaders refused to meet with him. He received massive news coverage because of the trip.

Lowery was a key organizer for a march on August 27, 1988, that commemorated the twenty-fifth anniversary of the historic March on Washington. The themes of the gathering were a tribute to King and his memorable "I Have a Dream" speech, as well as protest against the civil rights policies of the Reagan administration. Lowery told the crowd: "We fought too long, we prayed too hard, we wept too bitterly, we bled too profusely, we died too young to let anybody ever turn back the clock on racial justice. We ain't going back."

Lowery has repeated these lines several times as the federal government has cut back on many programs that were gained by the civil rights movement. On August 26, 1989, he helped the National Association for the Advancement of Colored People stage a reenactment of their famous "Silent March" of 1917 in Washington. The march took place down Fifth Avenue in New York to protest lynching and racial segregation. The 1989 march was designed to persuade Congress to reverse recent decisions of the U.S. Supreme Court that Lowery and others believed were weakening affirmative action and minority "set aside" programs. Lowery said he and those assembled were not ready to sit by and watch "the meager gains washed away by a flood of insidious insensitivity nor insidious individualism."

Lowery has campaigned for voting rights, fought the dumping of toxic wastes in black areas, met political leaders, and addressed the economic needs of young blacks. In all of these activities he has stayed close to the original vision he shared with King. He sees the role of the minister as an advocate, interpreter, and servant. He regards human rights not as add-ons to the ministry, but as a commitment to the kingdom of justice, equality, and peace.

Picked new issues for the 1990s

After thirty years in the civil rights movement, Lowery sees no reason to slow down. He says that today's problems are different and more complex than those faced in the 1960s. Many are wondering whether civil rights organizations, which contributed so much to black liberation in the past, must change their traditional agendas to bring about nonviolent social reform. To meet this aim,

Lowery and other SCLC leaders have campaigned against drugs, poverty, and violence. In an interview with *Ebony* magazine, Lowery commented: "We believe that much of our problem is that we are worshipping the material over the spiritual. That is why we are killing each other and that is why people are expendable, as long as the goal is money."

The SCLC has been involved with many wide-ranging programs since Lowery became president, including Operation Breadbasket, a joint venture with Shoney's Inc. that will raise $90 million for black colleges, restaurants, and hotels; a march from Selma to Washington, D.C., to publicize the renewal of the Voting Rights Act of 1982; and to fight for the rights of Haitians seeking asylum in the United states but jailed by the American government.

Lowery believes that programs such as these keep the SCLC as relevant as it ever was and will help African Americans with their sense of self-worth and determination of their own future.

Naomi Long Madgett

Poet, educator, publisher
Born July 5, 1923, Norfolk, Virginia

"I would rather be a good poet than anything else I can imagine."

S ince Naomi Long Madgett first started writing more than fifty years ago, she has had seven poetry books published and her poems have been included in more than eighty anthologies as well as in numerous newspa-

Naomi Long Madgett

pers and magazines. She has also made her mark as a public school teacher and university professor, and in 1974 became publisher and editor of the Lotus Press in Detroit.

Much of Madgett's poetry has a lyrical quality, reminiscent of the classic English poets, though her subject matter draws on her own experience and on African American themes. She once said, "I discovered Alfred Lord Tennyson and Langston Hughes about the same time ... and I think my poetry represents something of the variety of interest and style that these two widely divergent poets represent."

The young poet

Madgett was born Naomi Cornelia Long, the daughter of Clarence and Maude (Hilton) Long. Encouraged by her parents, she was an avid reader from a very young age. She can remember lying on the floor of her father's study when she was no more than seven or

eight, eagerly poring over poetry books. Her father was a Baptist minister, and as the minister's daughter she was often called on to recite poems she had learned. "I do not recall any time in my life when I was not involved in poetry," she later wrote.

Madgett lived in East Orange, New Jersey, until she was fourteen, when her father moved the family to St. Louis, Missouri. Here a whole new world was opened up to her. In East Orange she had studied at an integrated school, which largely ignored the black contribution, but at the all-black Sumner High School in St. Louis she learned about African American achievements and was encouraged to take pride in her heritage.

At Sumner, Madgett was also encouraged to continue with her writing. She had been composing poems almost as far back as she could remember, and in 1941 she collected a number of them together for her first book, *Songs to a Phantom Nightingale*. The book was published a few days after her graduation from Sumner.

Career and marriage

In the early 1940s, Madgett studied at Virginia State College, from which she graduated with a B.A. in 1945. She then started graduate studies at New York University, but left after one semester to marry Julian Witherspoon The couple settled down to married lif' Detroit, where Naomi found a job ? porter on *The Michigan Chronicle* riage ended soon after Madge' daughter Jill, was born in 1'

After taking a ye' baby, Madgett began

sentative at Michigan Bell Telephone Company, and she remained with the company until her marriage to William Madgett in 1954. Although this marriage, too, ended in divorce, she kept the name Madgett and continued to use it even after her marriage in 1972 to school principal Leonard Andrews.

In 1955, Madgett began teaching in the Detroit public schools while studying for a degree in education at Wayne State University. She received her M.Ed. in 1956, the same year that her second book of poetry, *One and the Many,* was published. This collection was more original than her first book, and it included a number of poems on African American themes. The most important poem in the book is "Refugee," which had been written more than ten years earlier and chosen by Langston Hughes and Arna Bontemps for their anthology, *The Poetry of the Negro: 1746–1949* (1949).

Madgett's next book, *Star by Star* (1965), contains the poem "Midway," originally written in 1959. This is probably Madgett's best-known poem, with its memorable lines:

> I've prayed and slaved and waited and
> I've sung my song.
> You've bled me and you've starved me
> but I've still grown strong.
> You've lashed me and you've treed me
> And you've everything but freed me
> But in time you'll know you need me
> and it won't be long.

These lines were much quoted at the height of the civil rights movement, for they expressed forcefully what many African Americans feeling.

Professor and publisher

While teaching school in Detroit, Madgett was appalled to discover that most black children knew almost nothing about their heritage, so in 1965 she began to give a course on African American literature—the first course on the subject ever given in the Detroit public schools. After taking the next year off to study as a Mott Fellow at Oakland University, Madgett continued with the course, making it a regular part of the school curriculum. It was largely because of this enthusiasm that in 1967 the Detroit English Club honored her as Distinguished Teacher of the Year.

In 1968, Madgett was appointed associate professor of English at Eastern Michigan University, a position she held until 1973 when she was promoted to professor. These were busy years for Madgett. As well as visiting Africa and bringing out another book of poetry, *Pink Ladies in the Afternoon* (1972), she and her husband, Leonard Andrews, took over the Lotus Press in 1974. Since then, Lotus Press has published more than sixty-five titles, including two more books of Madgett's poems, *Exits and Entrances* (1978) and *Phantom Nightingale: Juvenilia* (1981). The latter is a collection of poems written between 1934 and 1943, some of Madgett's earliest work.

Madgett retired from formal teaching at Eastern Michigan in 1984, becoming a professor emeritus, and in 1988 she published her seventh volume of poetry, *Octavia and Other Poems.* This book struck out in a new direction. In her earlier collections, Madgett had usually placed her Afro-American poems at the end, as if she considered them less important than the love poems and other lyrics on universal themes. By contrast, *Octavia* is strongly African American right from the start, consisting of three sections: a sequence of poems on Madgett's family history; a series of recent poems; and an appendix containing family pictures, biographies, and a family tree.

In 1993, Madgett was recognized by the Before Columbus Foundation with an American Book Award for literary excellence across "the entire spectrum of America's diverse and multicultural literary community." Madgett also became a senior editor at the Michigan State University Press, where she edits a new poetry series.

Like all poets, Madgett continues to write, for poetry is a central part of her life. She has passed on her talent to her daughter. "It pleases me tremendously," she has said, "that my social worker daughter is becoming a very good poet."

Malcolm X

Civil rights activist
Born May 19, 1925, Omaha, Nebraska
Died February 14, 1965, Harlem, New York

"I have sat at our Messenger's feet, hearing the truth from his own mouth, I have pledged on my knees to Allah to tell the white man about his crimes and the black man the true teachings of our Honorable Elijah Muhammad. I don't care if it costs my life."

"All negroes are angry, and I am the angriest of all," was a motto Malcolm X repeated time after time. He rebounded from a life of crime to become a powerful voice for right. As a member of the Lost-Found Nation of Islam and later with his own organization, Malcolm X attracted huge crowds. He spoke about the need for black unity, self-respect, and self-reliance. His militant stance caused both black and white Americans to fear him, and on February 14, 1965, he was shot by three men of his own race.

Experienced hate crimes to his family

Malcolm X was born Malcolm Little to Earl and Louise Little May 19, 1925, in Omaha, Nebraska. His father openly supported the views of Marcus Garvey, founder of the United Negro Improvement League, who believed blacks would never find peace in America and should return to Africa. In retaliation for Little's outspokenness, several white supremacists drove them from their home. They resettled in Milwaukee, Wisconsin, and eventually in Lansing, Michigan, where the Black Legion, a terrorist organization, burned the Littles' house in 1929. Two years later Earl was found on a streetcar track with his skull crushed and his body nearly cut in half. The police ruled it an accident, but the Littles believed he was killed by the Legion and placed on the tracks to look like an accident. After years of the turmoil Malcom X's mother was placed in a state mental hospital in 1937.

Malcolm X and his seven siblings were placed in foster homes and state institutions. Malcolm X proved to be a brilliant student and a class leader who dreamed of becoming a lawyer, but he dropped out of school after confiding his dream to a white teacher, who told him to be realistic and become a carpenter. Living in Boston with his half-sister, Ella, Malcom X began shining shoes at the Roseland State Ballroom. Not long after he became involved with a group of gamblers and thieves and was dealing bootleg liquor and illegal drugs. He soon moved to Harlem, New York, where, known as "Detroit Red," he ran a gambling operation, sold and used marijuana and cocaine, and hustled business for brothels. He returned to Boston and organized a burglary ring, which led to his imprisonment in 1946.

Began his turnaround in prison

In prison the other inmates called him "Satan" because he was so full of hate and anger. He began to read everything he could get his hands on and became interested in the philosophies of Elijah Muhammad. Leader of the Lost-Found Nation Islam, also known as the Black Muslims, Muhammad taught that whites were a "devil" race created to torment the black race. If blacks wanted to flourish, they would have to separate themselves culturally, economically, politically, and physically from whites.

Malcolm X improved his penmanship by copying out a dictionary and preached to prisoners about the Nation of Islam's theories about whites. The group that formed around Malcom X emphasized personal hygiene including cleanliness and perfect grooming, and forbade smoking, drinking, and eating pork.

When Malcolm X was paroled in 1952, he changed his last name from Little to X. He felt "Little" was the name given to him by slave owners and X would stand for his African tribe, the origin of which he would never know. Muhammad was so impressed with Malcolm X's intelligence and forceful personality that he ordained him a minister and gave him the position of assistant minister to Muslim Temple Number One in Detroit, Michigan. After studying under Muhammad, Malcolm X was sent to Philadelphia to establish a new congregation. He then served as leader of the Harlem mosque, but was frequently asked to start congregations across the country.

During the 1950s and 1960s, Malcolm X rallied the Nation of Islam from a small group of about 400 people to an organization with 10,000 official members and many other people who sympathized with the cause. His fiery, intense style made him the most effective and prominent preacher the Nation of Islam ever had. He was in constant demand at colleges, meetings of various organizations, and television and radio programs.

Broke away from Elijah Muhammad

Malcolm X spoke against what most people were used to hearing from black civil rights leaders. While Martin Luther King, Jr., was teaching blacks to fight racism with love, Malcolm X was telling them to understand their exploitation, to fight back when attacked, and to seize self-determination "by any means necessary." Malcolm X said blacks should use arms in self-defense against white hostility. With his militant style, he became feared not only by whites, but also by blacks. The media portrayed him as a dangerous outlaw.

As Malcolm X's popularity grew, other leaders of the Nation of Islam began to grow uneasy with his actions. Muhammad may have been looking for an excuse to get rid of him when Malcolm X described the assassination of President of John F. Kennedy as a case of "chickens coming home to roost" in a society that tolerated white violence against blacks. *Rolling Stone* magazine reported that many people believed Malcolm X had meant that the president deserved his fate, when he really "meant the country's climate of hate had killed the president." Muhammad suspended Malcolm X in December 1963 and prohibited him from speaking on behalf of the Nation of Islam for ninety days. Malcolm X believed he was being set up by jealous members of the Nation of Islam and that a member would eventually be convinced to assassinate him. On March 8, 1964, he broke from the Nation of Islam and formed two new groups—the Harlem-based Muslim Mosque Inc. and the multinational Organization of Afro-American Unity.

Murdered in front of his followers

Later that spring Malcolm X made a pilgrimage to the holy city of Mecca and stayed in the Middle East and Africa to study. He returned to the United States in 1964 a changed man. He converted to orthodox Islam and adopted a new name, El-Hajj Malik El-Shabazz. His new philosophy combined Islam with socialism, anticolonialism, and what eventually became known as black consciousness, a sense of pride in being black. He traded in his militant approach for a softer style and downplayed his menacing image. Admitting he had once been a racist, he claimed he no longer believed that

Malcolm X

whites are evil. Economics and not color was what kept blacks from succeeding. He also condemned separatism as counterproductive and expressed a willingness to work within the system to secure black rights.

For most of 1964 and early 1965 Malcolm X became increasingly critical of Muhammad and the Nation of Islam. He raised questions about finances, contacts with white supremacist organizations, and blasted Muhammad for being a fake, a racist, and a bigamist. Both sides began to dig in, and accusations were hurled back and forth. Malcolm X received countless death threats. On February 14, 1965, his house was firebombed, but his wife and four daughters were unharmed.

A week later, Malcolm X, his wife (pregnant with twin girls), and four daughters went to the Audubon Ballroom in Harlem, New York, to address several hundred of his followers. During the speech, three black men rushed up the center aisle and opened fire with a shotgun and two pistols. Malcom X was struck more than a dozen times and died a short time later while in surgery at a nearby hospital. The man with the shotgun was tackled by those in attendance, and the other two were apprehended a short time later. All three men had ties to the Nation of Islam, although one of them later claimed that he had been paid by someone else to kill Malcolm X. A jury found them guilty of murder, and they were sentenced to life in prison.

Inspiring a new generation of black Americans

Despite his death, Malcolm X has remained a powerful force in black America. His belief in black pride was admired by people from each end of the political spectrum. A renewed interest in his ideas has recently taken place through a film by Spike Lee. Malcolm X's likeness and slogans have begun showing up on clothes worn by black and white teenagers in major U.S. cities. After Lee began wearing a baseball cap featuring a large "X" on the front as a promotional tool, there was an explosion of interest in clothing and art bearing his image. Many rap musicians have also incorporated his words and messages into their songs.

Malcolm X gave blacks a sense that they had a right to feel anger and express the power of it, to challenge white domination, and to actively demand change. Not afraid to revise his ideas, he boldly admitted when he was wrong. But Malcom X never relented about the tenacious and pervasive restraints that years of racism had imposed on black Americans.

Annie Turnbo Malone

Beauty culture specialist
Born August 9, 1869, Metropolis, Illinois
Died May 10, 1957, Chicago, Illinois

"The significance of Malone as an entrepreneur, philanthropist, and founder of the first center for the study and teaching of beauty culture specifically related to African Americans ... is rarely mentioned in general black American histories."—Bettye Collier-Thomas

Annie Turnbo Malone, the beauty culturist who developed a successful hair straightener, was the first African American woman to become a millionaire. At the peak of her career in the 1920s, she was said to be worth $14 million, though her fortune was reduced to a few hundred thousand by the time she died.

One of the reasons for the loss of Malone's fortune was her incredible generosity. She gave away vast sums of money to almost every known charity. Black orphanages and universities received large grants from her each year, and at one point she was supporting two full-time students at every black land-grant college in the United States. She was the first major African American philanthropist.

Although Malone is less well known than her successful rival, Madame C. J. Walker, it was she who was the pioneer. She played a key role in experimenting with some of the processes that Walker later developed, and she formed the first African American center for teaching beauty culture.

Hair-straightening pioneer

Annie Minerva Turnbo was the tenth of the eleven children of Robert and Isabella Turnbo, both of whom died when she was very young. She was brought up mainly by an older sister in Peoria, Illinois, and it was there that she first became interested in hair texture.

Many of her neighbors straightened their curls with soap and heavy oils that were not good for the hair. Some used processes that harmed the hair follicles or burned the scalp. Malone decided to try and find something better, and during the 1890s she experimented with chemicals to create a substance that would straighten hair without harming it. By 1900, she had developed a selection of products: hair straighteners, hair growers, and hair oils, as well as ointments for treating scalp diseases. Her best-known product was called Wonderful Hair Grower. The pressing iron and comb is also said to have been developed and patented by her in 1900.

In 1902, Malone moved her business from Illinois to St. Louis, Missouri. With three assistants, she sold her products from door to door, attracting clients by offering free hair and scalp treatments. Her formulas sold so well that she began to expand her services throughout the country. By advertising in the major black newspapers and going on promotional tours, she soon gained a large clientele and hired hundreds of women as agents to sell the products. One of these women was Madame C. J. Walker, who established an office in Denver in 1906 and began to sell similar formulas in a similar way, with door-to-door agent-operators.

In an effort to protect herself from what she called "fraudulent imitations," Malone copyrighted her products and merchandising systems under the trade name Poro in 1906. Thus, although several other companies soon began to sell hair straighteners and complexion creams, the Poro Company retained a large share of the business.

Educator and philanthropist

In 1917, Malone established Poro College at Poro Corner in St. Louis. This was a sumptuous complex of buildings supplied with equipment and furnishings costing more than $1 million. The main building and its annex contained classrooms, barbershops, laboratories, an auditorium, a dining room, a cafeteria, an ice cream parlor, a bakery, a theater, and a roof garden. Here Malone taught her students how to use her products and how to present themselves well. She taught them such graces as how to walk, talk, and eat in the approved manner, as well as the specific details of how to apply the various oils and creams.

By 1926, the college had a staff of 125 people, and it claimed to have trained 75,000 Poro agents, who were selling Malone's products not only in the United States but throughout the Caribbean and in other parts of the world. However, the Poro empire was already beginning to crumble. One of the problems was that, as a successful and notoriously generous businesswoman, Malone was constantly being invited to African American conventions, church functions, and social gatherings. Organizations such as the National Association of Colored Women also sought her out. Since she gave her time as freely as her money, she was not in a position to concentrate on her business, and it had begun to suffer from poor management.

The chief manager and president of the company was her husband, Aaron Malone, whom she had married some years earlier. Her first marriage—to a Mr. Pope—had ended in divorce because of his interference in her business affairs, and there was much the same problem with Aaron Malone. In a messy divorce suit in 1927, Aaron claimed one-half of Poro's assets on the grounds that it was his business sense, not his wife's, that had made the company so successful. Although he did not win his case, the publicity surrounding the divorce did great harm to the Poro company's image.

During the 1930s, Annie Malone was faced with several more lawsuits, including one brought by a former employee who claimed the credit for Poro's success. This lawsuit proved so costly that Malone had to sell the St. Louis property. She moved the Poro business and college to Chicago, where she reestablished it on 44th Street in what came to be called the Poro Block. Meanwhile, her money troubles were on the increase, for she was being sued by the government for the excise tax she owed. In the 1920s, the federal government charged a 20 per cent tax on all ,cosmetics, and Malone often had not paid this sum. By 1943, she owed almost $100,000 in taxes, and in 1951 the government took control of Poro.

Annie Turnbo Malone

In the midst of all these problems, Malone's reputation as a philanthropist stood firm. People were overwhelmed by her generosity, which started with her employees. At the annual Christmas banquets, she gave diamond rings to five-year employees, gold awards to real estate investors, and numerous other gifts, including prizes for punctuality and regular attendance at work. Needless to say, these gifts cost the business a large amount of money each year.

Then there were her other charities, some of which received very large grants. To Howard University Medical School she gave more than $25,000, which was worth far more then than it is today. Up to that time, no African American had ever given such a large sum to a black college. In 1924, she gave a similar sum to the St. Louis Colored YWCA. Tuskegee Institute was another regular beneficiary of Malone's generosity, as were other colleges for African Americans.

Whether or not Annie Malone is remembered as a pioneer in African American hair products, nothing can obliterate the contribution she made by supporting so many colleges and charitable institutions. Thanks to her generosity, tens of thousands of young African Americans were given their first start in life; they were given the special care or education that set them on the path to a promising future.

Eugene A. Marino

Former archbishop
Born May 28, 1934, Biloxi, Missouri

"Once we put our trust in God when we didn't have a thing on earth. Now some of us have achievements. But we can't forget the God who brings us salvation."

When the Roman Catholic Church needed strong black leadership in the United States, they turned to Eugene A. Marino. In a fast-track career, Marino was the first African American to hold the number two post in a religious order, and after a brief spell as auxiliary bishop of Washington, he became the archbishop of Atlanta. As the highest ranking African American Catholic in the country, Marino was expected to be a role model for young African Americans considering a career in the church. Despite these high expectations, Marino's career came crashing down in 1990 when it was revealed that he had been secretly married two years earlier. He now lives with his wife and daughter in Georgia.

Deep religious roots

Marino was born on May 29, 1934, in Biloxi, Missouri, to Jesus and Irnen Marino. His mother was from Biloxi and his father, a baker, moved there from Puerto Rico. He was raised in a cultural and religious tradition that stemmed from the early French Catholic and Spanish settlers. Even during his childhood days he was attracted to the church. "I took in my faith like my mother's milk," he said in a *Time* interview. "Some of my earliest recollections are of my family kneeling around the bed praying to Mary, when I was too small even to be really a part of it."

Marino attended a segregated school and by his teen years he realized he wanted to be a Catholic priest. He was one of only a handful of blacks in a Diocesan seminary, and in 1962 he was ordained in the Josephite order of priests, which was founded in the nineteenth century to serve blacks. Although its leadership had always been white, Marino became its vicar-general (second-in-command), the first African American to hold such an office in any religious order.

Church officials in Rome began to notice him. In 1974 he was consecrated as a bishop and assigned as an auxiliary in Washington, D.C. In 1985 he was elected secretary of the American bishops' national conference, a sign that his colleagues held him in high regard.

The previous year, Marino had been one of the authors of a letter sent to the Pope by African American Roman Catholic bishops. The letter expressed concern about the lack of black leaders in the Church. In 1987 a Washington conference of 1,250 black Catholics repeated the plea that more blacks should run dioceses instead of being auxiliaries under white bishops. With only 12 of 400 U.S. bishops being black, Pope John Paul II decided to take action. On May 5, 1988, Marino was named to succeed Thomas A. Donnelan as head of the archdiocese of Atlanta, making him the first African American to become an archbishop.

"I would see my appointment as a great sign of hope to black Catholics in our country and to all people of good will," Marino was quoted in *Sojourners*. "It means that the church recognizes the wealth within its ranks, that it is a church of many significant minorities."

Most Catholics viewed Marino's appointment as an act of good faith by the Pope. Archbishop Pio Laghi, the Pope's personal representative, told *People* that he was impressed with the turnout of more than one hundred bishops at Marino's consecration. "That means the selection by the Holy Father ... is the right one."

A rising career falls

As the head of the Atlanta archdiocese, Marino presided over 156,000 Catholics, both in the city and in sixty-nine northern Georgia counties. He also became metropolitan of an ecclesiastical province, with influence over four other dioceses in three states. Marino placed an emphasis on pastoral rather than administrative duties. For example, during a trip to visit his new flock, he made a special effort in the midst of a hectic schedule to visit Our Lady of Perpetual Help Home, a nursing home for the free care of terminal cancer patients.

Marino appeared to be a perfect role model for young blacks interested in the

Eugene A. Marino

church, but in May 1990, Marino's career began a downward spiral. That month he suddenly went on leave for what spokesmen termed was cardiac stress and exhaustion. In July he became one of the few archbishops ever to resign, saying in *Time* he needed "spiritual renewal, psychological therapy and medical supervision." In early August, Atlanta's WAGA-TV reported that Marino and Vicki Long, a twenty-seven-year-old aspiring singer, were having an affair. The TV station stated that Marino and Long attended social functions together and that Marino had named her as beneficiary in a flight insurance policy. It was also reported that he helped her buy a house and paid her $1,500 a month in living expenses. The archdiocese later confirmed the reports and assured Catholics that Church money had not been used to aid Long, except for unspecified medical bills.

Two days after the reports, a second priest—Rev. Michael Woods, pastor of St.

Jude the Apostle in suburban Sandy Springs—confessed in an open letter to his parish that he too had an affair with Long. Through her attorney, Long denied any misconduct with Woods, who had served at her church in nearby Hapeville for more than a decade. She stated he was the godfather of her child and a close family friend, but she never had anything to do with him sexually.

In another twist to the case, Long's four-year-old daughter, LaDonna, figured in yet another of her alleged sexual relationships with priests. In 1987 Long filed a paternity suit against Reverend Donal Keohane, formerly of the diocese of Savannah, naming him as LaDonna's father. A court-ordered blood test in 1988 revealed that Keohane was not the father, but the church reportedly had promised to pay Long compensation.

Seclusion and divorce proceedings

Throughout the episode, Marino and Long were subjected to intense media scrutiny. Long said Marino seduced her when she went to see him for counselling. Their relationship eventually culminated in marriage on December 27, 1988, during a trip to New York City. The revelations to the media splintered their relationship, they both went into seclusion and divorce proceedings began. Some reports indicated that Marino, a recovered alcoholic, and Long attempted to commit suicide.

By early 1993, the two had decided to continue their relationship as husband and wife. "The divorce petition was dismissed," Long told *Jet*. "We agreed to reconcile our marriage and we are back together again."

Marino, Long, and LaDonna moved into a home somewhere in Georgia. To make the transition as easy as possible, they underwent therapy to put the past behind them. Long told *Jet* Marino would be a father figure for her daughter. "She knew Marino for two years. He was very much a father figure in her life ... she always cared a lot about him. We'll all be going to family therapy. She's at the age where she really misses a father figure. She knows we love her and we're going to do this as a family. Come what may, we'll get through it okay."

Branford Marsalis

Jazz saxophonist, composer
Born August 26, 1960, New Orleans,
  Louisiana

"Each record, I try to sound like a different influence because critics are so apt to pigeonhole you. With me, I don't want it to be so easy. I want them to grapple for a way to define me."

Since releasing his first solo album in 1984, Branford Marsalis has gathered thousands of fans with his superb performances on the saxaphone. He usually plays in a style known as "neoclassical" or "postbop" and is considered by many to be the greatest jazz saxophonist since John Coltrane.

Marsalis has made recordings with such jazz greats as trumpeters Dizzy Gillespie and Miles Davis, as well as with his brother Wynton Marsalis, another famed trumpeter. In

1985 he began recording with Sting, the British pop-rock star. Marsalis's other recordings include an album of classical music, which he made with the English Chamber Orchestra. He has also appeared in several films, and in 1990 he and his quartet played on the soundtrack of two movies: the smash-hit *Mo' Better Blues* and the spy film *The Russia House*.

Came from a musical family

The eldest of six boys, Branford Marsalis comes from a family of musicians. His father is Ellis Marsalis, the jazz pianist/educator who is coordinator of the jazz program at Virginia Commonwealth University in Richmond, Virginia. Marsalis's mother, Dolores (Ferdinand) Marsalis, was a jazz singer and teacher in her early years.

Branford began learning the piano when he was four years old, and at the age of seven he took up the clarinet so that he could play in the school band. At fifteen he began learning the alto saxophone. "I didn't want to play tenor," he said, "because everybody else was playing tenor." Although the alto sax is considered the most difficult saxophone, Marsalis mastered it quickly and performed so well that within six months he was chosen for the all-state band.

When Marsalis was a sixteen-year-old high school student, he and his brother Wynton formed a funk-rock band called the Creators. But it was too funky to be popular and had only a short life. On graduating from high school in 1978, Marsalis enrolled at Southern University in Baton Rouge, Louisiana, where he did so well in his music studies that one of his teachers suggested a transfer to the Berklee

School of Music in Boston. Marsalis studied at Berklee from 1979 to 1981.

When Marsalis started at Berklee, he had not yet set his mind on becoming a professional jazz player. It was Wynton's success that swung him round. Although Wynton was younger, he was already performing as a musician. He had joined a group called the Jazz Messengers, which came to play in Boston during summer 1980. "I was so proud, so happy," Marsalis said, recalling his brother's performance. "When I saw him, I got fired up and thought, 'Man, I want to do this, too.'" That summer and the following one, Marsalis toured with the Jazz Messengers, playing baritone saxophone, and in August 1981 he joined Wynton's newly formed quintet as a tenor saxophonist.

Talent recognized
with grammy awards

Marsalis performed with the quintet on Wynton's first album, which was released in 1982. During the next few years he played on three more of the Wynton's albums, as well as performing on *Keystone 3* (1983), a Jazz Messenger album that was nominated for a Grammy Award.

Although Marsalis was doing well, he was not happy. It seemed to him people thought he was a member of the group because he was Wynton's brother, not because he could play well. To establish a reputation of his own, he recorded the solo album *Scenes in the City* in 1984. The album featured Marsalis playing both tenor and soprano saxophone, and it contained three of his own compositions. That same year Marsalis formed a

Branford Marsalis

quartet with drummer Marvin Smith, bassist Charnett Moffett, and pianist Larry Willis.

During the three years Marsalis had played with Wynton's quintet he had from time to time recorded with other players, including trumpeter Miles Davis. But the big break from Wynton came in 1985 when Marsalis agreed to play on *The Dream of the Blue Turtles,* the first solo album of the British pop singer Sting. Marsalis's playing received rave reviews, and the album rose to number two on the pop charts, selling over a million copies. However, Wynton and other jazz purists disapproved of Marsalis's switch from jazz to pop-rock.

In the summer of 1985 Marsalis performed with Sting in the famous "Live Aid" concert organized for the relief of famine victims in Africa. He then went on an eight-month tour with Sting, in which the band played throughout the world, attracting huge audiences. This was very different from the

audiences Marsalis had experienced as a member of Wynton's quintet. "On a Wednesday night," said Marsalis, "I was playing with Wynton in New Jersey in front of 800 people, and on Saturday morning I was at Wembley [England] playing in front of 90,000."

Marsalis did another tour with Sting in 1988, and he has since performed on more Sting albums. His association with the rock group brought him great publicity, but he decided he "didn't want to be playing rock-'n-roll forever." On returning from his first tour in 1986, he therefore formed another jazz quartet, and he recorded two albums, *Royal Garden Blues* and *Romances for Saxophone.* A number-one hit on the jazz charts, *Royal Garden Blues* brought Marsalis a nomination for a Grammy Award for best solo jazz instrumental performance. *Romances for Saxophone* was entirely different—a recording with the English Chamber Orchestra, with pieces by Claude Debussy and other classical composers—but it too was a hit, remaining in the top five of *Billboard*'s classical music charts for more than two months.

Since these two very different successes, Marsalis has brought out an album almost every year. All have scored high on the charts, including *Random Abstract* (1988) and *Crazy People Music* (1990), which received Grammy nominations. Marsalis also won a Grammy nomination for his playing of "Cottontail" on the Duke Ellington Orchestra's album *Digital Duke* (1987).

Like most musicians, Marsalis tours extensively—he spent about 300 days on tour in 1990. He has also appeared in films, including *Bring on the Night* (1985), *School Daze*

(1987), and *Throw Momma from the Train* (1987). He was offered a role as a saxophone player in Spike Lee's *Mo' Better Blues* but turned it down because he thought he couldn't do justice to the part. Instead, Marsalis performed the music for the sound track—and his 1990 album of the film music brought him yet another Grammy nomination.

One of the attractions of Marsalis's albums is that each one is different, for he is constantly experimenting. *New York Times* critic Peter Watrous captured this quality when reviewing Marsalis's 1991 album, *The Beautiful Ones Are Not Yet Born:* "Like his previous records, it's an investigation of different styles and jazz approaches. There are moments of music that verge toward free jazz, others that are straight-ahead swinging, and Mr. Marsalis himself sounds like a variety of improvisers."

Since 1985 Marsalis has been married to actress Teresa Reese. They have one son, who is named Reese, after his mother.

Wynton Marsalis

Trumpet Player
Born October 18, 1961, New Orleans,
   Louisiana

"I love the music, above anything else. That's all I answer to."

As the winner of eight Grammy Awards, Wynton Marsalis has left an indelible mark on the music profession. Heralded by some critics as the best trumpet player of all time, Marsalis is the consummate jazz and classical musician. Besides receiving praise for his concerts and records, Marsalis also strives to educate the next generation of possible jazz players on the contributions of past jazz masters. To some he is the savior of modern jazz.

Received his first trumpet at age six

Marsalis was born on October 18, 1961, in New Orleans, Louisiana, to Ellis and Delores Marsalis. His father was a music professor and played piano in a band which included the great Dixieland trumpeter Al Hirt. His mother was a former jazz singer and substitute teacher. When Marsalis was six, Hirt gave him his first trumpet, although he did not begin playing it in earnest for six more years, when he heard a recording by jazz trumpeter Clifford Brown. Marsalis then began studying with John Longo, who showed him the classical repertoire of the instrument.

It did not take him long to master it. By fourteen he was a featured soloist with the New Orleans Philharmonic Orchestra. Three years later he was invited to a summer session at the famed Berkshire Music Center at Tanglewood, Massachusetts, which waived its normal eighteen-year-old age requirement.

Marsalis was an exceptional high school student, graduating with a 3.98 grade point average, and was a finalist for a National Merit Scholarship. He accepted a scholarship in 1979 to the elite Juilliard School of Music in New York City. In his spare time he played with several orchestras, including the Brooklyn Philharmonic. During his summer vacation in 1980, Marsalis toured with Art

Blakey, a famous jazz drummer. He walked away from Juilliard during his second year to tour with jazz pianist Herbie Hancock's V.S.O.P. quartet. Later that year he received a recording contract with Columbia Records to record both jazz and classical music, prompting him to form his own jazz band.

Music ranged from a blues lament to a baroque exaltation

In time, Marsalis's reputation grew. He was noted for being able to play music that ranged from a blues lament to a baroque exaltation. Marsalis was equally at home at a small, smoky New York jazz club or in Washington's prestigious Lincoln Center.

Jane O'Hara pointed out in *Maclean's* that "Marsalis's classical training may have offered a temporary refuge from the black ghetto, but there is no question about the prodigal son's real musical home: 'I have studied Bartok and Stravinsky and I love them ... but jazz is in the present tense.'" Marsalis expanded upon this idea to Howard Mandel of *Down Beat:* "Jazz is the most precise art form of this century [because of] the time.... What the musicians have figured out is how to conceive, construct, refine and deliver ideas as they come up, and present them in a logical fashion. What you're doing is creating, editing, and all this as the music is going on. This is the first time this has ever happened in western art. Painting is painted. Symphonies are written. Beethoven improvised, but by himself, over a score. When five men get together to make up something, it's a big difference."

Marsalis's outspokenness has not gone unnoticed by critics, but he always maintains

Wynton Marsalis

that it is easier for a young musician to master classical music than jazz. Whitney Balliett remarked in the *New Yorker,* "Technique, rather than melodic logic, still governs his improvising and the emotional content of his playing remains skittish." *Down Beat* stated that Marsalis "seems to be detached from his prodigious maturity by not having experienced abandon.... Musicians, like artists, must live if they are going to make significant contributions."

Marsalis has lived

Marsalis seems to have taken the advice of *Down Beat,* and most critics will admit he has "lived." *Time* stated that even Marsalis "admits that the shoot-from-the-lip style of his early years went too far at times: 'I was like 19 or something, man—you know, wild. I didn't care.'" The article added that he has since become "less strident and more articulate for the cause. Says pianist and composer

Billy Taylor: 'Wynton is the most important young spokesman for the music today. His opinions are well founded. Some people earlier took umbrage at what he said, but the important thing is that he could back it up with his horn."

Marsalis has spoken on the proper understanding and respect for jazz since his early years because he believes jazz is not just another style of popular music, but a major American cultural achievement and a heritage that must not be lost. Marsalis told *Time*, "It (jazz) shows you how much the individual can negotiate the greatest amount of personal freedom and put it humbly at the service of a group conception."

Firm in his beliefs, Marsalis wants to educate the next generation of possible jazz musicians about the contributions of past jazz masters. He visits schools, and in 1987, he helped launch a three-year jazz education program in the Chicago school system. He often stays in contact with the students he meets, offers them tips over the phone, invites them to sit in on his gigs, and sometimes even gives them his instrument. This is in stark contrast to Marsalis's early days when he did not know anything about jazz masters Ornette Coleman, Duke Ellington, or Thelonius Monk. His dad tried to make him listen to Louis Armstrong, but Marsalis felt that Armstrong was an Uncle Tom.

Although early critics faulted Marsalis's work for lacking emotion, his later recordings have been lauded. He has won eight Grammy awards for best solo jazz instrumental in 1983 for *Think of One;* for *Hot House Flowers* in 1984; and *Black Codes*, 1985. He won Grammy awards for best solo classical per-

formance with orchestra in 1983 for *Trumpet Concertos;* and *Baroque Trumpet Music,* 1984. He also won Grammy awards for best jazz instrumentation performance with a group in 1985 for *Black Codes; J Mood*, 1986; and *Marsalis Standard Time Vol. 1*, 1987. Marsalis is the only person in history to have won back-to-back classical and jazz Grammys in two consecutive years.

Down Beat stated *J Mood* was "an intimate revelling in sensuous sounds, the sense of quirky unpredictability in the original melodies and the solo lines (no cliches here), an unexpected quietude and austerity on many tracks." *Rolling Stone* felt *Marsalis Standard Time Vol. 1* "tugging at the beat with willful elasticity and venturing out with confident improvisations heightened by the clarity of his technique." Another article in *Rolling Stone* stated *Majesty of the Blues* was "an artistic quantum leap forward." If "whorehouses still played jazz in the front room, this is what it would sound like."

Besides the high praise for his jazz, Marsalis has also received strong reviews for his classical music. The *New Yorker* stated the *Haydn/Hummel/Mozart Concertos* is "a beautiful record, full of the silver and bells and sunlight of perfectly played brass." *Down Beat* added that Marsalis "has a natural flair for the witty exuberance, jazzy metrics, and peripatetic lines" of the concertos on the *Jolivet/Tomasi* recording.

From his recordings, educational programs, concerts, and interviews, critics have been able to define Marsalis. The book, *Black Music in America: A History Through Its People,* noted that "because of his versatility,

Wynton Marsalis brought a highly technical sense to his jazz playing and a vividness and immediacy to his classical playing that no one else had ever been able to do." *Time* stated that Marsalis's effect extends beyond any individual ability or achievement: "It is the fact that, largely under his influence, a jazz renaissance is flowering on what was once barren soil." The best way to sum up Marsalis's impact may be a quote from a member of his group, Wes Anderson in *Time:* "Wynton is someone who can guide us. He's one of the shepherds of this music."

Paule Marshall

Writer
Born April 9, 1929, Brooklyn, New York

"I realize that it is fashionable now to dismiss the traditional novel as something of an anachronism, but to me it is still a vital form."

The author of four novels and two collections of short stories, Paule Marshall writes thoughtful, compassionate books that draw on her heritage as an African American of West Indian origin. Rejecting racism as subject matter, Marshall writes rather about the black community itself. She first began to do so because she felt this aspect was missing from African American literature.

"I had a sense that a whole dimension was missing," she said, "that in the face of racism, in the face of oppression, there was a black community that blacks had been able to elaborate.... And that our lives were not solely defined by racism, that we did most of the time love our children, our husbands and our wives and we had a family life, and these were things that had to be celebrated."

Learned the narrative art in "the wordshop of the kitchen"

Paule Marshall's parents, Samuel and Ada Burke, emigrated from Barbados in the early 1920s and settled in Brooklyn, New York, among other families from the Caribbean. Marshall absorbed many aspects of the West Indian culture as she grew up, becoming familiar with traditional rituals and customs.

Most of her mother's friends worked as domestics in white homes, and in the evenings they often gathered round her mother's kitchen table to discuss the day's events and recount their experiences. "They taught me my first lessons in the narrative art," Marshall later recalled. "They trained my ear. They set

Paule Marshall

a standard of excellence. This is why the best of my work must be attributed to them; it stands as testimony to the rich legacy of language and culture they so freely passed on to me in the wordshop of the kitchen."

When Marshall was nine years old she visited Barbados, an experience that affected her profoundly and inspired a series of poems she later wrote. Educated in American public schools, Marshall attended Brooklyn College, where she majored in English and in 1953 earned her B.A., graduating magna cum laude and Phi Beta Kappa.

Served writing apprenticeship with first novels

Marshall began her career as a researcher for *Our World,* a small black magazine in New York City. The only woman on the staff, she often felt that "the men were waiting for me to fall," but in fact she did so well that she was soon promoted to staff writer and sent on assignments to Brazil and the Caribbean. Marshall left the magazine in 1956, for by then she was deep into writing her first novel, *Brown Girl, Brownstones,* which she had been working on in the evenings. She and her husband, Kenneth Marshall, moved to Barbados in 1957, and the completed novel was published in 1959.

Marshall has often said that when she created *Brown Girl, Brownstones,* she was still learning how to write, still finding the best way to present her characters and give them authentic voices. She decided to use the voices she knew so well—the West Indian speech of her family and friends. The novel is largely autobiographical, following the experiences of Selina, a black Brooklyn girl whose parents are West Indian immigrants. Essentially the story is about Selina's search for identity, which she eventually resolves by deciding to go to Barbados, her parents' homeland. Much of the strength of the book lies in the characterization—the vividly drawn portraits of Selina, her parents, and their friends, all of whom are true individuals and entirely different from the usual stereotypes.

Marshall's first book did not sell particularly well, even though it received some good reviews. Nevertheless, Marshall now felt totally committed to being a writer, and she was soon hard at work on her next book, a collection of four stories published in 1961 under the title *Soul Clap Hands and Sing.* Marshall wrote the group of stories shortly after the birth of her son—Evan, her only child. Finding it difficult to work with a baby in the house, she hired someone to look after Evan each day while she wrote at a friend's apartment. Her husband did not approve, and the couple divorced in 1963. Marshall later embarked with Nourry Menard, her second husband, on what she called "an open and innovative marriage," which allowed her the time she needed to devote to her work.

Of the several short stories Marshall wrote in these years, one eventually was featured as the title story of the collection *Reena and Other Stories,* published years later, in 1983. Reena is a middle-aged American woman of West Indian origin who is confronted with all the complex problems that face educated black women. However, Marshall's second novel, *The Chosen Place, the Timeless People,* saw publication before her stories. Released in

1969, the novel is set on a fictional island, which Marshall symbolically located between Africa and the New World. The plot focuses on the relationship between the traditional island society and a do-good agency, the Center for Applied Social Research, which purports to help the people of the island move into the twentieth century. Marshall said about the book that "I was finally able … to bring together what I consider to be the two themes most central to my work: the importance of truly confronting the past, both in personal and historical terms, and the necessity of reversing the present order." She succeeded in doing this with such effect that a reviewer for the *New York Times Book Review* hailed *The Chosen Place, the Timeless People* as "the best novel to be written by an American black woman" and "one of the two most important black novels of the 1960s." However, other reviewers were less enthusiastic and the book sold only moderately well.

Acclaimed novelist of "passionate understanding"

Marshall's next novel, *Praisesong for the Widow* (1983), at last brought her a large readership—and also won her the Before Columbus Foundation American Book Award. *Praisesong* follows the adventures of Avey Johnson, a wealthy widow in her sixties, who goes on a cruise to the Caribbean each year. On one of these cruises she has a dream about her childhood which so affects her that she decides to leave the ship. As the story unfolds, Avey separates herself from the North American culture—in which she has lived so comfortably and correctly for the past forty years—

and rediscovers the culture and history of her ancestors.

As with all Marshall's books, the words flow along easily, building detail on detail to create a totally absorbing story. "I realize that it is fashonable now to dismiss the traditional novel as something of an anachronism," Marshall has stated, "but to me it is still a vital form. Not only does it allow for the kind of full-blown, richly detailed writing that I love (I want the reader to see the people and places about which I am writing), but it permits me to operate on many levels and to explore both the inner state of my characters as well as the worlds beyond them."

Marshall achieved this effect again with her fourth novel, *Daughters* (1991), which, as usual, links black America and the Caribbean. The heroine, Ursa Mackenzie, has roots in both worlds. Her mother is an American schoolteacher, while her father, Primus Mackenzie, is a leading politician on the fictional island of Triunion. Ursa is a successful young career woman in New York City, and much of the story focuses on her struggle to come to terms with her family back in Triunion after having stayed away from them for so long.

Like all Marshall's books, *Daughters* took many years to write. "One of the reasons it takes me such a long time to get a book done," Marshall once explained, "is that I'm not only struggling with my sense of reality, but I'm also struggling to find the style, the language, the tone that is in keeping with the material." To support herself while working on her books, she teaches at the university level, such as at Yale, where in 1970 she was appointed a lecturer in creative writing. Since the early

1990s she has been professor of English at Virginia Commonwealth University in Richmond, Virginia.

Although Marshall's early books attracted few readers when first published, they have since been reprinted and she has become an extremely popular author. Many people now agree with the *San Francisco Chronicle,* which called her "one of our finest American novelists." Author Tillie Olsen went further, explaining why so many people read and re-read Marshall's books. "This beautiful and lasting writer," she said of Marshall, "has that rarest of capacities—to create characters with such passionate understanding and radiant art that they remain with us permanently."

Thurgood Marshall

Supreme Court justice
Born July 2, 1908, Baltimore, Maryland
Died January 24, 1993, Bethesda, Maryland

"Equal means getting the same thing, at the same time, and in the same place."

Thurgood Marshall has been called "one of the greatest Americans of this century." As a lawyer, appeals court judge, solicitor general of the U.S., and Supreme Court justice, he spent his life fighting for the cause of civil rights. As a result of his efforts, segregation and discrimination declared illegal in schooling, housing, voting, and many other areas, to the benefit of millions of Americans.

Marshall's greatest triumph occurred in 1954 when he was a lawyer representing the National Association for the Advancement of Colored People (NAACP). In a case before the Supreme Court, *Brown v. Board of Education,* he argued that the current system of education, which provided for "separate but equal" public schools, was a violation of the Fourteenth Amendment to the U.S. Constitution. The Supreme Court agreed with his arguments and ruled unanimously that segregated education was unconstitutional, thereby giving all American children the right to attend desegregated public schools.

Later in life, when Marshall himself was a Supreme Court justice (1967–1991), he continued his efforts to bring an end to discrimination. He was the first African American appointed to the Supreme Court, and in many ways he served as the court's conscience—a vigilant watchdog, staunchly insisting that the United States live up to its Constitution.

A lawyer in the making

Thurgood Marshall was named after his great-grandfather Thoroughgood, who was captured in the Congo and brought to Maryland as a slave. Thoroughgood is said to have won his freedom through his "rebellious nature," a trait that was inherited by his descendants. Thurgood's father, William Marshall, possessed this quality in good measure and passed it on to his son. "In a way, he was the most insidious of my family rebels," Thurgood Marshall once said. "He taught me how to argue, challenged my logic on every point, even if we were discussing the weather."

Marshall's father started work as a Pullman porter and eventually became head steward at an all-white country club on the shores of Chesapeake Bay in Maryland. The family lived in a comfortable home in a pleasant part of Baltimore, where Thurgood and his elder brother played with white as well as black children, though they had to go to all-black schools. Similarly, it was at a black elementary school that their mother, Norma (Williams) Marshall, pursued her career as a schoolteacher.

After graduating from Douglas High School, Thurgood enrolled at all-black Lincoln University in Oxford, Pennsylvania. He intended to study dentistry, but changed his mind and decided to train as a lawyer. This was partly the result of his success with the debating team. He had discovered that he had a talent for building up a case and presenting it in a convincing manner—an essential ability for a practicing lawyer.

On graduating with honors in 1930, Marshall applied to the University of Maryland Law School, which at the time was an all-white institution and which confirmed this fact by turning him down. He therefore enrolled at the small all-black law school at Howard University in Washington, D.C., and in 1933 gained his LL.B., graduating first in his class. He was admitted to the Maryland bar the same year.

Civil rights lawyer

While he was still a teenager, Marshall had married Vivian Burey, who was studying at the University of Pennsylvania while he was at Lincoln University. Now that he was a fully qualified, he opened a law practice in Baltimore. He made far less money than most lawyers, for he soon found himself specializing in civil rights cases, often on behalf of people who could not afford to pay him. In one of his first cases he turned his sights on the University of Maryland Law School—the school that had to refused to admit him—and forced it to admit its first black student.

Marshall's activities soon brought him to the notice of the NAACP, and in 1936 he moved to New York City to work as the organization's lawyer, first as its assistant counsel and then as chief counsel. In an effort to bring an end to segregation, Marshall and others formed the NAACP Legal Defense and Education Fund in 1939, of which Marshall was made director. Their aim was to work through the courts to get segregation declared illegal, especially segregation in the schools.

American public schools had been segregated since 1896, when a judicial ruling had authorized "separate but equal" education for black and white children. Marshall set out to overturn this law, arguing that separate education did not ensure equal education. "Equal means getting the same thing, at the same time, and in the same place," he said. He encouraged fellow lawyers to challenge the ruling in court, and when the lower courts upheld the 1896 ruling, Marshall appealed to higher courts.

Marshall's most important case was *Brown v. Board of Education* in 1954, which resulted in the U.S. Supreme Court's unanimous decision that "separate educational facilities are inherently unequal" and that racial segregation in public schools is unconstitutional. This landmark case ended half a century of segregated schooling—at least, in theory. Despite the legal victory, Marshall found that much of his remaining work for the NAACP involved lawsuits forcing schools to comply with the Supreme Court ruling.

Throughout these years, Marshall also fought segregation in other areas, such as housing and voting, following the same strategy. He had his team of lawyers challenge the constitutionality of the laws on a case-by-case basis, appealing to higher courts when necessary. As a result, Marshall argued thirty-two cases before the Supreme Court, and he won twenty-nine of them.

While Marshall was involved with these pivotal events, his wife Vivian was seriously ill and died in 1955. The following year he married an NAACP secretary, Cecilia Suyat, by whom he was to have two sons. Thurgood, Jr., trained to become a lawyer like his father, while John entered the Virginia State Police.

Justice Marshall

In 1961, President John F. Kennedy appointed Marshall to the U.S. Court of Appeals for the Second Circuit in New York. There was a year's delay before Marshall could take up the position because a number of Southern senators did their best to block the appointment. Four years later, in 1965, President Lyndon Johnson appointed Marshall solicitor general of the United States. In this position, Marshall represented the government in cases before the Supreme Court, and in the two years he held the office he won fourteen of the nineteen cases he argued.

Marshall's strength as a lawyer lay in the logic of his argument. Rather than relying on emotion, he always built up his cases step by step, using such commonsense reasoning that it was difficult to disagree with him. His most important achievement as solicitor general was to get acceptance of the *Miranda* rule, which requires police to inform suspects of their rights.

The position of solicitor general was an obvious step toward being made a Supreme Court justice, and it was no great surprise when President Johnson appointed Marshall to the Supreme Court in 1967. In that era of civil rights activism, Johnson could hardly have picked a more acceptable candidate. Not only was Marshall an African American, but he had gained wide respect as a pioneering lawyer who had helped strike down segregation in schools, universities, housing, public accommodation, voting, juries, and in many other areas. Marshall's appointment was confirmed by the Senate in a vote of sixty-nine to

Thurgood Marshall

eleven, despite strong opposition from some Southern senators.

During Marshall's twenty-five years on the Supreme Court, he remained a staunch champion of the underdog, speaking up for the rights of the poor, of women, and of all who had difficulty defending themselves. Consistent with his support for civil liberties, he took a strong stand against the death penalty.

As the years passed, Marshall had less and less support from his colleagues on the Supreme Court as the more liberal-minded justices retired and were replaced by the conservatives appointed by Presidents Nixon, Reagan, and Bush. During his last years, Marshall was the only true liberal left on the nine-member court, and for this reason he refused to step down and did not retire until he was in his eighties and his health was failing. When Marshall died in 1993, 20,000 people paid their respect by filing past his coffin at the Supreme Court. Four thousand dignitaries attended his memorial service.

America saw many changes during Thurgood Marshall's life, and he helped bring about many of them. In the 1930s, he fought for civil rights long before there was such a thing as the civil rights movement. Fifty years later, he was still fighting for civil liberties and the rights of the individual. In his determination to make his country live up to its Constitution, Thurgood Marshall brought about an almost bloodless revolution, which, in the words of the *Detroit News*, "extended liberty and dignity to a large segment of the American population."

Biddy Mason

Humanitarian
Born August 15, 1818, Hancock County, Mississippi
Died January 15, 1891, Los Angeles, California

"Mason's transformation from slave to successful businesswoman created a secure future for her family and provided inspiration for those who came into contact with her."—Oscar L. Sims

B orn a slave on a Southern plantation, Biddy Mason walked all the way to California, where she became a leading member of the Los Angeles black community. She was one of the first black women to own land in Los Angeles.

Mason is remembered especially for her charitable work. During her years as a slave she was trained as a midwife and nurse, and in Los Angeles she cared for the needy of all races, including prisoners in the jails. She also founded the Los Angeles branch of the First African Methodist Episcopal church. An indomitable woman who fought courageously to obtain her freedom and who then used it to help others, Mason was an inspiration to all who knew her.

Moved out west with false promise of freedom

Biddy Mason's full name was Bridget Mason. Her parentage is unknown, but the records show that as well as being of African origin she was descended from Seminole, Geegi, and Choctaw Indians. Born into slavery, she spent her childhood on the Smithson family's plantation in Mississippi, where she worked as a household slave and was given training as a midwife and nurse.

When Mason was eighteen, her owner's cousin married Robert Smith, and Mason was given to the young couple as a wedding present. The couple also received three other slaves, one of whom was named Hannah. Robert Smith was to have three children by Biddy Mason and nine by Hannah in addition to the six his wife bore him. Mason's children were all girls: Ellen, Ann, and Harriet.

Sometime in the 1840s Robert Smith was converted to Mormonism, and in 1847 he decided to migrate to Utah Territory, where the Mormons were building Salt Lake City. Mason and Hannah went with him, having been told they would be given their freedom if they accompanied the family on the trek westward.

Some 56 whites and 34 slaves formed the column that set off for Utah in 1847. They completed the 2,000-mile journey in March 1848. Mason and her children were right at the tail of the column, walking in the dust from the wagons ahead of them. During the journey Mason coped with a multitude of tasks. She herded the Smith family's two yoke of oxen, seven milk cows, and eight mules. She made camp at the end of each day and then cooked the main meal of the day at crack of dawn next morning. She acted as midwife to several women who gave birth during the journey, and she also cared for her own baby, her youngest daughter, Harriet. After all this, Mason was not given her freedom as promised.

Sued for freedom

The Smiths lived in Utah for the next three years, and their slaves remained with them. Then Robert Smith heard of a new Mormon community that had been started at San Bernardino, California. In 1851 he took his family and slaves there, unaware that the 1849 California constitution forbade slavery and that California had been admitted as a free state when it joined the Union in 1850.

Despite this, there were quite a number of slaves and slaveowners in California, since nobody was sure what the position was with regard to existing slaves. But Smith was not happy with the situation. To be sure of keeping his slaves, he planned to move to Texas, a slave state. Mason was greatly upset when she heard of these plans, since they dashed her hopes of ever being free. In a bold move for a

Biddy Mason

slave, she decided to take action against her master.

Mason recruited the help of the Owens family. Mason's eldest daughter, Ellen, was being courted by Charles Owens, a free black who was son of the influential Los Angeles businessman Robert Owens. On hearing of Mason's troubles, father and son went to the sheriff and arranged for a writ to be served on Smith. Through the ensuing lawsuit, Mason gained her freedom in 1856. Thirteen other slaves of Smith were given their freedom at the same time. The lawsuit was extremely significant since it set a precedent establishing the rights of African American settlers in the West.

Prospered as a midwife in Los Angeles

Although Mason and her daughters were now free, they had no means of support and nowhere to live, so the the Owens family invited them to stay. Before long the two families became one when Ellen Mason and Charles Owens married. Meanwhile, Biddy Mason had started practicing as a midwife in Los Angeles. Serving all races, including the local Indians, she quickly gained a name as a highly skilled practitioner.

For many years Mason worked with Dr. John Griffin, serving as his nurse and midwife throughout the Los Angeles area. Earning $2.50 a day, she managed to save a large portion of her salary until she had enough to buy a lot on Spring Street. She later bought other land, some of which she sold in 1884 for $1,500. With this money Mason built a commercial building, which she rented out as office space. Despite having been allowed no

money of her own during the first part of her life, Mason proved to be a highly efficient businesswoman. Her descendants have exhibited these talents: One of her grandsons was said to be the richest African American in Los Angeles.

While Mason was making a success in the business world, she was also doing a great deal of unpaid work. She visited and nursed prisoners in jails, the sick in hospitals, and the mentally disturbed in asylums. She established a daycare center for the the children of African American workers. If anyone was in need of help or care, they could count on Biddy Mason. One of her most lasting efforts was the branch of the First African Methodist Episcopal church she and a group of friends established in Los Angeles in 1872.

More than a century later Biddy Mason is still honored in Los Angeles. In 1988 Mayor Tom Bradley and some 3,000 members of the First African Methodist Episcopal church held a ceremony to place an impressive tombstone on her grave. The following year, November 16 was declared Biddy Mason Day, and at the Broadway Spring Center a memorial was unveiled recording the major events in the life of this remarkable women and her many contributions to the city of Los Angeles.

Willie Mays

Former professional baseball player
Born May 6, 1931, Westfield, Atlanta

B orn to play baseball, the legendary Willie Mays was playing catch with his father not long after he learned to walk. By the time he was thirteen he was playing semi-professional ball, and he joined the big leagues when he was twenty. In his twenty-two-year-long career he excelled at every aspect of the game. He hit for average and for power, stole bases, played center field with magical grace, and set several records for durability. Although his playing days came to an end in 1973, he remains the standard by which many young players measure themselves.

Learned the game from his father

Mays was born on May 6, 1931, in Westfield, Alabama, to William and Ann Mays. His father, a steelworker, played center field for the Birmingham Industrial League semipro team, and his mother was a high school track star. At an early age Mays began exhibiting athletic ability. When he was three years old, his parents divorced, but Mays continued to live with his father. He learned to play catch by the time he was six, and the more he played baseball, the more he realized it was the ticket out of a life in the steel mills. He played ball whenever he could and would sit in the dugout with his father's Industrial League teammates and listen to baseball strategy and techniques. Mays literally grew up on the baseball field, and by the time he was thirteen he was playing on a semiprofessional team called the Gray Sox.

Mays was such a gifted outfielder that his friends urged him to try out for the Birmingham Black Barons, a local team in the Negro League. This league was the top level for black athletes, since they were barred from playing in the white leagues. Negro League teams played throughout the South and in some northern cities, often to large crowds, but they could not play in the "big leagues."

Played for a team in the Negro League

Mays joined the league when he was fifteen and took over center field on a team dominated by men ten years his senior. He received a salary of $250 a month, far more than he would have earned with a part-time job as a high school student. He eventually finished high school, but he did so as a professional baseball player.

Piper Davis, the manager of the Black Barons, became an important tutor to Mays. Davis recognized Mays's abilities and helped perfect them, while serving as father-figure for him. The team traveled as far as Chicago and New York, often riding all night in a

Willie Mays

secondhand bus to make the next day's game and lodging in mediocre hotels in the "colored part" of each town. Despite its unglamorous side, Mays thrived on the competition.

Baseball legend Jackie Robinson was the first black player to crack the colored barrier in major league baseball, opening doors for other blacks to follow. Scouts began watching the Negro League for future talent, and a New York Giants scout spotted nineteen-year-old Mays. A short time later the team offered Mays a $4,000 bonus and $250 per month to play for their Class A team in Sioux City, Iowa. Racial problems in that city prevented Mays from joining the team in 1950, so he played for a team in Trenton with the Class B Interstate League. He was the first black to play in that league, and he won the batting title with a .353 batting average.

Broke records in the major leagues

The next season Mays played with the Minneapolis Millers in Class AAA. After the first sixteen games he had a sparkling .608 batting average, with amazing plays in the outfield to his credit. Word of his success soon reached the ears of Leo Durocher, manager of the New York Giants. Then having an unspectacular season, the Giants promoted Mays, bringing him on as starting center fielder on May 25, 1951, and number three hitter in the lineup. Mays got off to a poor start—only 1 hit in 25 at bats—but Durocher had confidence in him. By mid-August it appeared neither the Giants nor Mays were going anywhere fast. The team was 13 $\frac{1}{2}$ games out of first place, and while Mays showed flashes of brilliance, he was still only a rookie. But the team suddenly got hot and caught the first-place Brooklyn Dodgers on the last day of the regular season. The Giants won a best-of-three playoff series but then lost the World Series in seven games to the New York Yankees. Mays only hit .182 in the series, but he was named the National League's Rookie of the Year for 1951 in light of his 20 home runs and .274 batting average.

At only twenty years of age Mays became one of the most talked about ball players in the league. His baseball career had to be put on hold for two years, however, when he was drafted by the army, which used him as an instructor on their baseball teams. Many feared the two-year hiatus would hurt his career, but those fears were soon dismissed. Mays led the Giants to a world championship, hit .345, slammed 41 home runs, and won the Most Valuable Player Award. He led the league in batting average, and in the first game of the World Series he made such a spectacular catch that he became known as "the catch." Mays became a popular star and appeared on the "Ed Sullivan Show" and the "Colgate Comedy Hour." He spent the winter playing ball in Puerto Rico for the Giants. He lead that league in hitting and slugging percentage, and the Giants' management offered him a new high-paying contract.

Mays played his first full season in 1955 and became only the seventh player in the history of the game to slug 50 or more home runs (he hit 51) in one season. He also led the National League in triples and slugging percentage, was second in stolen bases, and led all outfielders with 23 assists.

Categorized as one of the game's greatest

Since most home run hitters were mediocre outfielders and often slow runners, it was a surprise that Mays could do everything so well. It was said he could alter the number of home runs he hit according to the team's needs. In 1955, for example, Durocher told Mays to supply the team with more power, so he hit 51 home runs. The year before he told Mays to stop worrying about hitting home runs and concentrate on just hitting the ball. Mays hit only 5 homers during the last third of the season but won the batting title.

Bill Rigney replaced Durocher in 1956, and Mays hit 36 home runs and led the league with 40 stolen bases. He would go on to lead the league in stolen bases for the next three years. Mays also married Marghuerite Wendell in 1956, just before his twenty-fifth birthday. They adopted a boy, Michael, in 1958, but they divorced in 1962.

The Giants relocated to San Francisco in 1957, and Mays found the transition difficult. At first, the new fans did not idolize him like those in New York, and the press was only lukewarm to him. It was difficult for him to gauge the widely shifting winds at Candlestick Park, where the Giants played. As Mays became more familiar with the area, things improved. He won over the fans with his outstanding play at the bat and in the field. In 1961 he became the fifth player ever to hit 4 home runs in a single game; in 1962 he led the Giants back to the World Series with a career-high 141 runs batted in; and he clubbed his 400th career homer the next year.

Since Mays was such a hard-driving player, he occasionally suffered from bouts of exhaustion. In spite of this problem, Herman Franks, the new Giants manager, used Mays as the team captain and unofficial coach during the 1962 season. Franks would often consult with Mays on player personnel and strategy, and Mays responded with 52 home runs and his second Most Valuable Player award.

The only milestone left for Mays to beat was Babe Ruth's record of 714 career home runs. He had passed the records of many of the game's all-time great players but stood 170 homers behind the Babe. May's hard-driving approach began to take its toll after the 1966 season, and his home run and batting average began to diminish. He finished his career with the New York Mets in 1973 and left the game as one of its greatest all-around players.

George Marion McClellan

Poet, short story writer, educator
Born September 29, 1860, Belfast, Tennessee
Died May 17, 1934

"McClellan, like many other writers of this period, black and white, took what was essentially a sentimental approach to literature."—Dickson D. Bruce, Jr.

Although George Marion McClellan followed a career as a school teacher and Congregational minister, he is remembered chiefly for his writings. He was the author of *Poems* (1895), *Songs of a Southerner* (1896), *Old Greenbottom Inn and Other Stories* (1906), and *The Path of Dreams* (1916). He also wrote an article on "The Negro as a Writer," which was published in 1902.

In his poetry McClellan followed the conventions of his day, writing in a sentimental tone about love, death, and nature. He so seldom chose African American themes that many readers believed the verses were written by a white poet. McClellan's short stories, on the other hand, show a keen awareness of the issues that faced African Americans around the turn of the century. Racism was an underlying theme in most of the stories, and many had sad endings.

Published poems in the sentimental style of the day

McClellan was the son of George and Eliza (Leonard) McClellan. Little is known about his childhood, but it is evident from his poems that he grew up in a middle-class environment and was given a good basic education that included a study of English literature. In 1885 he graduated A.B. from Fisk University in Nashville, Tennessee, and enrolled at Hartford Theological Seminary in Connecticut, where he studied for the ministry for the next three years. In 1887 he moved to Louisville, Kentucky, where he took up his duties as a Congregational minister.

The year after beginning his ministry in Louisville, McClellan married Mariah Rabb, with whom he was to have two sons. Around 1890 the couple returned to Fisk, where Rabb became a member of faculty while McClellan completed his master's degree. The following

George Marion McClellan

year he earned a B.D. from Hartford Theological Seminary.

McClellan held the position of financial agent for Fisk University from 1892 to 1894, and for the next two years he served as chaplain to the State Normal School in Normal, Alabama. It was during McClellan's years in Alabama that he published his first two works: *Poems* (1895) and *Songs of a Southerner* (1896). Both were published at his own expense, as were all his works. *Poems* was by far the more important of the two. *Songs of a Southerner* was simply a reprint of some of the material from *Poems*.

Despite its title, *Poems* contained prose as well as poems. One of the prose pieces, "The Goddess of Penitentials," gave McClellan's views on poetry. He said that the writing of poetry involved feeling deeply—experiencing "exquisite sensibilities"—and then putting those feelings into suitable words. The feelings he chose to express in his verses were the same as those of white nineteenth-century poets—wonderment at the the beauty of nature, musings about love, and so on. Sentimental and conventional, the poems were well executed, but they were not at all original in thought.

Even the few poems on racial subjects were sentimental and romantic. "The Octaroon's Farewell," for example, is a lament by a young woman of color that she cannot fulfill her love for a white man. The tone is genteel and the approach conservative. Like many other black writers of his generation, McClellan hoped to be assimilated into the white cultural world and thus made a continual effort to show that black culture was just as refined as white culture. He was not one of the few turn-of-the-century black intellectuals who were calling for a distinctive black literature.

Explored "Negro life and character" in his short stories

Sometime before 1900 McClellan returned to Louisville, where for the next twenty years he had a successful career as a teacher in the public school system. He was teaching at Central Colored High School in Louisville when his article "The Negro as a Writer" was published in *Twentieth Century Negro Literature* (1902). In this article McClellan praises Paul Laurence Dunbar and Charles Chesnutt—the only black writers whose works were popular with whites—but condemns the writing of most other black writers as mediocre. However, for the first time he expresses an awareness that there may be a future for a black literature based on African American life.

The stories in his next book, *Old Greenbottom Inn and Other Stories* (1906), all focused on African Americans and were set in real places that McClellan knew personally, such as Fisk University. But even though McClellan was writing about "Negro life and character, thought and feeling," he was still doing so in the sentimental and romantic style of the white literary tradition.

The most powerful story in the book is the title story, "Old Greenbottom Inn," which is about interracial love. The heroine, a refined young woman of mixed race, falls in love with a white man—with tragic consequences. Since they cannot marry, the young couple make love secretly and the woman becomes pregnant. This leads to the murder of the white man by a jealous African American, who is then lynched in retribution. Yet this is not a protest story, raging against injustice. It is too quiet and accepting for that. Basically it is a comment on the complications of living in a segregated environment.

McClellan's final work, *The Path of Dreams* (1916), was published during a sad period of his life. Although he was doing well in his career and had been appointed principal of Dunbar Public School in Louisville, all was not well in his personal life. His youngest son, Theodore, was dying of tuberculosis, and McClellan could not get suitable treatment for him, for apparently racial reasons. The volume is dedicated to Theodore, who died the year after it was published.

The Path of Dreams is a collection of forty-three poems and five short stories and is mainly recycled material from McClellan's earlier books. Only ten of the poems had not appeared previously, and only one story, "Gabe Yowl," was new. "Gabe Yowl" deals with race relations in the framework of a mystery story about a white man's murder.

In the 1920s McClellan said he was working on a book called *The History of American Literature*, but no trace of it has ever been found. Little is known of his final years, though he seems to have continued his work as a teacher. As a writer he falls far short of such giants as Paul Laurence Dunbar, yet he was a skilled poet, and his short stories give an interesting view of attitudes at the turn of the century.

Hattie McDaniel

Actress, singer
Born June l0, 1895, Wichita, Kansas
Died October 26, 1952, San Fernando Valley, California

"I portray the type of Negro woman who has worked honestly and proudly to give our nation the Marian Andersons, Roland Hayeses and Ralph Bunches."

A witty and good-humored performer, Hattie McDaniel gathered thousands of fans during her career in show business. She made a name as both a singer and an actress and appeared in virtually every type of setting, from the crowded tents of travelling vaudeville shows to sophisticated radio and television studios and Hollywood film sets. In 1939 she became the first African American to win an Oscar when she was named best

Hattie McDaniel

supporting actress for her role as Mammy in *Gone With the Wind*.

McDaniel performed in some three hundred movies all told, though she received credit in only about seventy of them. Usually she played a "mammy" or maid who humorously catered to the whims of her white employers. One of her best-known roles, and the one that brought her the most fans, was the maid Beulah in the radio and television shows of that name.

While McDaniel was sometimes criticized for playing such stereotypical roles, she injected so much character into her performances that she gave lie to the stereotype. Moreover, as she pointed out, "It's better to get seven thousand dollars a week for playing a servant than seven dollars a week for being one." At a time when it was hard for black actors to find work, McDaniel was not only getting parts but was using her earnings to help others. She was involved in a number of causes, including one that provided educational scholarships for young African Americans.

Singer and vaudeville performer

Hattie McDaniel was the thirteenth child of the Baptist minister Henry McDaniel and his wife Susan (Holbert) McDaniel. Soon after Hattie was born, the family moved to Denver, Colorado, where the children attended the local elementary school and East Denver High School. Hattie was a student at the high school when, at the age of fifteen, her recital of "Convict Joe" won her a gold medal in dramatic art from the Woman's Christian Temperance Union. However, she began her professional career as a singer, not an actress.

McDaniel's brother, Otis, led a traveling vaudeville group, and McDaniel joined his company in her late teens, writing her own songs and performing them in tent shows in the small towns they visited. She made recordings of some of her songs, and in 1915 she sang on a Denver radio show with Professor George Morrison's Negro Orchestra. McDaniel was the first African American woman to sing on radio. During the following years she sang with a number of vaudeville groups and at one point had her own act in Kansas City. She also sang at conventions, and in 1925 she moved into the theaters when she landed a part in the operetta *Showboat,* which toured major cities throughout the country.

Although the tour brought McDaniel to a wide audience, she found herself out of work in Milwaukee a few years later. To fill the gap until she could join another show, she took a job as a maid at Sam Pick's Suburban Inn. This gave McDaniel the experience she was to use time and again in her film and broadcasting career, though in fact she did not remain a maid long. Auditioning to join the Suburban Inn's variety show, she sang "St. Louis Blues" with such effect that she won a starring role. She remained with the show for the next two years.

Hollywood actress and radio star

In 1931 McDaniel moved to Hollywood, where she had immediate success as Hi-Hat Hattie in "The Optimistic Donuts Show" on Los Angeles radio. The following year she played in her first movie, *The Golden West* (1932). This was the beginning of a film career that kept McDaniel busy for the next quarter of a century.

McDaniel's most noted movie roles were in *Blonde Venus* (1932), *Babbit* (1934), *The Little Colonel* (1935), *Music Is Magic* (1935), her Oscar-winning *Gone With the Wind* (1939), *They Died With Their Boots On* (1941), *Reap the Wild Wind* (1942), and *Since You Went Away* (1944). She also gained widespread praise for her role as Mammy in the classic production of *Showboat* (1936), which starred Paul Robeson.

Although McDaniel's movie career was built on the image of a "mammy" who was at the beck and call of whites, she used her expressive face and voice to shape her characters so deftly that they often seemed stronger and wiser than the white people they served. McDaniel took the same approach in her role as Beulah on CBS radio. When signing her contract for "The Beulah Show" in 1947, she insisted on being allowed to alter any script that she did not like, and she said she would not speak in dialect. The producers agreed on both counts.

"The Beulah Show" brought McDaniel to an even wider audience than her film career had. The program was immensely popular, and McDaniel became so identified with her character that she often received mail addressed to "Beulah McDaniel." When the show moved to television in 1950, actress Ethel Waters was at first chosen to play Beulah, but there was such a public outcry that Waters bowed out in 1951, and the part was given to McDaniel. Since McDaniel died the following year, this was her only television role, but she appeared in a number of radio shows, including "The Rudy Vallee Show" (1941) and "Amos 'n Andy" (1945).

Although McDaniel gained her greatest fame in the role of a servant, she was not at all subservient in real life. Married four times, she was a woman of strong character who was prepared to fight for causes she believed in. When she wanted to buy a house in a white neighborhood in California, she fought—and won—an antidiscrimination suit against those who tried to stop her. She supported numerous good causes, especially those that helped African Americans, and in World War II she organized entertainment for black troops.

During her life McDaniel had often led the way for other African Americans—the first black woman to sing on radio in the United States, the first black actor to win an Oscar—and in her death she also scored a first. She was the first African American to be buried at Rosedale Cemetery in Los Angeles. McDaniel was given a lavish farewell there by her many friends in the movie business and by thousands of fans. Some fans lined up for twelve hours to pay a last tribute to their beloved Beulah.

Claude McKay

Poet, novelist
Born September 15, 1889, Sunny Ville, Jamaica
Died May 22, 1948, Chicago, Illinois

"Our Negro newspapers were morbid, full of details of clashes between colored and white, murderous shootings and hangings.... During this time 'If We Must Die' exploded in me."

Claude McKay is best known for his poem "If We Must Die," in which he calls on his kinsmen to resist oppression. "If we must die, O let us nobly die." he wrote. "Like men we'll face the murderous, cowardly pack/Pressed to the wall, dying, but fighting back!"

First published in 1919, the poem was much quoted in the 1960s at the height of the civil rights movement, and it brought a renewed interest in McKay himself, who was the most radical poet of the Harlem Renaissance of the 1920s. Over the years his poetry had fallen out of fashion, but twenty years after his death, his powerful verses against racism swept him back to popularity. McKay's poems are now found in many anthologies and his three novels are also being read once more. Like most of his poetry, his prose works focus on the problems and frustrations faced by black people in a white society.

A Jamaican upbringing

Festus Claudius McKay was the youngest of the eleven children of Thomas and Ann (Edwards) McKay. His father, who was descended from the Ashanti people of West Africa, farmed a small plot of land in Sunny Ville, in Jamaica's Clarendon Mountains. Although Africa was far away, it was very much part of McKay's home life, for his father often recounted the folk tales told him by *his* father. McKay's grandfather had been born in Africa, where he had been seized and taken away as a slave, and McKay heard many stories of the cruelties of slavery. Even as a young child he developed a strong distrust of whites, along with a fierce pride in his African roots.

The boy's distrust of whites did not include Walter Jekyll, an Englishman who had come to Jamaica to study the local folklore. Jekyll encouraged McKay to read poetry and gave him the run of his library. The boy also received encouragement from his schoolteacher brother, Uriah. As a result, he came to know the works of all the major English poets, as well as many other English writers. His early poems reflected their style until Jekyll suggested that instead of imitating the English classics, he should write in the Jamaican dialect.

When McKay was seventeen, he left Sunny Ville to become an apprentice to a cabinetmaker in Brown's Town, but he did not like the work and two years later he moved to Kingston to join the police force. Until he went to Kingston, McKay had always lived in areas where blacks were the majority, but in the capital there were far more whites than blacks, and for the first time in his life he ran up against overt racism. As a policeman, he saw that the people with the darkest skins always received the worst punishments. Similarly, those with the darkest skins had to make do with the worst jobs. McKay stuck it out for almost a year before giving up in disgust and returning home.

Back in Sunny Ville, he collected together the poems he had been writing, and with Jekyll's help he sent them to England, where they were published as *Songs of Jamaica* (1911) and *Constab Ballads* (1912). Both collections were written in dialect. *Songs of Jamaica* was based on the poet's childhood experiences and showed a great love for the way of life of the average Jamaican. By contrast, the works in *Constab Ballads* were angry, expressing McKay's hatred of Kingston.

The firebrand poet

Songs of Jamaica won McKay a medal from Jamaica's Institute of Arts and Sciences. He was the first black Jamaican ever to received this award, and he used the money that came with it to pay for his journey to the United States. Arriving there late in 1912, he enrolled at Tuskegee Institute in Alabama, where he studied for two months before moving on to Kansas State College as an agriculture student. Over the next two years, McKay gradually came to the conclusion that he did not want a career in agriculture, and by 1914 he was in New York City, working at various jobs while writing some very strong poetry.

Claude McKay

In New York, McKay once again encountered the racial bigotry and blatant unfairness that had so angered him in Kingston, and it fired him to express his rage through his poems. Some of his verses were so outspoken that they were refused by *Crisis,* the literary magazine of the National Association for the Advancement of Colored People (NAACP). However, McKay found a sponsor in Frank Harris, the Irish-American writer and publisher. Harris was himself an outspoken man, and he was so impressed by the hard-hitting way McKay wrote about racial prejudice that he sought him out and published some of his poems in *Pearson's Magazine.*

McKay had chosen the pen name Eli Edwards when he first had his poetry published in the United States, but at Harris's suggestion he began to call himself Claude McKay. It was under this name that "If We Must Die" was published in the *Liberator* in 1919. McKay was inspired to write the poem because of recent outbreaks of violence, which had caused many African Americans to fear for their lives. Although he was speaking for black Americans at a particular period in history, the poem has had a universal appeal in that it touches all who are oppressed in any age and in any part of the world. However, when it first came out, the poem found its audience largely among the black community, who hailed McKay as an important new writer.

Writer and traveler

The next few years saw McKay publishing two more volumes of poetry, *Spring in New Hampshire and Other Poems* (1920) and *Harlem Shadows* (1922), which contains some of his best-known verse. During this period, he spent over a year in Europe before returning to the United States in 1921 to become an associate editor of the *Liberator.* The editor of the *Liberator* was the white Marxist writer Max Eastman, who had been a friend of McKay for some time and had convinced him to become a communist. McKay twice visited Russia and was a guest at the Fourth Congress of the Communist party in 1923, but he became less enthusiastic about communism as the years passed.

By the end of 1923 McKay was in Paris, and he stayed in Europe for the next ten years, living in France, Germany, Spain, and also in Morocco. His three novels, *Home to Harlem* (1928), *Banjo* (1929), and *Banana Bottom* (1933) were written during these years, as was the collection of short stories, *Gingertown* (1932). While all these books did well, *Home to Harlem* was especially successful. Reprinted five times in its first two months, it was the first novel by a black writer to appear on the bestseller lists.

McKay spent his last years in the United States, and his major work during this period was his autobiography, *A Long Way from Home* (1937). As the book makes clear, he was by then totally disillusioned with communism. Toward the end of his life he became a Roman Catholic, and some of his later poems reflect his religious conversion. Whatever his views, McKay never ceased to compose strong and eloquent poetry. His talent for expressing the feelings of fellow African Americans has assured him a permanent place in American literature.

Floyd B. McKissick

Former CORE national director
Born March 9, 1922, Asheville, North
　Carolina
Died April 28, 1991, Durham, North Carolina

"Black Power is no mere slogan. It is a movement dedicated to the exercise of American democracy in its highest tradition; it is a drive to mobilize the black communities of this country in a monumental effort to remove the basic causes of alienation, frustration, despair, low self-esteem, and hopelessness."

N orth Carolina district court judge Floyd B. McKissick dedicated his life to the cause of black civil rights. He was the first black admitted to the law school at the University of North Carolina, and he used his legal talents to end segregation in the South.

As the head of the Congress of Racial Equality (CORE), McKissick helped determine the direction of the Black Power movement of the 1960s. He urged his members to spearhead a nonviolent revolution to widen civic, political, and economic opportunities for blacks. Later in life he received federal aid to begin Soul City, a North Carolina community dedicated to black business opportunities.

Felt the sting of racism

McKissick was born on March 9, 1922, in Asheville, North Carolina, to Ernest and Magnolia McKissick. Asheville was a popular tourist spot for the wealthy, and McKissick's father was the head bellhop in one of the luxury hotels. The family lived comfortably, but his father's position meant he was subservient to the whims of the guests. He told his sons that success could only be achieved through education.

McKissick's later talents as a speaker and a leader may have developed by watching his grandfathers. His paternal grandfather was a Baptist minister, his maternal grandfather a Methodist minister. McKissick was deeply devoted to the Baptist faith and served as a deacon and a youth leader.

Although a model student, McKissick experienced racism as a youngster growing up in the South. When he was a twelve-year-old Boy Scout, he was assigned to direct traffic during an all-black, roller skating tournament. A policeman saw him directing traffic, knocked him down, and then arrested him.

McKissick gained extra income by delivering groceries and newspapers and by shining shoes. He graduated from high school at the beginning of World War II and was drafted into the army. He was sent to Europe, received the Purple Heart for being wounded in action, and rose to the rank of sergeant. After the war he used the GI bill to help him attend college. He started at the all-black Morehouse College in Atlanta and later transferred to North Carolina College in Durham to finish his degree.

Sued the University of North Carolina for admission—and won

To help combat racism, which was an everyday occurrence in the South, McKissick joined the National Association for the Advancement of Colored People (NAACP). While he was still in college he became the youth chairman of the North Carolina NAACP, and he was an early member of the Congress of Racial Equality, an interracial organization that aimed to publicize the plight of blacks through nonviolent means. In 1947 McKissick met CORE founder James Farmer on the Journey of Reconciliation, an integrated bus ride through parts of South.

In the early 1950s McKissick decided to become a lawyer and applied to the University of North Carolina at Chapel Hill Law School. When the university denied him admission because of his race, McKissick turned for help to Thurgood Marshall, the NAACP lawyer who later became the country's first black Supreme Court justice. Marshall won the NAACP's suit against the college, and McKissick became the first black law student at the university to earn an LL.B. degree.

After graduating McKissick decided to battle racial injustice full time, for he realized that getting an education was not enough to

Floyd B. McKissick

guarantee success for blacks. As he told a reporter for the *New York Post:* "I was as educated as any white lawyer in my area. Do you think I had the opportunity to be a judge?... You can educate the black man [but] you've got to overcome the racism to get him the job. There's got to be some counterpart in education of that portion of the white community that is bigoted."

McKissick decided to challenge existing laws in several all-white schools in Durham, North Carolina, by using his own children. He also defended CORE demonstrators on trial for sitting at lunch counters and in theaters for "whites only." By the early 1960s, his law firm was handling 5,600 cases at one time, for which McKissick was traveling nationwide.

Distinguished with judicial appointment

When he was a high-ranking member of CORE, McKissick declared that the economic gulf was widening between blacks and whites. He believed that the gains made by the civil rights movement in the areas of school and public facilities did not address the real issues. Many other civil rights leaders shared his views, and as the 1960s progressed, blacks became increasingly impatient with the rate of social change. CORE responded by replacing national chairman Charles R. Oldham with McKissick in 1963. In his acceptance speech McKissick hinted that if blacks could not obtain their rights through the courts, they must resort to direct action. He warned that if the white majority ignored nonviolent black protests, then blacks would turn to direct action. His predictions came true when many violent riots broke out a few years later.

In January, 1966, McKissick succeeded James Farmer as CORE's national director. Thereafter he lobbied the federal government for aid to inner cities and became a fierce opponent of the Vietnam War. Under his direction CORE supported the Black Power movement. McKissick believed Black Power would mobilize blacks to overcome their feelings of alienation, frustration, despair, and low self-esteem. He wanted CORE to bring political economic power to blacks, especially those in the ghetto.

McKissick resigned from CORE in 1968 to support Republican Richard Nixon's candidacy for president. He was rewarded for his support when he received federal funds from the New Communities Act to build a new town in North Carolina. Named Soul City, it was to be a black-run metropolis with business and industrial opportunities for minority businesses. McKissick predicted the community would have 40,000 residents by the end of the century. However, his plans have yet to be realized, and by the end of the 1970s the government ended its funding of the project. In 1991 it was estimated that Soul City had a population of approximately 200.

In 1990 the governor of North Carolina named him a judge to the state's ninth district court. By then he was already suffering from lung cancer, which resulted in his death on April 28, 1991. He is buried in Soul City, just several blocks from the house he shared with his family.

Terry McMillan

Novelist
Born October 18, 1951, Port Huron, Michigan

"Even though a lot of 'professional' men claim to want a smart, independent woman, they're kidding themselves."

Watch Terry McMillan. She's going to be a major writer," commented *Cosmopolitan* magazine in its review of McMillan's first novel, *Mama* (1987). In the few years since this prediction, McMillan has lived up to expectations by producing two more blockbusters, *Disappearing Acts* (1989) and *Waiting to Exhale* (1992). She has sold movie rights to both books.

McMillan's novels all feature strong-minded women like herself, though her own achievements far outshine those of her heroines. Her most successful book, *Waiting to*

Exhale, sold hundreds of thousands of hardback copies before McMillan won a whopping $2.64 million for the paperback rights. Very seldom has any author been paid so much for paperback rights. McMillan still finds it all rather overwhelming. "It's wonderful, it's a writer's dream," she says, "but it doesn't really feel like it's happening to me."

Discovered books on the job

Born into a working-class family, McMillan was the eldest of the five children of Madeline and Edward McMillan. She grew up in the small town of Port Huron, about sixty miles northeast of Detroit. McMillan says that she learned from her mother "how to be strong and resilient." McMillan's father was an alcoholic who often became violent. In this stressful situation McMillan's mother not only struggled to cope at home but became the main wage earner in the family, bringing in a small but regular income as a worker in an auto plant.

When McMillan was thirteen, her mother divorced her father. McMillan helped out by taking a part-time job shelving books in the local library. She had never been interested in books—there were seldom any at home—but handling so many of them in the library soon turned her into an avid reader. McMillan was surprised one day when she came across a book by James Baldwin and saw from the cover photo that he was black. She had not realized that African Americans wrote books.

At the time, McMillan had no ambition to be a writer, but during the next few years she gradually developed an interest in African American writing. When she was seventeen she left Michigan for California, where she worked as a secretary in Los Angeles while taking a course on Afro-American literature. McMillan started to write almost by accident—composing a poem to ease her feelings after an unhappy love affair. Before long she was trying her hand at prose as well.

Having realized how much she enjoyed writing, McMillan enrolled at the University of California at Berkeley, where she studied journalism for three years. She graduated with a bachelor's degree in 1976, the same year she first had a short story published. She then moved to New York City to study for a master's degree at Columbia University but soon dropped out, because she found the school so racist. This was a difficult period for McMillan, since she was also having problems in her relationship with Leonard Welch, the man she lived with. To help support them both she took a job word processing. Meanwhile, she joined the Harlem Writers Guild, and it was there she gained the impetus to get started on a novel.

Best-selling novelist sued by former lover

McMillan's first novel, *Mama,* was based to a large extent on her mother's experiences. The story of a woman who raises five children in difficult circumstances, McMillan completed the first draft shortly before her son Solomon Welch was born in 1984. She then spent more than a year perfecting the manuscript—only to have her agent suggest a number of changes. Annoyed at this interference, McMillan decided to act as her own agent, which she did with great success: the manuscript was ac-

Terry McMillan

cepted by Houghton Mifflin, the first publisher she showed it to.

Since Houghton Mifflin would not mount a large publicity campaign for a first novel by an unknown author, McMillan took matters into her own hands. "I've never been passive, and I'm not going to start now," she announced. To advertise the book she wrote to more than 3,000 bookstores, universities, and colleges, and then scheduled her own publicity tour, which included giving thirty-nine readings. The publicity blitz paid off. Within six weeks of publication in 1987, *Mama* went into its third printing.

That same year McMillan left New York for Laramie, Wyoming, where she had an appointment as visiting writer at the University of Wyoming. Her son's father, Leonard Welch, did not accompany her. Their relationship had come to an end. But it was to reappear in print in McMillan's next novel, *Disappearing Acts,* the story of a love affair between Zora, an ambitious young musician, and Franklin, a high school dropout. Some of the story is told by the woman, Zora, and some by Franklin.

The editors at Houghton Mifflin were so impressed by the way McMillan was able to think like a man when writing Franklin's sections that they suggested she write the whole story from his point of view. This annoyed McMillan. She felt she was being used to prove a point: "Black woman writes story from black man's point of view, it's never been done, blah, blah, blah, blah, blah." She took the manuscript away from Houghton Mifflin and offered it to Viking Penguin.

When *Disappearing Acts* was published by Viking Penguin in 1989, it was an instant success, garnering excellent reviews and selling hundreds of thousands of copies. It seemed that everyone was reading the book. All this infuriated Leonard Welch, who saw himself in many of the scenes and asserted that McMillan had written the story to revenge herself on him. In 1990 Welch filed a $4.75 million defamation suit against McMillan and her publishers, but when the case came to trial two years later, it was decided against him. The judge declared that, although there were many similarities between Welch and the fictional character, "the man in the novel is a lazy, emotionally disturbed alcoholic who uses drugs and sometimes beats his girlfriend.... Leonard Welch is none of these."

McMillan's third novel, *Waiting to Exhale* (1992), took up one of the threads of *Disappearing Acts* in that it again featured strong-minded, intelligent women. The story is about four professional black women who have everything going for them except a good relationship with their men. This is a subject McMillan feels strongly about: "Even though a lot of 'professional' men claim to want a smart, independent woman, they're kidding themselves." She maintains that what the men really want is a passive woman who will give in to them and allow them to feel superior.

McMillan herself is anything but passive, and she responds tartly when attacked for such things as the foul language in her books: "I've never read a review where they complain about the language that male writers use!" In 1989 McMillan was appointed professor at the University of Arizona at Tucson. Soon after her arrival, she turned her attention to promoting the works of other black writers and in 1990 published a collection of short stories, *Breaking Ice: An Anthology of Contemporary African American Fiction*. In the introduction to this collection McMillan wrote that her generation of black writers is "a new breed, free to write as we please."

Thelma "Butterfly" McQueen

Actress
Born January 8, 1911, Tampa, Florida

"Each of us is born 'perfect'; we acquire habits of hate."

Thelma McQueen's career as a stage and screen actress spans more than fifty years. She took the stage name Butterfly McQueen in 1935 when she made her debut in the "Butterfly Ballet." Four years later she won world fame as the slave girl Prissy in the movie *Gone with the Wind*. Since then McQueen has appeared in numerous plays and films, as well as on television and in musicals. Despite her talent, McQueen found that her film career came to an abrupt halt when she objected to being given only "black woman" parts, such as maid and servant. In the lean years that followed, while McQueen took what work she could get, she also put herself through college. She graduated at the age of 64 with a B.A. from City University of New York.

Of all her achievements, McQueen is most proud of her community work. She teaches at recreational centers and is involved in projects to protect the environment. "Community work comes first," she says. "I don't like people to call me a star. I'm not a star. I'm a community worker." Nevertheless, she is indeed a star—a highly talented actress. This was obvious many years ago when she first attracted attention with her witty performances and deliciously piping voice.

Attracted to dance and acting

An only child, McQueen was raised alone by her mother, after her father, a stevedore at the Tampa docks, left home when McQueen was five. They moved from city to city in search of work until her mother found a permanent job as a cook in Harlem. In 1924 they moved again, settling this time in Babylon on Long Island.

As a result of her unsettled childhood, McQueen was educated at number of different schools, which ranged from St. Benedict's Convent in Augusta, Georgia, to a school at

Thelma "Butterfly" McQueen

Walker Baptist Church. In Harlem she attended the local public school, and she completed high school in Babylon, after which she took a course in nursing at Lincoln Training School in the Bronx. But already McQueen was looking toward the stage. Soon after graduating from high school she joined a dance group—the Negro Youth Group run by Venezuela Jones—and she also became a member of a dramatic club.

Dance and drama soon won out over nursing, and during the next few years McQueen studied under the famous Katherine Dunham and other teachers of dance and acting. Her performance in the "Butterfly Ballet" in 1935 whetted her appetite for a stage career, and in 1937 she appeared on Broadway in the murder drama *Brown Sugar.* McQueen was cast as a maid—the stereotype role she would rebel against when she was older—but she played it for only four days before the show was closed. Her next role, in *Brother Rat,* lasted for more

than a year, and in 1938 she appeared in *What a Life,* remaining a member of the cast when the show went on tour.

Played the role of Prissy in *Gone with the Wind*

Although all McQueen's roles were very small, she played them with a whimsical humor and delightful charm that invariably evoked laughter in her audiences. It was these qualities that caused her to be picked for the role of Prissy in *Gone with the Wind.* In Margaret Mitchell's book on which the movie was based, the slave girl Prissy was portrayed as slow and dull-witted. While McQueen kept faithfully to this image, she succeeded in presenting Prissy with a delicacy that was pathetic as well as humorous. With her high-pitched voice, ready smile, and large expressive eyes, she made the timid slave girl into a memorable character.

Her performance delighted Margaret Mitchell's agent, who wrote to the author: "I can hardly wait for the picture to be shown so you can laugh at the scenes where Prissy does her stuff. Butterfly McQueen is a good actress.... Every time Prissy worked in a scene we have a grand time."

However, McQueen did not always have a grand time when making the movie. She had to put up with racist jokes from a director, who thought it funny to pretend she really was a slave. He used to threaten to "sell her South" if she didn't follow his instructions. Then there was the time the script called for her to be slapped by the actress Vivien Leigh, who was playing Scarlett O'Hara. Leigh slapped too hard, causing McQueen to protest: "I'm not a stunt man, I'm an actress." She refused to take any more slaps, and in the second shooting of the scene Leigh had to make do with a "pretend" slap.

McQueen showed her metal in several other ways too. She refused to be filmed eating watermelon and spitting out the seeds—it was insultingly stereotype, she said—and she was part of the delegation of black actors who insisted that the restrooms be desegregated. She also objected when the white stars were provided with limousines while the black actors were made to share one crowded car. Nevertheless, *Gone with the Wind* was a high point in McQueen's career, bringing her worldwide acclaim.

Career experienced revival in 1980s

McQueen's performance in *Gone with the Wind* led to more movie roles, and the 1940s saw her appearing in *Affectionately Yours* (1941), *Cabin in the Sky* (1943), *Mildred Pierce* (1945), *Flame of Barbary Coast* (1945), and several other pictures. She was nearly always typecast as a maid, which she found increasingly objectionable, and toward the end of the 1940s she refused to accept any more maid parts. Since few other roles were offered to black actresses in those days, McQueen did not act in another film for about twenty years.

McQueen survived the hard years by acting in the theater whenever possible and by taking all sorts of jobs, which ranged from running a restaurant to selling toys at Macy's. She used some of her savings to stage her own one-woman show in Carnegie Recital Hall in 1951. Meanwhile, she played in a number of other shows, including the all-black production of *The World's My Oyster* (1956). In 1957 McQueen gained a following on television for her role in *The Green Pastures* (1957), and this led to other television appearances. As well, she performed in musicals, including her own musical revue, *Butterfly McQueen and Friends,* which opened in New York in 1969. In 1976 she staged another one-woman show, *Prissy in Person,* and a few years later she toured in the musical *Showboat.*

The 1970s saw McQueen at last getting back into films with a few small roles, but her real comeback occurred in the 1980s as a result of the celebrations marking the fiftieth anniversary of the publication of *Gone with the Wind.* Once more in the limelight, McQueen was invited to numerous showings of the movie. She was a guest on television talk shows and was sought eagerly by film and television producers. In 1986 she played Ma Kennywick in *Mosquito Coast,* and in 1989 she appeared in two movies, *Polly* and *Stiff.*

The wheel had come full circle. Stage and screen star Butterfly McQueen was once more reaching large and enthusiastic audiences.

James Meredith

Civil rights activist
Born June 25, 1933, Kosciusko, Mississippi

"I will be, in the future, the most important black leader in America and the world. I have a divine responsibility to lead the black race to its rightful destiny."

When James Meredith showed up to register for classes at the all-white University of Mississippi in 1962, little did he realize he would be the cause of a mammoth riot that saw hundreds of people injured and took twenty-two thousand troops to end. Four years later he embarked on a solitary "walk against fear" from Memphis, Tennessee, to Jackson, Mississippi, to encourage black voter registration, and this time he was felled by a shotgun blast. More than two decades later, Meredith continues to march to his own drummer, supporting North Carolina Senator Jesse Helms, a staunch conservative who came to Congress in 1972, and former Ku Klux Klansman David Duke.

James Meredith

Eight hours to school and back

Meredith is the son of Cap and Roxie Meredith, who owned eighty-four acres and raised a variety of crops. He spent eight hours each day walking to and from school, and was known as the smartest and strongest boy at his Negro training school. When he was seventeen years old, his father sent him to live with an uncle in St. Petersburg, Florida, so he could attend a better high school. He immediately set out to win the respect of his classmates. He beat up two bullies, the first using a stick lined with nails, the second with his bare fists.

Meredith wanted to prove his academic qualities by entering an American Legion essay-writing contest. The paper was supposed to be about why he was proud to be an American, but Meredith wrote that he was proud of what American could become, not of what it was. His teachers rejected it, saying it was not good enough to represent the school, but he went over their heads and submitted it anyway. His paper won the contest.

After high school, Meredith served nine years in the U.S. Air Force, then enrolled at Mississippi's all-black Jackson State College. He attended class wearing an army uniform, a black leather biker jacket, pea cap, and cane. Meredith completed his degree requirements, but he did not graduate from Jackson State because he refused to pay a $4.50 diploma fee.

To show his opposition to the second-class status of blacks in Mississippi, Meredith decided to become the first black to apply for admission to the prestigious University of Mississippi (known as Ole Miss). Meredith believed that President John F. Kennedy needed the Negro vote if he wanted to win re-election in 1964; if the Mississippi state legislature would not grant him admission to Ole Miss, then Kennedy would have to step in or risk being called a hypocrite over his civil rights reforms. Meredith was denied admission to the spring semester, so he wrote to the U.S. Justice Department for assistance. He also contacted the National Association for the Advancement of Colored People, which promised him legal assistance. Meredith filed suit in federal court, but the judge ruled against him. He then appealed to the U.S. Court of Appeals for the Fifth Circuit, which finally ruled in his favor on June 25, 1962. Governor Ross Barnett of Mississippi then instructed state education and university officials to ignore the court orders.

Riots at Ole Miss

President Kennedy did enter the fray by issuing a proclamation damning the actions of Barnett and other state officials who opposed the court orders. He also issued an executive order authorizing the Secretary of Defense to use armed force if necessary to get Meredith to school. Flanked by federal marshals, highway patrolmen, and school officials, Meredith entered his dormitory room on September 30, 1962. But he was not home free. A riot erupted outside. People fired guns, and tear gas choked the air. Two men were shot and killed. National guardsmen came in to restore order, and at the president's request, twenty-two thousand army troops moved in. By 8 A.M. the next day, Meredith had formally enrolled as a political science major, 175 people had been injured, and 212 were arrested. Meredith was front-page news across the country, and people admired his courage and determination.

Meredith made headlines again four years later when he decided to embark on a solitary "walk against fear" from Memphis, Tennessee, to Jackson, Mississippi, to inspire black voter registration. When curious onlookers asked him what he was trying to do, Meredith replied that if he could walk unarmed through Mississippi during primary-election week, then he might just soothe the fears of black people and get them to the polls. When he was about twenty miles south of the Mississippi/Tennessee state line, somebody reported a white man hiding in a gully with a gun waiting to kill him. The report was ignored. James Norvell stepped out of the woods, called Meredith's name, and then started shooting. His first shots missed, but his second and third ones found their mark, and Meredith was shot in the legs and back. Norvell was quickly captured by the police. Meredith eventually recovered without any long-term effects.

After graduating from the university, Meredith was offered a scholarship from the Nigerian government. He stayed there for several months, but the money he was promised never came. In an *Esquire* interview he said, "I didn't know how I was going to make it, and that was when a woman came on campus looking for me. I didn't know her, but she found me. A white woman. She endorsed 3,600 British pounds to me in ... traveller's checks. She had a knapsack on her back. She left and I never heard from her again."

After Africa, Meredith went to Columbia Law School and earned his degree. In 1971 he returned to Mississippi and incurred the wrath of many blacks by failing to endorse Charles Evers for governor. Evers was a mayor and the first black to run for the governor's office.

Meredith settled in Jackson and began managing a nightclub. From 1972 to 1979 he ran for public office unsuccessfully five times.

He also started his own church called the Reunification Under God Church, which tried to teach black men how to grow their own food. Meredith occasionally staged a protest walk, but received little attention from the press.

In 1979 Meredith's wife, Mary June, died at age forty of a heart attack, leaving Meredith with three sons to raise. His brother, Arthur, told *Esquire* that after losing his wife, "I noticed the greatest change in James. He cried a lot, and I couldn't remember him ever doing that. Daddy used to say, 'No use crying when somebody dies.'"

Troubles in Ohio

Meredith tried several times to get a college teaching job in Mississippi (including at Ole Miss). In 1984 the University of Cincinnati gave him a year-long contract to be a lecturer in Afro-American studies. He moved to Ohio with his new wife, television reporter Judy Alsobrooks, and two of their children. It was not long before Meredith found himself in trouble. He charged the university with failing to graduate any black athletes since 1964, when the truth was that more than twenty had graduated over the previous decade. He also complained that blacks were not adequately represented on the city's school board, when in fact three of the board's seven members were black. In another incident, police had to escort him out of a health club when he failed to produce a membership card. He later filed charges against the police, saying he was picked on because he was black.

After a year the University of Cincinnati decided not to renew his position, and

Meredith moved to San Diego because he felt he could obtain a high-level position in the Republican party. North Carolina Senator Jesse Helms offered him a position to do research and write papers. Meredith and Helms eventually parted company, and Meredith threw his support behind David Duke's unsuccessful bid for the Republican party's 1992 presidential nomination.

Although Meredith now remains on the periphery of the American political scene, he intends to play a key role in the black movement. "I will be, in the future, the most important black leader in America and the world," he once said. "I have a divine responsibility to lead the black race to its rightful destiny."

Ron Milner

Playwright
Born May 29, 1938, Detroit, Michigan

"There used to be a lot of screaming and hate.... It was reacting to white racism.... We're no longer dealing with 'I am somebody' but more of who that 'somebody' really is."

A major force in promoting theater that is specifically by and for African Americans, Ron Milner has drawn wide attention since his first play was staged in the 1960s. His plays represent a change in approach in black theater, a shift from angry and violent dramas to less aggressive works that make the same points in a subtler and quieter manner.

One of Milner's aims as a playwright is to create a greater sense of understanding and unity within black families and within the black community in general. His plays are concerned with moral principles and promote such virtues as honesty and integrity. This has caused some critics to call Milner a preacher, a label he does not at all mind. Milner has said that he wants his works to educate the audiences as well as entertain them. "When people call me a preacher," he says, "I consider it a compliment.... When you get an emotional response it's easier to involve the mind."

Turned to playwriting

Ronald Milner grew up in Detroit, where he attended Northeastern High School and then spent a brief period at Highland Park Junior College and the Detroit Institute of Technology. He decided to become a writer during his teenage years, though his first attempt was a novel rather than a play.

"The more I read at high school," he once said, "the more I realized that some tremendous, phenomenal things were happening around me." On Hastings Street, where Milner's family lived, he saw many of the same things described in the novels of William Faulkner. "I thought why should these crazy people Faulkner writes about seem more important than my mother or my father or the dude down the street. Only because they had someone to write about them. So I became a writer."

In 1962 Milner won a fellowship to complete a novel called *Life with Father Brown,* though he did not manage to get it published. Two years later he went to New York to attend a writing workshop at Columbia University. He became involved in the theater through his association with director and actor Woodie

Ron Milner

King, and in 1965 he joined up with King at the newly formed American Place Theater in New York. The following year Milner's first play was produced there. Entitled *Who's Got His Own,* the play was later taken on tour of colleges in New York State, after which it returned to New York City, where it was shown at the New Lafayette Theater in 1967.

Who's Got His Own was about relationships within a family and the efforts of the various family members to get on with one another. An underlying theme was the problems faced by African American men as a result of the subservient role they had been forced into for so many generations. This was also a major theme in Milner's next play, *The Warning—A Theme for Linda* (1969), in which he explored male behavior through the eyes of the heroine. Milner's third play, *The Monster* (1969), again dealt with black manhood, though in this case the setting was a college campus rather than a family.

By 1970 Milner was widely recognized as a skilled playwright who had something important to say. He was particularly well known in colleges and universities, where his plays were frequently performed and where he himself was a familiar figure as a guest speaker and visiting playwright. Milner once remarked, "I've taught at college more than I've attended." He was writer-in-residence at Lincoln University 1966–67 and he taught at Michigan State University in 1971–72. He later led a playwriting workshop at Wayne State University.

Succeeded wildly with *What the Wine Sellers Buy*

In the early 1970s Milner returned to Detroit, where he founded his own theater company, the Spirit of Shango. His main aim in doing so was to get young African Americans involved in theater, both as actors and audience. This was a long-standing concern of Milner, who had written a number of essays pointing out the need for black playwrights to attract a black audience, in much the same way as black musicians had done in the development of jazz.

Milner was particularly writing for black teenagers in his next play, *M(ego) and the Green Ball of Freedom,* a brief skit that included music and dance. By means of a story line about a revolutionary who had escaped jail after many years inside, the play showed young people the changes that had taken place in the black community since the early 1960s. *M(ego)* was first staged at the Spirit of Shango theater in 1971, and it has since become a staple of the theater's repertoire.

In Milner's best-known drama, *What the Wine Sellers Buy* (1973), he was again speaking to the black community and especially to black teenagers. The story centers on seventeen-year-old Steve Carlton, who lives in Detroit and is persistently tempted by the unprincipled Rico. Smooth-talking Rico tries to persuade Steve to make money by turning his girlfriend into a prostitute. Steve resists the temptation—what could he buy with the money that would be even half as valuable as his girlfriend?—but he is then faced with other difficulties.

Milner was motivated to write the play by his hatred of prostitution and drugs and the way they are glorified in movies such as *Superfly:* "I've actually seen a 10-year-old boy sniffing salt … because he wanted to look like Superfly. You see enough cases of this and it suddenly becomes important enough to write about."

What the Wine Sellers Buy opened at the New Federal Theater in New York in May 1973 and was so popular with black audiences that a new production was launched in Los Angeles in October. The following year saw it playing at the Lincoln Center—the first play by an African American ever to be performed there. A shorter version of *What the Wine Sellers Buy* then went on a nationwide tour, with record-breaking results. In city after city the drama played to packed houses for weeks on end, racking up huge profits. In Chicago alone it is said to have taken in more than a million dollars.

Part of the appeal of the play lay in its superb characterization. The evil Rico was thoroughly convincing and was recognizable as a the worse type of American businessman—"the people who pollute the air and water for profit." As Milner pointed out, when Rico "talks about everything for profit, trading everything for money, he's talking about society."

Created a body of African American plays

Milner's later dramas have continued to fulfill his aims of attracting black audiences and appealing to young people. To heighten the appeal and emphasize the relevance of his works, he has often used music and dance, as in the popular *Jazz-set* (1980) and *Crack Steppin'* (1981). Another popular success was *Don't Get God Started,* which opened on Broadway in 1987.

Because of Milner's plays and the energetic way he has promoted black theater, African Americans are no longer subjected to large doses of white American culture when they want a night out at a show. Milner summed it up nicely when he said: "'Theater' and 'play' have always meant going to see somebody else's culture and seeing how you could translate it into your own terms. People always felt they were going to a foreign place for some foreign reason. But now there's a theater written to them, of them, for them and about them." He added: "Theater lifts a community in more ways than one. The idea of seeing yourself magnified and dramatized on stage gives you a whole perspective on who you are and where you are." It is this credo that has inspired Milner to reach a growing African American audience with his insightful dramas.

Thelonious Monk

Pianist, composer, bandleader
Born October 10, 1917, Rocky Mountain, North Carolina
Died February 17, 1982, Englewood, New Jersey

"My music is not a social comment on discrimination or poverty or the like. I would have written the same way even if I had not been a Negro."

One of the founding fathers of modern jazz, Thelonious Monk came into his own in the 1960s after being treated as an outcast for many years. His jarring music with its dissonant melodies was too "different" to gain immediate appeal. But by the 1960s Monk's compositions no longer seemed strange, and by the time of his death in the 1980s he was recognized as a brilliant and highly original musician. His best-known compositions include "Round about Midnight," "Blue Monk," "Epistrophy," and "Little Rootie Tootie."

Watching Monk perform was almost as good as listening to him. He was famed for his oddball behavior on stage. Hunched over the piano, he played the keys with his elbows as well as his fingers, and he often left the piano stool to do a shuffling dance. Nobody was ever sure what type of hat he would be wearing—fur cap, baseball cap, Chinese coolie hat, or others. With his goatee beard and bamboo-framed glasses, Thelonious Monk was the extreme eccentric—and a superb jazz musician.

Banned from Apollo Theater contests—because he always won

Thelonious Sphere Monk, Jr., was the youngest of the three children of Thelonious and Barbara (Batts) Monk. He was fascinated by the piano from his earliest years. "If anybody sat down and played the piano, I would just stand there and watch 'em all the time," he has said. He began picking out tunes almost as soon as he could walk, and he was only about five years old when he learned to read music by looking over his sister's shoulder during her piano lessons.

Monk grew up in New York, where his family settled when he was four. He was raised by his mother, for his father stayed only briefly before returning to North Carolina. Although Monk's mother earned a very small income, she saved up to buy a baby grand piano—which filled half their two-room apartment—

Thelonious Monk

and she paid for Monk to start piano lessons when he was eleven.

For two years Monk played the piano and organ at the Baptist church where his mother sang in the choir. But the music he really liked was jazz. He haunted the local jazz clubs and modeled his playing on that of popular pianist James P. Johnson. By the age of thirteen Monk was playing in the local bars as well as at "rent parties," where bands performed to raise rent money for neighbors who were out of work. Monk became such a good player that he was banned from the weekly talent contests at Harlem's Apollo Theater. It wasn't fair on the others, the manager said, because Monk always came away with the prize.

Enjoyed enormous success as a jazz pianist

When Monk was sixteen he left high school to tour the country with a woman faith healer and preacher. "She healed and I played," he later told a journalist. On his return to New York he worked as a pianist in various Harlem clubs, and in 1939 he formed his first group.

By the early 1940s Monk had become well enough known to land a job as house pianist at Minton's Playhouse, a famous Harlem club. Minton's was the main place where the type of jazz known as bepop was developed by trumpeter Dizzy Gillespie and saxophonist Charlie Parker. They would stay on after the club closed and improvise in all-night jam sessions. As the regular pianist at Minton's, Monk took part in the jam sessions, and his imaginative playing inevitably contributed to the shaping of bebop. But Monk was too much of an individual to stick to one style. He remained on the fringes of the movement, a loner doing his own thing.

Monk became even more of a loner in 1951 when he and a friend were arrested for possessing heroin. Although Monk was not a heroin addict, he went to jail for sixty days rather than let his friend down. As a result of the drug charge, Monk's cabaret license was revoked, which meant he could not play in any of the New York nightclubs. Although his wife Nellie was able to bring in money by working as a clerk, he had a very difficult time until his license was restored six years later.

During these years Monk did have one powerful friend—the Baroness de Koenigswarter, a millionairess who was passionately keen on jazz and had helped out several jazz musicians. On more than one occasion she housed Monk and his family in her apartment, and he often composed his music there. Although Monk was barred from New York clubs, he was able to write and record music, and he composed some of his classic numbers at the time. He also recorded his first solo album, *Pure Monk,* which was released in 1954, the same year he gave a series of concerts in Paris, France.

When Monk's license was renewed in 1957, he came back in style. Leading his own quartet, which included the brilliant saxophonist John Coltrane, he opened at the Five Spot Café in Greenwich Village. Jazz lovers thronged to hear him, for his records had begun to attract a following. Soon his quirky

behavior and curious dances on stage became notorious, attracting ever larger audiences. Meanwhile, his reputation was increased through such inspired albums as *Thelonious Himself* and *Monk with Coltrane,* both of which were released in 1957. But just when things seemed to be looking up for Monk he was arrested for disturbing the peace. Once again his license was removed. He was barred from playing in the clubs from 1958 until 1960.

This time, though, Monk did not languish in oblivion. He had made too much of a splash, and there were now hundreds of thousands of fans who raved over his music. In addition to his quartet, he led a ten-piece band, for which he could charge as much as $1,000 for a single performance. He was a major draw at jazz festivals, and he played to a packed audiences at Carnegie Hall and Lincoln Center and other large concert halls. He also had thousands of fans overseas, and in the early 1960s he made some enormously successful overseas tours—to Japan in 1963 and Europe the following year. By 1964 Monk was so famous that he was featured on the cover of *Time* magazine, a very rare honor for a jazz musician.

For the next ten years Monk remained at center stage, famed for his highly innovative music, eccentric performances, and brilliant recordings. But by the mid-1970s his health was failing, and he became too weak to carry on as a performer. In 1976 he gave his last concert at Carnegie Hall. He spent his final years at the New Jersey home of the Baroness de Koenigswarter.

Audley Moore

Feminist, civil rights activist
Born 1898, New Iberia, Louisiana

"They stole our language, they stole our culture. They stole our mothers and fathers and took our names away from us.... The United States will never be able to pay us all they owe us."

Audley Moore has spent her life working for causes she believes in, especially those that help African Americans and women. During her more than ninety years, she has been involved in almost every important American group that has fought for civil rights, women's rights, and Pan-African nationalism—and when there wasn't an appropriate group, she founded one.

Moore's deep commitment to rights had its roots in her childhood in the South, where her grandfather was lynched by a white mob and other men were regularly rounded up so that the police would be free to rape their wives. Moore carried these memories with her through the years that followed as she tried to create a society in which African Americans would be protected by the law and could live in safety and dignity.

Early years in the South

Audley Moore was the oldest daughter of Henry and St. Cyr Moore. Her mother died when she was five, whereupon she and her two sisters, Eloise and Lorita, were taken in by their grandmother while their father moved to New Orleans. The girls joined their father a few years later, but he died soon afterward, leaving his three daughters stranded in New Orleans. As the eldest, Audley Moore took it upon herself to support her sisters, which she did by lying about her age so that she could take work as a hairdresser.

During World War I, the Moore sisters moved to Anniston, Alabama, where Audley continued to earn a living as a hairdresser. Her sisters, who were now teenagers, were so appalled at the conditions in which the black soldiers were forced to live that they collected food and supplies for them from members of the black community. The center they set up for the men in an abandoned church building was likely the first United Services Organization (USO).

On her return to New Orleans at the end of the war, Moore married and opened a small store with her husband. In 1919 she took her first steps as an activist when the police tried to prevent the black nationalist Marcus Garvey from giving a talk during his visit to New Orleans. Moore joined the crowd that flocked to the hall, determined to hear Garvey speak. Most of the crowd were armed, and Moore herself had two guns—"one in my bosom and one in my pocket book." When the police moved in, she stood on the benches and waved her guns as the others were doing, calling on Garvey to speak. Faced with such a strong opposition, the police retreated.

This incident had a profound effect on Moore. As well as discovering that citizen action could achieve results, she was greatly affected by Garvey's lecture itself. Garvey lit a fire in her, sparking her lifelong crusade for fairness and justice, and giving her great pride in her African origins. "He raised in me a certain knowledge of the history of the wealth of Africa," she said.

Working for others

Hoping for a less racist atmosphere, Moore and her husband and sisters left the South, and in 1922 they settled in Harlem. Moore soon discovered that the conditions there were no better than in New Orleans. So many Southerners had recently moved to Harlem that it was desperately overcrowded, and few people had jobs. Moreover, black women were exploited by white women, who hired them as domestics for as little as fifteen cents a day. Declaring that their working conditions were no different from slavery, Moore formed the Harriet Tubman Association to give the Harlem women some protection from their employers.

In 1933 Moore joined the Communist party, because it seemed to be the only political movement that genuinely cared about improving conditions for African Americans. With the help of the party, she successfully organized some rent strikes in New York: "Getting the landlord ... to roll back rents from where he had them, I went from apartment to apartment and rolled back the people's rent." As well, Moore worked as campaign manager for Benjamin Davis, a black Communist leader who served on New York city council in the 1940s. But by 1950 she had become disillusioned and left the Communist party, declaring it was "racist to the core."

During this period Moore also joined such mainstream groups as the National Council of Negro Women. If any organization represented a cause she believed in, she was prepared not only to join it but to throw all her energies into working for it. Returning to Louisiana, she led a successful campaign to get twenty-three thousand poor people—white as well as black—put back on the welfare rolls after the state had cut them off. She also tried to get the death sentences of black prisoners overturned.

In 1955 Moore launched a campaign to try to get the U.S. government to compensate African Americans for the centuries of slavery they had suffered. "They owe us more than they could ever pay," she said. "They stole our language, they stole our culture. They stole our mothers and fathers and took our names away from us.... The United States will never be able to pay us all they owe us."

It was not money Moore sought so much as a restoration of the African American cul-

Audley Moore

ture. She formed several organizations to achieve this goal, including the World Federation of African People. Moore made her first trip to Africa in 1966 and returned many more times, attending the All-Africa Women's Conference (1972) and other conferences, and visiting with heads of state. In Ghana she was made "Queen Mother" of the Ashanti people, and in Ethiopia she was baptized into the Ethiopian Orthodox Church, of which she became an abbess (and, later, archabbess).

In the United States, Moore was one of the founders of the Ethiopian Orthodox Church of North and South America, as well as the Congress of African Peoples and the Republic of New Africa. In recent years she has campaigned for a national monument to be built in memory of the millions of Africans who died in slave ships crossing the Atlantic.

Of Moore's many contributions to people of African descent, one of the most personal was the Eloise Moore College of African Studies, named in honor of her sister. Although the school burned down in 1961, Moore still hopes to achieve its aims, one of which was to link America and Africa in an effective crosscultural relationship. As she explained to an interviewer, "We wanted to give our children skills that automation could not eradicate like soil conservation, skills like pruning trees, like landscaping, like poulty rearing.... Africa needs those skills. So if we could teach our children to be teachers—to go to Africa to teach the young ones their skills, we could have a flow of interests and collective work reaching across the seas."

Garrett Morgan

Inventor
Born March 4, 1877, Paris, Kentucky
Died July 27, 1963

"The device is also efficient and useful for protection to engineers, chemists, and working men who breathe noxious fumes or dust derived from the materials with which they work."

I t has been said that necessity is the mother of invention. If so, then Garrett Morgan must have needed a lot of things. An inventive genius, Morgan escaped from the poor mountainous regions of Kentucky to put his creative talents to use in Cleveland, Ohio. He invented the gas mask, the traffic light, a human hair straightener, a belt fastener for sewing machines, a woman's hat fastener, a round belt fastener, and a friction drive clutch. His inventions made him a wealthy man, and he counted among his friends John D. Rockefeller and J. Pierpont Morgan. He was also the owner of the *Cleveland Call* newspaper and ran for the Cleveland City Council.

Learns all about sewing machines

Morgan was born on March 4, 1877, in Paris, Kentucky. He attended school until grade five and left home at age fourteen to find work in Cincinnati, Ohio. He became a handyman for a white landowner, but quickly found himself bored. In 1895, he went to Cleveland, where he taught himself all about sewing machines

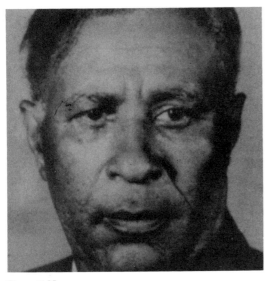

Garrett Morgan

and landed a job as a sewing machine mechanic and adjustor with the firm of Roots and McBride. Over the next few years he bounced from one sewing machine company to the next.

In 1901 Morgan invented a belt fastener for sewing machines that he sold for fifty dollars. Six years later he managed to save enough money to open his own sewing machine sales and repair store. Morgan was so successful that he bought a new home in his first year and moved his mother to Cleveland. The next year he married Mary Anne Hassek. By 1909 Morgan owned and operated a tailoring shop that employed thirty-two people, manufacturing dresses, suits, and coats.

The tailoring shop did a brisk business, but a mechanical problem developed that hurt the quality of his merchandise. The woolen material was frequently scorched by the heat generated when the sewing machine's needle moved up and down. Morgan decided to experiment with a chemical solution that would reduce the friction and prevent the material from scorching. One day he wiped the solution off his hands using a piece of wiry pony-fur cloth. When he returned, he saw that the wiry fuzz of the cloth had become straight. Morgan was intrigued with the results and tried the solution on a neighbor's wiry-haired dog. The solution worked so well on straightening the hair that the owner didn't recognize his own dog. Morgan then tried a little on his hair, then more, then gradually over his whole head without any ill effects. In 1913, he began manufacturing and marketing the first human hair straightener under the name G.A. Morgan Hair Refining Cream.

Invents the gas mask

Morgan filed a patent application for a new invention he called a "breathing device" on August 19, 1912. He later refined his invention into a gas mask that was used extensively in World War I. Morgan described the invention as a device that could "provide a portable attachment which will enable a fireman to enter a house filled with thick suffocating gases and smoke and to breathe freely for some time therein, and thereby enable him to perform his duties of saving life and valuables without danger to himself from suffocation. The device is also efficient and useful for protection to engineers, chemists, and working men who breathe noxious fumes or dust derived from the materials with which they work."

Morgan established the National Safety Device Company to manufacture and promote the new "safety hood." He was the only non-white officer in the company. He urged his fellow blacks to buy stock in the company, but many failed to listen. The stock shares sky-rocketed in value from $10 a share in 1914 to more than $250 per share two years later. As a master salesman, Morgan extensively adver-tised the safety hood and travelled around the country, demonstrating its effectiveness and trying to gain the interest of industrialists and firefighters.

Sometimes Morgan would start a fire in-side a canvas tent using a fuel made of tar sulphur, formaldehyde, and manure.The smoke produced was the thickest and most evil-smelling imaginable. Morgan would go into the tent wearing a safety hood. Despite the thick odor and smoke, he would linger in the tent for about twenty minutes without ex-periencing any discomfort. The safety hood soon became a big hit.

The biggest test for Morgan's safety hood took place on July 24, 1916, when an explo-sion ripped through a tunnel in the Cleveland Water Works. About two dozen men were trapped five miles out and more than 200 feet below Lake Erie, and the tunnel was quickly filling with smoke, dust, and poisonous gases. If immediate action was not taken, the men would surely die. Someone recalled Morgan's safety hood, and he was quickly summoned to the scene. Morgan and his brother, Frank, ar-rived, put on their safety hoods, and entered the tunnel. They descended more than 200 feet into suffocating darkness before finding one of the workers. They dragged him back to the surface and returned to find more workers. They made several trips until they had saved more than twenty lives. Morgan received a solid gold, diamond-studded medal from a group of prominent local citizens. The inscrip-tion read, "To Garrett A. Morgan, our most honored and bravest citizen." He also received a medal from the International Association of Fire Engineers and was made an honorary member of that association.

Due to the publicity, fire departments, po-lice departments, and mining companies flooded his office with requests for safety hood demonstrations. Knowing the racial prejudice of the South, he hired a white man to sell in that area. When the racial identity of the owner became known, sales declined.

The first automatic traffic light

Morgan was always concerned with the safety and well-being of citizens. It was this concern that prompted him to develop the first auto-matic traffic light. He filed a patent applica-tion on February 27, 1922, for a device that would control traffic at intersections. His in-vention came at a time when horse-drawn carriages had to share the road with automo-biles, and there were many collisions at inter-sections. Morgan obtained patent rights in the U.S., Canada, and Britain, and sold the rights to General Electric for the hefty sum of $40,000.

Dissatisfied with the newspaper coverage of black people and events, Morgan decided to establish his own newspaper, the *Cleveland Call* in the 1920s. The paper later changed its name to the *Call & Post,* and was published in Cleveland, Cincinnati, and Columbus, Ohio.

In 1931 Morgan entered politics by run-ning as an independent candidate for Cleveland City Council. His platform included relief for the unemployed, better administration, improved housing conditions, better lighting, improved sanitation, and improved city-owned hospital accommodations.

Morgan lost 90 per cent of his vision in 1943 after suffering a severe case of glaucoma. He still managed to keep busy by organizing a fraternity of black students at Cleveland's Western Reserve University. One of his last goals was to attend the Emancipation Centennial in Chicago in August 1963. He fell short of that goal, passing away after two years of illness on July 27, 1963.

Toni Morrison

Writer, editor
Born February 18, 1931, Lorain, Ohio

"I want my books to always be about something that is important to me, and the subjects that are important in the world are the same ones that have always been important."

One of America's leading novelists and the pre-eminent black novelist, Toni Morrison has won two of the nation's most prestigious literary awards, the Pulitzer Prize for Fiction and the National Book Critics' Circle Award. She also garnered international renown when she was awarded the Nobel Prize in 1993. She was the first African American writer to win this honored award. Morrison has been compared to classic authors such as William Faulkner because of her brilliance as

a storyteller and her rich and lyrical language. Her best-selling novels focus on small-town America and are steeped in African American folklore and mythology.

In addition to writing her own books, Morrison has promoted the works of other black writers, through the courses she has given on African American literature and through her work as a senior editor at Random House publishers. Since her first book was published in 1969, she has become one of the most respected figures in the literary world, proud to be known not only as an American writer but as a black woman writer.

A childhood rich in folklore

The African American folklore and history that play such a central role in Morrison's stories were part of her everyday life as a child. From her parents and grandparents she learned about black myths, music, and cultural rituals, and heard tales of black suffering and achievement.

Morrison was born Chloe Anthony Wofford, the second of the four children of George and Ramah (Willis) Wofford. She grew up in the small town of Lorain, Ohio, where her father worked as a shipyard welder while also holding down two other jobs. All the family were great storytellers, and one of Morrison's favorite pastimes as a child was to listen to the ghost stories her parents told. The stories seemed very real, for many people in her community had a powerful belief in the supernatural. Morrison's grandmother told wondrous tales of magic and strange happenings, and she kept a dreambook of symbols with which she interpreted her dreams.

541

Because Morrison so enjoyed the world of storytelling, she learned to read at a very young age. When she began first grade at her integrated school, she found that she was the only child in the class who could read, as well as being the only black child. Morrison read avidly throughout her school years and graduated from Lorain High School with honors in 1950. She then enrolled at Howard University, where she majored in English. It was at Howard that she began to call herself Toni, because people had difficulty pronouncing the name Chloe.

A writer in the making

While she was a student at Howard University, Morrison joined the college theater group, which toured the South during the summers, exposing her to some of the experiences she had heard about from her parents. After graduating with a B.A. in 1953, she went on to Cornell University, where in 1955 she gained her master's degree. She then embarked on an academic career, teaching for two years at Texas Southern University in Houston before becoming an instructor in English at Howard University. While teaching at Howard, she met and married the Jamaican architect Harold Morrison and gave birth to her two sons.

Up to this point in her life, Toni Morrison had been a reader rather than a writer. She has said that she never particularly wanted to be an author but that she "drifted into a writer's group while teaching at Howard University in 1962." The group had a rule that all those attending the monthly meetings must bring something they had written. One month when Morrison had nothing to bring, she wrote a short story about a little black girl who wanted blue eyes. This story became the basis of her first book, *The Bluest Eye,* which was published by Holt, Rinehart & Winston in 1969.

By the time the book came out, Morrison was working for a rival publisher, Random House. Her marriage had not been a success, and in the early 1960s she took her sons, Harold and Slade, home to her parents in Lorain. When she returned to work in 1965, it was as an editor with a branch of Random House in Syracuse, New York. Two years later she was promoted to senior editor and was transferred to New York City. Morrison wrote *The Bluest Eye* in the evenings after her sons had gone to bed, and this became the pattern of her life as she juggled three careers, for she soon added to her workload by becoming a visiting lecturer at Yale University.

Prize-winning novelist

The Bluest Eye received good reviews, though the reaction was mild compared with the enthusiasm that greeted Morrison's later novels. Each book she wrote added enormously to her reputation. Her second novel, *Sula* (1973) was nominated for the National Book Award, and her third novel, *Song of Solomon* (1977), won both the National Book Critics' Circle Award and the American Academy and Institute of Arts and Letters Award.

Song of Solomon was the first novel in which Morrison featured a man as the central character, and its story moves beyond the small-town black community that was the setting for her two earlier books. The hero, Milk-

Toni Morrison

man Dead, sets out on a journey south with the hope of finding long-lost family treasure, but instead of finding gold he discovers a wealth of family history. Myth and the supernatural weave in and out of the story, which is full of eccentric characters. The book was justly hailed as a masterpiece, raising Morrison to the stature of a major novelist.

The inspiration for *Song of Solomon* came partly from Morrison's work as an editor at Random House. In 1974 she had edited *The Black Book,* an anthology of photographs, newspaper clippings, advertisements, recipes, and other souvenirs of black life over the past three hundred years. *The Black Book* proved to be a celebration of black achievement, recording little-known success stories as well as the more familiar aspects of black history.

Morrison's fourth novel, *Tar Baby* (1981), was the first to give white people a major role. Much of the story takes place on a Caribbean island, and in true Morrison style it embodies a wealth of folklore and a mix of fantasy and realism. The book quickly became a bestseller, as did Morrison's next work, *Beloved* (1987), which won the Pulitzer Prize and the Robert F. Kennedy Book Award.

Beloved has been described as "a brutally powerful, mesmerizing story about the inescapable, excruciating legacy of slavery." Set in the nineteenth century, it centers on the life of Sethe, a runaway slave woman who tries to kill her children to prevent them being taken as slaves. She does succeed in killing one of them, and this daughter later returns as a ghost to haunt her mother. The strength of the story is increased by the way it is told, using flashbacks and differing viewpoints.

Morrison's next novel, *Jazz* (1992), has an entirely different setting, featuring the Harlem of the 1920s, but it too moves back into the past and delves deep into human emotions. As usual, the book immediately became a best-seller, hailed as another masterpiece from the hand of a superb writer. "Morrison has moved from strength to strength until she has reached the distinction of being beyond comparison," enthused *Entertainment Weekly.*

Over the years, Morrison has written several plays and numerous articles in addition to her novels. Her teaching role has expanded to include professorships at several universities, and in 1989 she was appointed Robert F. Goheen Professor of the Humanities at Princeton University. Meanwhile, she continues her work with Random House. In all these roles Morrison remains a major force in the literature of her day.

Constance Baker Motley

Lawyer, politician, judge
Born September 14, 1921, New Haven,
 Connecticut

"When I graduated in 1946, you would not have been able to find a single person willing to bet twenty-five cents that I would be successful in the legal profession."

Episodes of racism during her teenage years convinced Constance Baker Motley to become involved in the civil rights movement. She served as an associate counsel for the National Association for the Advancement of Colored People (NAACP) Legal Defense Fund for twenty years. Motley had a spectacular record of victories in the segregation cases she took to the Supreme Court. She represented some of the most important leaders of the civil rights movement of the 1960s and was rewarded for her efforts by being named a senior district judge for the Southern District of New York. She also served in the New York State Senate and was the first woman elected president of the Borough of Manhattan.

Encounters racism as a teen

Motley is the daughter of Willoughby and Rachel Baker. Her parents immigrated to the United States from Nevis, a Caribbean island. She first encountered racism when she entered New Haven High School at age fifteen. She and a group of friends went to Bridgeport,

Connecticut, for a picnic and were refused entry into a roller-skating rink. Another time she and her friends were barred from swimming at a local beach in Milford, Connecticut, because their group was interracial. These episodes prompted Motley to become involved in the civil rights movement, and she became president of the New Haven Youth Council and secretary of the New Haven Adult Community Council.

After graduating from high school in 1939, Motley wanted to attend college, but her family was too poor to support her. A year and a half later, Clarence Blakeslee heard her speak at a New Haven community center he built. As a man who had contributed to many African American causes, Blakeslee offered to pay Motley's college expenses. In February 1941, she enrolled at Fisk University in Nashville, before transferring in June 1942 to Washington Square College at New York University. She graduated in October 1943 with an economics degree. The next year she was one of a handful of women who enrolled at Columbia Law School. "When I graduated in 1946, you would not have been able to find a single person willing to bet twenty-five cents that I would be successful in the legal profession."

Motley excelled at law school and in her last year, she was selected as a law clerk for Thurgood Marshall, who was then the chief counsel of the NAACP Legal Defense and Education Fund, and would go on to become a Solicitor General of the United States and Supreme Court Justice. During the course of her work, Motley traveled around the country trying school and other types of desegregation cases.

One of her earliest cases involved the equalization of black teachers' salaries in 1949 in Mississippi. The local newspapers ran front page stories on the day the trial began because there were two black lawyers from New York who were going to try the case, and one was a woman. The courtroom was packed because this was the first trial in this century in which blacks in Mississippi tried to end segregation, and because a black female lawyer from New York was in attendance.

After World War II, Motley noticed a change in the momentum for civil rights. She felt the returning servicemen had a new sense of pride in being American, and this gave them the strength to unite in their struggle against discrimination and oppression.

Involved in school desegregation

In 1954 Motley helped write the briefs filed in the United States Supreme Court in the land-

Constance Baker Motley

mark school desegregation case, *Brown v. Board of Education*. The Supreme Court's decision helped pave the way to ending other areas of segregation. "The Brown decision was the catalyst which changed our society from a closed society to an open society and created the momentum for other minority groups to establish public interest law firms to secure their rights," Motley said. She believed it also provided the impetus for the women's rights movement, the poor people's movement, and other public interest concerns, including prisoners' rights, consumer rights, and environmental law.

During her career, Motley argued ten civil rights cases before the Supreme Court, winning nine. She represented James Meredith in his struggle to enter the University of Mississippi (*Meredith v. Fair*), Charlayne Hunter and Hamilton Holmes as they sought to enter the University of Georgia (*Holmes v. Danner*), and similar cases involving schools and colleges.

Motley was a keen and perceptive lawyer, who was forceful in her legal arguments. As associate counsel of the NAACP Legal Defense Fund, she appeared before state and federal courts in eleven southern states. She also argued cases involving public school desegregation, public and publicly aided housing, transportation, recreation, and sit-in cases in the District of Columbia. When Jack Greenberg succeeded Marshall in 1962 as NAACP Legal Defense Fund director-counsel, he called Motley the "anchor woman of his team." Motley and other NAACP lawyers represented Martin Luther King, Ralph Abernathy, Fred Shuttlesworth, and other influential members of the civil rights movement of the 1960s.

As Motley's reputation grew, she was elected to the New York State Senate in February 1964. She was the first African American woman to hold the office. During her first seven weeks in the state legislature, she began a campaign to extend civil rights legislation in employment, education, and housing.

Motley's stay in the state senate was brief. The New York City Council called a special election in February 1965, and Motley was elected to fill a one-year term as president of the Borough of Manhattan. She was reelected to a full four-year team in the city-wide elections of November 1965. Motley was the first woman and the third African American to hold the position, and she drew up plans to revitalize Harlem and other underprivileged areas of the city.

Appointed to United States District Court

Motley received national recognition for her civil rights achievements in 1966 when President Lyndon B. Johnson appointed her to the United States District Court for the Southern District of New York, which covers Manhattan, the Bronx, and six counties north of New York City. Her nomination aroused opposition from southern senators as well as from other federal judges. She was eventually confirmed in August 1966. Motley became the chief judge of her court on June 1, 1982, and served in that position until October 1, 1986, when she reached senior status.

Through her long and distinguished career, Motley received support and encouragement from her husband, Joel Motley, and their son, Joel Motley, Jr., a graduate of Harvard, now a lawyer and investment banker. Joel Motley told *Ebony* he maintained his own identity by "being considerate and understanding of his wife's career."

Motley feels that in the future, there will be an increasing demand for black lawyers. "Most of the problems blacks now face require political solutions. The most pressing need among blacks is the need for greater political power," she said in an interview. "Lawyers are natural leaders and activists in the black community. More and more blacks will become involved in policy making agencies, in government, in politics, in business and diplomacy—in areas where blacks have not been before and where decisions and changes are going to be made."

Willard Motley

Novelist
Born July 14, 1912, Chicago, Illinois
Died March 4, 1965, Mexico City, Mexico

"My race is the human race."

The author of four massive documentary novels, Willard Motley was often assumed to be white because his books focused on poor whites rather than on the problems of African Americans. He wrote what were called "raceless novels."

Motley's first book, *Knock on Any Door* (1947), was a powerful story about a juvenile delinquent from an inner-city ghetto. Hailed as a major work, the book sold phenomenally well and was made into a Hollywood movie starring Humphrey Bogart. Much was expected of Motley's later novels, but none quite lived up to the first. The other three were *We Fished All Night* (1951), *Let No Man Write My Epitaph* (1958), and *Let Noon Be Fair* (1966). The latter was published after Motley's death, as was the *Diaries of Willard Motley* (1979), which covered his life from his teenage years to his early thirties.

His writing talents emerged early

Although Willard Motley wrote of the poor and destitute in the slums of big cities, he himself was of middle-class origin. He was raised in a comfortable home on the South Side of Chicago. His mother, Mary (Huff) Motley, was the main influence during his childhood, for his father, Archibald Motley, was a Pullman porter on the Chicago-to-New York run, and his job kept him away from home much of the time. Motley's older brother, Archibald, Jr., was also a positive influence. Twenty years older than Motley, he was already gaining a reputation as a painter.

The Motleys were the only black family in their immediate neighborhood, yet they seldom encountered any discrimination, and during the 1919 Chicago riots their white neighbors rallied round to defend them. This relaxed interracial atmosphere may explain why Motley felt no need to write about racial injustice. It was other forms of injustice that he railed against.

By the time Motley was a teenager he had already decided to be a writer. At Englewood High School he contributed to the school newspaper, and when he was thirteen he sent a story to the *Chicago Defender,* which published it in three installments. The paper then hired Motley do a weekly children's column, which he wrote for the next two years, calling himself Bud Billiken. When he was sixteen he started a diary, which he kept until 1943. It is a fascinating document since it shows how his own experiences were incorporated into his novels.

Motley had a wealth of experiences during the next few years. Since his family could not afford to send him to college, he decided to travel and live rough in order to gain material for his writings. He bicycled to the East Coast, made two trips to the West Coast in an old car, and finally settled in a slum apartment near Chicago's Maxwell Street market. Motley supported himself by taking on all sorts of odd jobs—ranch hand, cook, shipping clerk, photographer. Then, in 1940, he joined the Works Projects Administration Writers' Project.

Best-selling novel indicted American penal system

Around the end of 1940 Motley began work on his novel *Knock on Any Door*. It was the story of a good boy who goes bad because of the influences he is subjected to. This was something Motley felt strongly about. While traveling rough, and while living and working in the seedy back streets of Chicago, Motley had come to know several juvenile delinquents. He had befriended one of them, hoping to get him to go straight, but without success. Motley was filled with fury at a society that could cause this type of situation. His

Willard Motley

aim in writing *Knock on Any Door* was to show the injustices of the penal system and to prove that reform schools actually turned boys into criminals.

The hero of *Knock on Any Door* is Nick Romano, an Italian American who is a model of virtue at the beginning of the story. But after experiencing ghetto life in a poor section of Denver, Colorado, he starts to go downhill—a process that is completed by a series of reformatories and prisons that turn him into a hardened killer. The book took Motley three years to write, during which he researched his subject thoroughly. He haunted Little Sicily, Chicago's Italian district, and steeped himself in its culture. He visited reform schools and even interviewed the warden of Cook County Jail to learn how executions were carried out.

Motley's careful research paid off, for the realism was a major factor in the success of *Knock on Any Door* when it was eventually published in 1947, after first being turned

down by several publishers. The book was a best-seller from the start. The critics gave it rave reviews, sparking an enormous amount of attention. Some 47,000 copies of the book were sold in the first three weeks, and within the next two years more than 350,000 copies were sold and a movie was made of the story.

Critics were less impressed with Motley's next book, *We Fished All Night* (1951), complaining that it was too preachy and too disjointed. While it was primarily about the adverse effects of World War II on three men, it also dealt with politics, labor unions, and other aspects of American life. Motley was more successful with *Let No Man Write My Epitaph* (1958), which was a sequel to *Knock on Any Door* and, like it, was made into a film. In this book Motley took a more positive look at ghetto life. He also introduced a racial element by having one of the Romano men fall in love with a beautiful black woman.

An African American, Motley often faced criticism for not writing about the many problems confronting his own race. However, the interracial love affair in *Let No Man Write My Epitaph* did not mean he was changing his approach. "My race is the human race," he told his critics. He believed very strongly that "people are just people."

Motley lived in Mexico after 1952, and he adopted a Mexican boy, though he never married. His final novel, *Let Noon Be Fair,* was set in Mexico and was an attack on American exploitation of the country. The story centers on the small fishing village of Las Casas (based on one of Motley's favorite Mexican communities), which is gradually spoiled as Americans move in and buy up property, build hotels, open brothels, and generally subvert the cultural and moral life of the community. Motley completed the book just two weeks before he died, so he was never able to polish it. Yet when it was published the following year it was praised by one reviewer as the "saddest and most skilful" of all Motley's books.

Motley's death was caused by gangrene for which he sought no medical attention until it was too late. The writer had been living meagerly off his declining royalties. Motley's writing style was considered out of fashion, for readers were focusing on the aggressive black writers who explored the civil rights issues of the 1960s. Against such a background, Motley's books did not seem very relevant. But as he so often said, "people are just people." His books remain strong and realistic statements about issues that are important to all people, and *Knock on Any Door* still ranks as a major contribution to American literature.

Elijah Muhammad

Leader of the Nation of Islam
Born October 7, 1897, rural Sandersville, Georgia
Died February 25, 1975, Chicago, Illinois

"Put your brains to thinking for self; your feet to walking in the direction of self; your hands to working for self and your children."

 s the religious leader of the Nation of Islam, Elijah Muhammad worked tire-

lessly to raise the economic and social standards of his black followers. He encouraged them to improve themselves by providing schooling and training in business enterprises. He promoted good health, self-improvement, and moral guidelines and prohibited the use of alcohol and tobacco. Muhammad almost singlehandedly stopped Americans from using the word *Negro,* with all its negative connotations, to adopting the expression *black people.* As his successor Louis Farrakhan said in *The Final Call*, "he more than any religious leader is responsible for causing us to refer to one another as brothers and sisters."

Great Depression causes unemployment

Muhammad's original name was Elijah Poole. His parents, Wali and Marie Poole, were former slaves who worked as sharecroppers. Muhammad went to school until grade four, learning the basics of reading, writing, and arithmetic, but was forced to leave school to work with his family in the fields. When he turned sixteen, he left home and six years later married Clara Evans. In 1923, he, Clara, and their two children moved to Detroit in search of work. Muhammad held a series of jobs, but the Great Depression hit the Detroit area hard and he found himself unemployed.

In 1930 he met Wallace D. Fard, the founder and leader of the Nation of Islam. The charismatic Fard used to sell raincoats and silks, charming his customers with tales of black history. Using his interpretation of the Bible, Fard was able to convince many customers that Islam and not Christianity was the religion of black people in Asia and Africa.

He started preaching his beliefs to gatherings in different homes, but as the group became bigger, they contracted a hall and named it the Temple of Islam.

Those who joined the temple had to write a letter asking for their original or Islamic name to replace the slave names the white man had provided. Elijah Poole's name was changed to Karriem. He quickly became Fard's most trusted assistant, and Fard renamed him Muhammad and appointed him chief minister of Islam.

In 1932 Muhammad was charged with establishing the Southside Mosque in Chicago, Illinois (later renamed Temple No. 2). Although successful in that venture, Muhammad ran into trouble with the law in 1934. He was arrested when he refused to transfer his children from the movement's school, the University of Islam, to a public school. He was tried in Detroit, found guilty of contributing to the delinquency of a minor, and placed on six months' probation.

Muhammad succeeds Fard

Fard disappeared in June 1934, and many felt Muhammad, as his chief minister, should be his successor. Since Detroit was filled with rival leaders, Muhammad returned to Chicago. Working out of Temple No. 2, he set up a new headquarters and began reshaping the movement under his own highly militant leadership. Although he was short in stature—five feet, five inches tall—his intensity and radicalism made up for it. Muhammad claimed that whites had created the poor economic conditions that caused blacks to suffer. Blacks were also at fault for allowing it to happen.

Separation was the only answer, and blacks should claim some of the land "our fathers and mothers paid for in 300 years of slavery." Muhammad used the Nation of Islam to foster black pride and self-sufficiency to its mainly young, male, lower-class members.

Muhammad's followers adhered to a set of guidelines that fostered good health, self-improvement, and high morals. Alcohol, tobacco, and the "slave diet" of pork and cornbread were prohibited. Members were encouraged to eat one meal of fresh fruit and practice marital fidelity. The males were expected to recruit new members. Muhammad provided business schooling and training in hopes that blacks could become self-sufficient. In *The Black Muslims in America,* he said, "put your brains to thinking for self; your feet to walking in the direction of self; your hands to working for self and your children.... Stop begging for what others have and help your-

Elijah Muhammad

self to some of this good earth.... We must go for ourselves.... This calls for the unity of us all to accomplish it!"

During the 1930s, Muhammad continued to build the Nation of Islam and constructed many temples in the midst of black urban ghettos. During World War II, many government officials felt Muhammad's separatist ideology was contrary to the war effort. In 1942 he was arrested and charged with sedition and violation of the Selective Service Act. Although he was cleared of sedition, he was charged with convincing his followers to avoid the draft and spent the rest of the war in a federal prison in Milan, Michigan.

Nation of Islam spreads

Muhammad managed to control the movement from his cell. He wrote a column in the *Pittsburgh Courier* that was widely read and discussed within the black community. In the late 1940s, Malcolm Little joined the movement and was renamed Malcolm X. A charismatic speaker, Malcolm X became Muhammad's chief disciple and spread Islam across the country. By 1960 the Nation of Islam had sixty-nine temples or missions in twenty-seven states. Although tiny compared to conventional churches, its growth began to worry many Americans. Even Thurgood Marshall, then chief counsel for the National Association for the Advancement of Colored People, said the group was run by a bunch of thugs from their jail cells.

Although frequently criticized, the movement did have a positive side. *Newsweek* once said, "the real heart of Muhammad's message was the worth, the competence and the soli-

darity of Black people. He urged them to express it through a meld of puritan morals (no cigarettes, liquor, drugs or non-marital sex) and Protestant work ethics."

Some say a rift developed between Muhammad and his chief disciple, Malcolm X, and that he was looking for an opportunity to silence him. His chance came in November 1963, when Malcolm X told a Black Muslim rally at Manhattan Center that the assassination of President Kennedy was a case of "the chickens coming home to roost." Muhammad said that kind of statement was against the movement, and he told Malcolm X that he couldn't preach for ninety days. Malcolm X accepted the punishment, but on March 8, 1964, he told the press he was leaving to form his own party. An article in the *New York Times* portrayed Muhammad's reaction as both angry and regretful. "Malcolm X's plans have had no effect at all on the movement. My work is divine work and people believe in what I am teaching is the resurrection from the death—the mental death of my people. Anyone who deviates from Islam is a hypocrite."

Malcolm X was assassinated in February 1965, prompting Muhammad to stay inside his Chicago mansion, giving few interviews and rarely appearing in public. If he did appear in public, it was with hundreds of volunteer security guards. He usually stayed in his office, planning recruitment drives and administering the group's network of businesses, farmlands, and restaurants.

The Nation of Islam received a black eye in January 1972 when a shootout took place between police and a Louisiana Nation of Islam splinter group. *Newsweek* reported that several young activitists were upset with the $1.5 million the Nation of Islam spent on mansions for Muhammad, his family, and his aides. In an interview with *Newsweek* Muhammad defended his actions. "I think there is some little splinter group that sometimes wants to go out for themselves and be big boys, and so they take chances sometimes, and sometimes they stub their toes and they have to go back home and bandage them up. By that time, we're back where we was."

Muhammad's failing health pulled him from the limelight during his last few years. He entered Mercy Hospital in Chicago on January 30, 1975, suffering from heart trouble, bronchitis, asthma, and diabetes. He died on February 25.

Eddie Murphy

Comedian, actor
Born April 3, 1961, Brooklyn, New York

"I wanna be like the Beatles, man. Like the Beatles were to music, that's what I want to be to comedy. That's my goal."

In the early 1980s, Eddie Murphy rocketed to fame to become one of the most successful actors in the movie business. Only three years after he first gained national attention on the television show "Saturday Night Live," he was hailed as a superstar, hero of the films *48 Hours* and *Trading Places*.

Murphy has since had hit after hit. His great talent is that he knows instinctively how to make people laugh, whether as a foul-mouthed wiseguy or as a gentler and more restrained character. Like all great comics, he has perfect timing, knowing exactly how long to hold a pose and how long to maintain a stone-faced stare. *Newsweek* has called him "the hottest performer in the land."

A born comedian

Edward Regan Murphy inherited his comic talents from his policeman father, Charles Murphy, who was a keen amateur comedian. Murphy's mother, Lillian, a telephone operator, was a more permanent influence on his life because his parents divorced when Murphy was three, and his father died five years later.

When Murphy was nine, he and his elder brother, Charles, had a new father figure when their mother married Vernon Lynch, a foreman at a Breyer's ice cream factory. Around this time, it was Murphy's great ambition to be the driver of an ice cream truck. Only later did he change his mind and aim for a career in show business.

Murphy's stepfather moved the family to a two-story ranch house in the predominantly black suburb of Roosevelt, and there Murphy became the family prankster, kidding around with his brother and baby half-brother, always ready to raise a laugh. At Roosevelt Junior-Senior High School, he practiced his wit on his classmates, becoming slicker and more sophisticated as he grew older. In sixth grade he put on an hour-long show, with impressions of teachers, students, and monitors. Meanwhile, the basement carpet at home was the imaginary stage on which he performed as Elvis or Stevie Wonder.

Murphy's first public performance took place in 1976, when at the age of fifteen he hosted a talent show at the Roosevelt Youth Center—and brought down the house with his impersonation of soul singer Al Green. If Murphy needed any confirmation of his choice of career, this was it. "Looking out at the audience," he later said, "I knew it was showbiz for the rest of my life."

The road to the top

While Murphy was still at school, he started calling on talent agents, who found him work in the local clubs. Before long he was so busy that his schoolwork began to suffer, and he failed tenth grade. He reacted with a concentrated burst of effort, attending summer school and night school, and doubling up on classes. As a result, he graduated only a couple of months late.

At his mother's urging, Murphy then enrolled at Nassau Community College to study theater, but he continued to play in the clubs (where he was still too young to buy a drink). Within a few months, he was making a good living as an entertainer, first in Manhattan's Comic Strip and then in clubs up and down the East Coast. The audiences loved his stand-up routine, which he had modeled after his favorite comedian, Richard Pryor. Like Pryor, Murphy gained many of his laughs with the foul language he used, and this became his hallmark.

Murphy enjoyed playing in the clubs, but he aimed to reach a far larger audience. His chance came when he learned that the producers of the late-night television show "Saturday Night Live" were looking for a black per-

Eddie Murphy

former for the 1980–81 season. Murphy was not the only person who had heard about this opening, and he was auditioned six times before he landed the part. Even then, he was hired only as an extra to appear from time to time. He did not get a regular spot in the show until late in the season.

That year's shows were not successful, and many of the cast were fired at the end of the season, but Murphy was kept on. The next year he stole the show with a raft of brilliant impersonations—of Muhammad Ali, Bill Cosby, Jerry Lewis, and Stevie Wonder—and with some new invented characters, such as Tyrone Green, the white-hating convict-turned-poet who wrote such semi-literate poems as "Cill My Lanlord." Most of Murphy's invented characters were thoroughly unpleasant, and he was criticized for giving such an unattractive picture of African Americans. But he insisted that his characters weren't meant to be taken seriously; they were simply meant to make people laugh. And that is what they did.

Capitalizing on his success, Murphy brought out his first comedy album, *Eddie Murphy,* in 1982. He also made his breakthrough into film, appearing as the co-star of *48 Hours,* which was released in December 1982.

Murphy the film star

In *48 Hours,* Murphy was cast as a convict who was let out of jail for two days to help a detective track down a murderer. Fast-paced and brilliantly funny in the way it played on the relationship between the two men, the movie was an instant hit and was quickly followed by *Trading Places* (1983), another smash hit. *Trading Places* was a madcap comedy of the old style, in which Murphy played a streetwise con-man posing as a wealthy businessman. These two films established Murphy as a major star and tremendous box-office draw. Paramount Pictures, which had produced the first two films, immediately signed Murphy to a $15 million contract for his next five films. In the first of these, *Best Defense* (1984), Murphy teamed up with Dudley Moore in a comedy about the arms trade, which did neither actor much good. Murphy's next film, *Beverly Hills Cop* (1985), was far more his style and was such a major hit that a sequel, *Beverly Hills Cop II,* was made two years later. In between, Murphy played in *The Golden Child* (1986), which was panned by the critics, though Murphy himself was praised for "trying to play the right guy in the wrong film." Nevertheless, it did very well at the box office, as did his next two productions: the

concert film *Raw* (1987) and the gently humorous romance *Coming to America* (1988).

Murphy left "Saturday Night Live" in 1984, and that year also saw him branching out in a new direction to record an album of songs, *How Could It Be?* Like almost everything he touched, the album was a success, selling more than a million copies, even though Murphy was judged to be not a great singer. There was a similar opinion about his first attempt at directing a film. Murphy often wrote the scripts of his films, and he usually played a major role in shaping them, but in *Harlem Nights* (1990) he served as director as well as writer and star. He was therefore held totally responsible by the critics, who roundly condemned the film as ineffective. Despite the bad press, the movie did well in the theaters, as did *Another 48 Hours* (1990), a sequel to the original blockbuster.

By 1990, Murphy's pictures had grossed more than $1 billion worldwide, and in 1992 he had two more hits, *The Distinguished Gentleman* and *Boomerang*. This gave credence to the claim made when Murphy launched his film career in the 1980s, "Eddie Murphy is an industry."

Along with his huge and adoring public, Murphy does have some critics in addition to the occasional film critic. Gay rights groups have denounced him for his continual jokes about homosexuals. Others have criticized him for using his comedy simply to amuse instead of seeing it as a vehicle for serious social comment. Through it all, Murphy goes his own way, racking up more hits as well as a number of awards, including a Grammy for his 1983 comedy album. As the naughty little good-bad boy, he wins over the hearts of the public time and again.

Pauli Murray

Lawyer, activist
Born November 20, 1910, Baltimore,
  Maryland
Died July 1, 1985

"(I was) biologically and psychologically integrated in a world where the separation of the race was upheld by the Supreme Court of the United States."

Although many would be satisfied with succeeding in one career, Pauli Murray was not one of them. She was well-known as a lawyer, poet, scholar, author, educator, administrator, religious leader, and an activist in the civil rights and women's movements. She once operated her own law office and later worked for a nationally recognized firm. She authored several books, taught at several universities, and was a founder of the National Organization for Women. During her last decade she served several parishes as an Episcopal priest.

Mother died of a cerebral hemorrhage

Murray was the daughter of William and Agnes Murray. Her father, a graduate of Howard University, was a teacher and school principal. Her mother died of a cerebral hemorrhage in 1914. Murray went to live with her grandparents and aunt, Pauline Fitzgerald, in Durham, North Carolina, while her other brothers and sisters went to live with their father's sister and unmarried brother. Murray's father suffered from the effects of typhoid fever and was eventually committed to Crownsville State Hospital where he died in 1923.

Fitzgerald was a forty-three-year-old school teacher when she took Murray to live with her. Murray was confirmed in the Episcopal Church when she was nine years old and was adopted by her aunt later that year. In 1926 Murray graduated at the head of her class of forty at Hillside High School in Durham.

Since she did not have enough credits to attend Hunter College in New York City, Murray decided to enroll in a New York high school and gain the necessary academic qualifications. After graduating from her New York high school, she returned to Durham and worked for a year before entering Hunter College in 1928. When the stock market crashed during her sophomore year, she was forced to leave the university. In 1931, Murray returned to New York to resume her studies at Hunter College and graduated in January 1933, with an English major and history minor.

During the 1930s Murray was employed by the Works Progress Administration (WPA) as a teacher in the Remedial Reading Project in the New York City public schools and then in the WPA Workers' Education Project. Through the years she continued to write poems and articles that were published in various magazines.

In 1938 she applied to the graduate school at the University of North Carolina. She received a letter from the dean informing her that "members of your race are not admitted to the University." Her determination to enter the university became public news since an earlier Supreme Court decision had ruled that the state must furnish graduate and professional training to all state residents. Her case was reported in the black newspapers, the student newspaper, and eventually white newspapers across the country. Her case was the first of its kind to receive national attention, and she opened the door for many other black students.

Found guilty of disorderly conduct

Murray's interest in law was sparked after she was arrested and thrown in jail in March 1940. She and her friend, Adelene McBean, were charged with disorderly conduct and creating a public disturbance after they refused to move further back on a bus to a broken seat where the driver had directed them. Despite the best efforts of lawyers from the National Association for the Advancement of Colored People (NAACP), they were found guilty and had to pay a fine.

In the fall of 1941, Murray enrolled at the Howard University Law School with the intent of becoming a civil rights lawyer. She continued with the movement by working with the NAACP and the Congress of Racial Equality (CORE). She also organized and led sit-in demonstrations aimed at desegregating restaurants in Washington. During her senior year Murray was elected president of her class and chief justice of the Court of Peers at Howard University. In 1944 she graduated cum laude from Howard and won a Rosenwald Fellowship for graduate study in law at Harvard Uni-

Pauli Murray

versity. She was rejected from Harvard because of her gender, so she entered the Boalt Hall of Law at the University of California, Berkeley. In 1945 Murray received an LL.M. degree in law and passed the California bar examination. The next year she was named the first black deputy attorney general of California, but she left due to a personal illness and her aunt's sickness.

Murray worked as a law clerk for several years before she gained admission to the New York bar. She opened a law office in New York City and in 1949 ran unsuccessfully for a New York city council seat.

She published her first book in 1951, entitled *States' Laws on Race and Color*. Justice Thurgood Marshall of the Supreme Court said it was the bible for civil rights lawyers who were fighting segregation laws. In 1956 she published *Proud Shoes: The Story of an American Family*, a biography of her grandparents and their struggle against racism.

In 1956 Murray was hired as an associate attorney in the prominent law firm of Paul, Weiss, Rifkind, Wharton and Garrison in New York City. As the only female attorney in the firm, she often suffered discrimination. In 1960 she spent eighteen months in Ghana teaching constitutional and administrative law as a senior lecturer at the Ghana School of Law. In the fall of 1961 she began graduate study at Yale Law School. The next year she was appointed to the Committee on Civil and Political Rights, one of seven study committees established by the President's Commission on the Status of Women.

Forms NOW

Murray received the degree of doctor of judicial science from Yale Law School in 1965. She met women's rights advocate Betty Friedan that fall, and the next year they formed the National Organization for Women (NOW), an independent national civil rights group for women.

Over the next few years Murray held a variety of positions. She was vice-president of Benedict College in Columbia, South Carolina; a consultant at the Fourth Assembly of the World Council of Churches in Uppsala, Sweden; and a professor of American Studies at Brandeis University. She had always felt a calling toward the church, and in 1973 she was admitted to holy orders and entered the General Theological Seminary.

During the last decade of her life, Murray wrote her autobiography, was ordained in the Episcopal Church, and lectured across the country. In 1976 she received the master of divinity degree and was ordained to the Holy Order of the Deacons of the Episcopal Church, USA. The next year she was ordained an Episcopal priest.

Murray served as priest of the Episcopal Church of the Atonement in Washington, D.C., priest of a "floating parish" for the hospitalized and shut-ins in Alexandria, Virginia, and priest of the Church of the Holy Nativity in Baltimore. In January 1984, she retired and moved to Pittsburgh, Pennsylvania. She died of cancer on July 1, 1985.

Gloria Naylor

Writer
Born January 25, 1950, New York, New York

"I wanted to become a writer because I felt that my presence as a black woman and my perspective as a woman in general had been underrepresented in American literature."

G loria Naylor has had the type of success most young writers dream of. Her first novel, *The Women of Brewster Place* (1982), not only got published, it also became a best seller, won the American Book Award, and was made into a television movie. Since then Naylor has written three more novels, which combine with the first one to form her "novel quartet"—four books portraying African American life from different angles.

Writing as both a woman and an African American, Naylor can see plenty of faults in the world around her, yet she writes less bitterly than many of her contemporaries. "It is refreshing to read a book by a black woman in which black men are not objects of ridicule or instruments of torture," commented a *Washington Post* reviewer. Nevertheless, Naylor's characters have the usual human frailties and are entirely convincing. Her books give a clear-sighted view of black life, which is evoked in wonderfully lyrical language that is often nearer to poetry than to prose.

Started college at the age of twenty-five

When Naylor was a child she read at least one book a day. "I used to be thrilled by just the smell and touch of books, the sights of them lined up in rows and rows on the library shelves," she wrote in an article about her life. Her mother, Alberta (McAlpin) Naylor, had grown up in the South, where African Americans were not permitted to borrow books from the public library. She made sure her daughters were given every opportunity to read as much as they liked. Naylor and her two sisters had their own library cards when they were as young as four years old.

Although both her parents came from the rural South, Naylor was raised in a middle-class environment in New York City. Both her parents went out to work, her mother as a telephone operator and her father, Roosevelt Naylor, as a transit worker. Naylor was a shy child who didn't easily talk to people, so her mother gave her a diary when she was twelve and told her to write down the things she felt and saw. Naylor became used to putting her thoughts on paper even before she went to high school.

At high school she gained a love of language by reading the English classics—authors such as Jane Austen and Charles Dickens. She did not read African American literature because she did not know it existed: "Growing up in the North in integrated schools, I wasn't taught anything about black history or literature." When Naylor later discovered such writers as Zora Neale Hurston and Toni Morrison, a whole new world opened up for her. However, she did not discover these writers until she was twenty-seven.

In the intervening years, Naylor was a missionary for the Jehovah's Witnesses. Shocked by the assassination of civil rights leader Martin Luther King, Jr., this was her way of trying to make the world a better place. But by the time she was twenty-five she was ready to move on to other things. Married and divorced by then and with only a high school education, she felt the need to be better qualified. So in 1975 she enrolled at Brooklyn College of the City University of New York. To support herself during her studies she worked as a hotel switchboard operator.

Won American Book Award for first novel

It was at Brooklyn that Naylor first read the major works of African American literature. They had a profound effect on her: "I wanted to sit down and write about something that I hadn't read about, and that was all about me— the black woman in America." In fact, her first book, *The Women of Brewster Place* (1982), follows the lives of seven black women in America. Varying widely in character and age, they all live in a dead-end street called Brewster Place, where they valiantly struggle to overcome such daily problems as poverty and racism. According to Naylor, the ugly wall at the end of the street symbolizes the wall of racism that blocks off black women from the larger world.

The book was based on a short story Naylor had written some years earlier, though she enlarged it and added other stories as she shaped the whole into a novel. She did the writing in whatever time she could find between attending classes and operating the hotel switchboard, and she completed the final editing while working on the midnight shift, when there were few phone calls. By the time the book was published, Naylor had graduated with a B.A. degree and had won a scholarship to Yale University, where she earned her M.A. in 1983. In the meantime, she had the excitement and encouragement of being a best-selling author and winning the American Book Award for best first novel of 1982.

The phenomenal success of her first novel brought Naylor offers of university positions, and she has since taught at several universities, including Cornell, where she was appointed a senior fellow in 1988. She has also founded her own film company, One Way Productions. The television version of *Brewster Place* (1989) was such a success that Naylor is considering making movies of other books in her "novel quartet."

The next of these to be published was *Linden Hills* (1985), which is set in a wealthy black suburb. In exposing the corruption and materialism found there, Naylor portrays the community as a form of hell. The farther up the hill the people live, the nearer they are to the center of hell. In structure she modeled the

Gloria Naylor

book on the journey through hell recounted by the medieval Italian writer Dante Alighieri in his famed *Inferno*. This was an ambitious device to attempt, yet Naylor carried it off most effectively, producing a powerful and highly imaginative work.

Naylor's first two books are linked by a woman who has lived at both Linden Hills and Brewster Place, and there is a similar character link between *Linden Hills* and Naylor's third novel, *Mama Day* (1988). This time the setting is the island of Willow Springs off the coast of Georgia and South Carolina. Again there is a classical connection, but with William Shakespeare rather than Dante. Willow Springs is an enchanted island, like the island in Shakespeare's play *The Tempest*.

The fourth book of the quartet, *Bailey's Cafe* (1992), has a more familiar setting—a roadside diner. The story focuses on the customers and the strange stories they tell. As in the three preceding books, the writing is masterly and the characters wonderfully drawn. This is what Naylor's readers can expect as she settles further into her life as an author, drawing sensitive and astute portraits of the society she understands so well. As *Publishers Weekly* pointed out, Gloria Naylor is a highly perceptive writer: "She does not simply tell a story but brings you face to face with human beings living through the complexity, pain, and mystery of real life."

Huey Newton

Civil rights activist, author
Born February 17, 1942, Munroe (some say New Orleans), Louisiana
Died August 22, 1989, Oakland, California

"The ultimate goal of the Black Panther Party is to organize for armed revolution in America."

The organization Huey Newton co-founded, the Black Panthers, is remembered for its members dressed in black berets and black leather jackets, with fists raised in angry defiance. The Black Panther Party attracted thousands of young blacks as members and was designed to aid the black community and protect its young and old from what it termed a tyrannical and insensitive government. Many whites thought the Panthers were a violent, revolutionary gang bent on anarchy, and in many ways, the history of the Panthers reflected the history of Huey Newton, who overcame illiteracy, poverty, and jail to organize the Panthers. He sought to improve black education, employment and housing, and to end police brutality. Despite his high ideals, Newton's violent nature resulted in jail on several occasions, and like the Black Panthers, Newton eventually faded from the limelight.

Started Black Panthers to expose racism

Newton was born on February 17, 1942, in Munroe, Louisiana (although some sources say New Orleans) to Walter and Armelia Newton. He grew up in a large family with his father working as a sharecropper and a Baptist minister. The family was raised in Oakland, California, where Newton had his first run-ins with authority. He was suspended from school about thirty times, broke open parking meters, and was arrested when he was fourteen years old for gun possession. Alienated from his teachers, he eventually graduated from high school functionally illiterate. Despite this condition, he had a keen admiration for his older brother, who earned a master's degree in social work, and wanted to prove his teachers wrong in their assessment of him by obtaining a college education.

He received an associate's degree in social science from Merritt College in Oakland, then took courses at the University of San Francisco Law School. Huey's behavior prompted more run-ins with authority, and he served a six-month sentence after brandishing a knife during a political argument at a party. Most of Huey's discontent stemmed from his vehement objection to racism and its resulting impoverishment of blacks in ghettos. Many of his views were shared by Bobby Seale, a fellow Merritt student, and in October 1966 the two formed the Black Panther Party, based on the beliefs of former Chinese ruler Mao Tse-tung, black scholar W.E.B. Dubois, and civil rights activist Malcolm X. They picked their name on the notion that, like a black panther, they would not attack unless they were attacked first. Newton wrote the party's platform, which demanded racial equality in education, employment, and housing, and stated that blacks should be exempt from military service and called for end to police brutality.

Incited police animosity with unconventional methods

The party used a California law that allowed guns to be carried in public, and they patrolled the Oakland streets at night looking for police abuse of blacks. If they saw a policeman with a black suspect, Newton would get out of the car with a law book and, armed with a sawed-off shotgun, explain the legal rights to the black suspect. Animosity soon rose between the black community and the police. On May 2, 1967, thirty armed Black Panthers disrupted the California state assembly in Sacramento to protest a proposed gun control law. After that, police increased their surveillance and harassment of the party.

Matters boiled to a head on October 28, 1967, when Newton and a passenger were stopped for a traffic check by an Oakland police officer at 5 A.M. Another officer soon arrived on the scene. What happened next is not clear, but one officer was shot dead with his own gun, and Newton and the other officer were wounded. Newton was charged with first degree murder, and his trial became a rallying point for the party. Blacks on college cam-

puses cried "Free Huey!" and a poster of Newton—dressed in a Panther uniform, sitting on a rattan chair, holding a spear in one hand and an M-1 rifle in the other—appeared everywhere. Party memberships soared, and new chapters sprang up across the country. Thousands of demonstrators surrounded the courthouse when Newton's trial began, yet eight weeks later he was found guilty of voluntary manslaughter and sentenced to a maximum of fifteen years in prison.

Newton's lawyer appealed the verdict, and he was freed after two and a half years in prison. He returned to lead the party, only to find that memberships in forty-five cities had dropped below 1,000 because of arrests, killings, and defections. The party was further hampered by in-fighting and eventually split into two factions—one led by Newton, the other by Elridge Cleaver, the party's minister of information.

Huey Newton

Cleaver, who was living in exile in Algeria to avoid criminal charges, wanted the party to pursue violent revolutionary tactics to attain social reform. Newton took a softer approach shortly before his release from prison and wanted the party to become a political and social issues organization. Panthers who believed in Newton helped develop several social programs in the black community, including a nationwide children's breakfast program, an accredited elementary school, a bus service for relatives visiting prison inmates, and free health clinics.

Pursued self-destructive behavior

Although Newton's motives were good, he pursued unconventional methods to raise funds. He would ask for donations, not only from black businesses to support their programs but also from drug dealers, pimps, prostitutes, and other crooks. Newton himself was also using cocaine and was known to burst out into unintelligible rants. He brought enthusiasm and humor to the civil rights movement, but his own violent streak was his undoing. Newton was charged in the fatal shooting of a 17-year-old prostitute for not recognizing him and in the pistol whipping of a tailor. He fled to Cuba in 1974 rather than face charges, then returned in 1977, but the murder charge was dismissed after two trials ended with deadlocked juries. The assault charge ended in acquittal when the tailor refused to testify against Newton.

He then returned to school and earned a doctoral degree in social philosophy from the University of California at Santa Cruz in 1980. The Black Panthers by then had been reduced to a small and insignificant organization, and Newton was following the same path. By his own admission Newton was drinking two quarts of cognac a day and abusing cocaine, heroine, and Valium. He tried and failed a drug abuse program in 1984, and he went back to prison for various offenses, including possession of a handgun and possession of narcotics paraphernalia. In 1989 he was convicted of embezzling funds intended for a Panthers-sponsored school run in the early 1980s.

Newton's self-destructive living ended in 1989 when he was shot and killed by a twenty-five-year-old drug pusher trying to win favor and promotion in a drug distribution gang called the Black Guerrilla Family. Ironically Newton was killed on the same streets where he began the Black Panther Party twenty-three years earlier.

Jessye Norman

Opera and concert singer
Born September 15, 1945, Augusta, Georgia

"As for my voice, it cannot be categorized— and I like it that way, because I sing things that would be considered in the dramatic, mezzo or spinto range. I like so many different kinds of music that I've never allowed myself the limitations of one particular range."

Since the early 1970s Jessye Norman has ranked among the world's greatest opera and concert singers. Her impressive appearance and dramatic stage presence add an extra dimension to her powerful yet beautifully controlled singing and her wonderfully expressive voice.

Norman's rich, velvety voice is usually described as soprano, though she also sings mezzo-soprano and contralto parts. She told *Stereo Review:* "When I began singing, I had three separate voices. My work over my professional life has been to connect them. I feel that I've made some progress in that respect, and it's now more comfortable to use all parts of my voice."

Learned her craft from famous teachers

As a child Jessye Norman used to listen over and over again to the records of Marian Anderson and Leontyne Price, though she never thought she would follow in the footsteps of these world-famous singers. She first heard opera on the Metropolitan Opera Company's radio broadcasts when she was doing her Saturday afternoon chore—scrubbing the kitchen floor for her mother. An instant convert, Norman could not get enough opera, even if it was mainly through records. Her favorite was an album of Leontyne Price singing *Aida.* Norman thought Price's voice was the most heavenly sound she had ever heard.

Norman was raised in a middle-class family, one of five children of Silas and Janie (King) Norman. Her father was an insurance salesman and her mother a secretary for the Democratic party. Both parents were musical, and all their children were taught the piano. Norman's father sang at Mount Calvary Baptist Church in Augusta, and Norman won a prize there in a children's singing contest when she was seven. Throughout her childhood she sang in choirs as well as at Girl Scout meetings and other events.

When Norman was sixteen her singing teacher at Lucy Craft Laney High School took her to Philadelphia to compete in the Marian Anderson Music Scholarship Competition that was held each October. Norman was far younger than the other contestants and did not win a prize, but on the way home she stopped off in Washington to sing for Carolyn Grant, a voice teacher at Howard University. Grant was so impressed by Norman's voice that she recommended her for a scholarship, and Norman enrolled at Howard the following year.

While studying voice, piano, and music education at Howard, Norman performed with the university chorus. She also sang in local choirs, including that of Lincoln Temple United Church of Christ, which hired her as a paid soloist. In 1965, at the age of twenty, she gained her first important award when she won the National Society of Arts and Letters singing competition.

Norman graduated with a bachelor of music degree with honors in 1967. She continued her studies at the Peabody Conservatory and then at the University of Michigan, where she earned her master's degree in 1968. At Michigan she had the good fortune to be taught by Elizabeth Mannion and the French baritone Pierre Bernac—both famed teachers. From them Norman gained a thorough grounding in a wide range of songs so that she began her career with an exceptionally broad repertoire.

Became a star abroad

Norman's career started off with four resounding triumphs, one after the other. The first was

Jessye Norman

in 1968 when she was picked for a U.S. State Department tour of South America and the Caribbean. While on the tour she learned she had won a scholarship to travel to Germany to take part in the International Music Competition sponsored by Munich radio. At the competition in September she won first prize. This brought her such renown that she was sought out to give concert performances in Europe, and in 1969 she was offered a three-year contract by the Deutsche Oper Berlin, the famous opera company in West Berlin.

Although Norman had never actually performed in an opera, she knew the music well and had no difficulty in adapting to the stage. She was a sensation right from the beginning, though her role was an exremely challenging one—she was cast as Elisabeth in Richard Wagner's *Tannhäuser*. Even in this first opera, Norman showed tremendous stage presence— a looming presence that matched the richness of her voice.

The success of Norman's debut in opera led to other major roles, as well as invitations to perform elsewhere. In 1970 she appeared in several operas in Italy, as well as in Mozart's *Marriage of Figaro* at the Berlin Festival. In 1971 she sang the role of the countess in the British Broadcasting Corporation's recording of *Figaro*. This recording brought Norman to the attention of a wider audience, not only in Europe but in the United States, where she was not yet well known. Like many other American opera singers, Norman was a star in Europe before she gained fame at home.

An adored and world-famous opera star

The year 1972 was a triumphant one for Jessye Norman. After performing in Verdi's *Aida,* both in Berlin and at Italy's famous La Scala opera house in Milan, she sang in a concert version of *Aida* at the Hollywood Bowl in Los Angeles. After several other enormously successful concerts in the United States she returned to Europe, where she performed at the Royal Opera House in London, England, and at the Edinburgh Festival in Scotland.

One of Norman's most famous appearances was in 1973 when she gave a song recital at the Lincoln Center in New York City. This was her first major concert on the East Coast, and it was greeted with cheers of praise. Norman spent much of 1973 touring in Europe, but she was back in the United States for the 1973–74 season, during which she performed on both coasts to approving audiences.

During the mid-1970s Norman gave up opera so that she could concentrate on concert appearances, but she returned to opera in 1980 with a performance of Richard Strauss's *Ariadne auf Naxos* in Hamburg, Germany. In 1983 she sang for the first time with the New York's Metropolitan Opera Company, which she had listened to so often as a child. "A soprano of magnificent presence who commanded the stage at every moment," enthused the *New York Times.*

In 1987, when Norman appeared at the Tanglewood Festival with the Boston Symphony Orchestra, her performance so moved the audience that they gave her ten minutes of thunderous applause. The performance included a scene from Strauss's opera *Salome,* which produced a glowing review from the *Times* music critic: "Ms. Norman's voice seems to draw from a vast ocean of sound.… No matter how much volume [conductor] Seiji Ozawa requested from his orchestra during the fiery scene from 'Salome,' it seemed little match for her voice. Yet, as always, what made the soprano's performance particularly remarkable was the effortlesseness with which she could hover over long, soft notes.… And there is also the quality of sound she produces: even the loudest passages are cushioned by a velvety, seductive timbre."

It is these qualities that have made Norman such an outstanding performer. She has become such a world-famous star that in 1989 the French invited her to sing their national anthem, "La Marseillaise," at the bicentennial celebrations of the French Revolution. Norman's honors at home include several Grammy awards and honorary degrees as well as the Outstanding Musician of the Year Award in 1982. However, her greatest award is the continuing adulation of her audiences—not only in the United States, but in Europe, Japan, the Middle East, or wherever her wonderous voice is heard.

Hazel O'Leary

Secretary of the U.S. Department of Energy
Born May 17, 1937, Newport News, Virginia

"In the public sector I've regulated industry broadly. In the private sector, I've been forced to live with those regulations and, perhaps more importantly, I've seen how those regulations if not carefully crafted and balanced can impact jobs and lives and economies of people who expected and hoped for better from their government."

Although the appointment of Hazel O'Leary as the United States secretary of energy surprised many Washington insiders, she has a proven track record in the industry. She is a former regulator in the Ford and Carter administrations and later became a member of an energy consulting firm. Before her appointment, she served for three and a half years as the executive vice president of the Northern States Power Company, where she developed new corporate culture and environmental policies.

Talented at overhauling corporate culture

O'Leary was born on May 17, 1937, in Newport News, Virginia. In 1959 she graduated from Fisk University in Nashville, Tennessee, and earned a law degree at Rutgers University seven years later. She was an assistant New Jersey attorney general, a prosecutor in Essex County, New Jersey, and a partner in the Washington office of the accounting firm of Coopers & Lybrand. She then worked at the Federal Energy Administration under President Gerald Ford and in the Energy Department under President Jimmy Carter. During this time she was a member of the Economic Regulatory Administration, which dealt with oil prices and allocation controls. This body was designed to protect U.S. consumers from foreign oil producers and encourage consumption. In 1978 she was credited with having helped write regulations for the Powerplant and Industrial Fuel Use Act, which prohibited natural gas use in new industrial boilers under the assumption that the United States had nearly exhausted its conventional gas resources.

She joined O'Leary Associates, a Washington-based energy consulting firm in 1981 as vice president and general counsel. In 1980 she married John F. O'Leary, the firm's founder. John, who served as deputy energy secretary in the Carter administration, died in 1987. They have a son, Carl G. Rollings, a lawyer in Washington.

In 1989 O'Leary became executive vice president of corporate affairs at Northern States Power Company in Minnesota. She oversaw the utility's legal and personnel affairs department, environmental affairs, public relations, and lobbying. O'Leary worked to change the NSP's corporate culture in an effort to prepare the utility for the competitive challenges of the 1990s. NSP needed changing after the Minnesota Public Utilities Com-

Hazel O'Leary

mission's (MPUC) auditors directed the company to reorganize its fifteen year old accounting system. MPUC told the utility to change its system from one based on line budgets to one that used functional budgets. O'Leary implemented a discipline she used while working at the Department of Energy (DOE)—assigning budget responsibilities to the lowest possible management level. "In the early days at DOE, the people doing the work developed the budget" O'Leary told *Electrical World.* "Being keepers of your own budget is a very powerful thing in a company."

The new budget system was combined with O'Leary's ideas for an employee empowerment program. Her program grew out of a training program for line managers. It allowed company executives to step back from the day-to-day management of personnel and allowed employees to develop corporate goals through departmental projects. With executives developing long-range planning, the staff are allowed to work with greater freedom. O'Leary also developed a system of productivity goals called "key performance indicators." This process allows staff, management, and corporate officers to have a concrete list of departmental goals and a tracking system for a review of a project's process.

Her ideas worked well. NSP's South Dakota regional office developed a customized collection method that gave the field office the lowest ratio of bad credit risks in the NSP system. In another instance, a research effort was coordinated by the benefits department in which a countrywide poll was taken of companies that were considered leaders in keeping health-care costs down. Eventually new recommendations were adopted that resulted in a new program of health care services.

As a member of NSP's board of directors, O'Leary assisted in the development of policies that resulted in the utility's coal-burning power plants exceeding national standards for clean air requirements. She also helped develop programs promoting energy conservation.

Appointed U.S. Secretary of Energy

In late 1992, a week after the company named O'Leary president in charge of the company's natural gas operations, President Bill Clinton nominated her to be the new secretary of energy. The announcement came as a surprise to many Washington insiders. She took over a department with almost 18,000 employees that had been put on the back burner by the Bush and Reagan administrations. President Clinton indicated he wanted the department to make

the industry more efficient and cleaner, to create jobs in environmental business, and to reduce the nation's dependence on coal and oil.

The biggest part of the department's budget goes to supervise the nation's nuclear bomb complex—reactors, factories, and laboratories. This complex has experienced safety and pollution problems costing billions of dollars each year to clean up. Some environmentalists have urged the Clinton administration to shift these responsibilities away from O'Leary's department to the Department of Defense or the Environmental Protection Agency.

"In the public sector I've regulated industry broadly," O'Leary said at a news conference announcing her appointment. "In the private sector, I've been forced to live with those regulations and, perhaps more importantly, I've seen how those regulations if not carefully crafted and balanced can impact jobs and lives and economies of people who expected and hoped for better from their government."

President Clinton has stated that, as the secretary of energy, O'Leary's top priority will be to transfer technologies developed for the military cleanup to the private sector.

Shaquille O'Neal

Basketball player
Born March 6, 1972, Newark, New Jersey

"I haven't had a chance to show all my talents. The NBA is more my game—banging and pushing, but man against man."

asketball player Shaquille O'Neal has the potential for superstardom on level with Wilt Chamberlain, Kareem Abdul-Jabbar, Magic Johnson, and other professional players who have dominated the league. O'Neal signed a multimillion dollar contract with the Orlando Magic when only twenty years old. His college credentials were impressive: he led the NCAA in rebounding and finished near the top on scoring, blocked shots, and shooting percentage. University of Texas coach Tom Penders told the *Atlanta Constitution,* "He's as big as Jabbar, if not bigger, stronger than Chamberlain and runs like Magic Johnson." If all the predictions of greatness come true, O'Neal will dominate the National Basketball Association for years to come.

Met LSU coach Dale Brown at basketball clinic in Germany

O'Neal was born on March 6, 1972, in Newark, New Jersey, to Philip Harrison and Lucille O'Neal. Since his parents didn't marry until he was three, O'Neal took his mother's maiden name. The young family lived in the rough areas of Newark and nearby New Jersey City, and when O'Neal was twelve, his father transferred to an army base in Wildflecken, West Germany. That was when O'Neal underwent a big growth spurt, and by the time he was thirteen he was 6 ft. 6 in. and wore size seventeen shoes. His father Philip Harrison told *Sports Illustrated,* "We'd buy him pants on the [army] post on Saturday and the next Friday they wouldn't fit." The family turned to ordering custom-made clothes from the United States, but sometimes they would arrive late and no longer fit.

When he was thirteen, O'Neal met Dale Brown, head of the Louisiana State University (LSU) basketball team. Brown was in Germany conducting coaching clinics, and O'Neal attended, hoping to improve his vertical jump. Brown realized O'Neal had considerable potential and told him to keep LSU in mind when it came time for university.

While he was a high school junior, O'Neal used to get into many fights. He had a bad temper and almost got thrown out of school, but his father soon set him straight. Harrison gave him "a few lickings" and that improved his attitude. One time Harrison grabbed O'Neal during halftime at a high school basketball game and ordered him to tuck in his shirt. "I always told Shaquille the world has too many followers," Harrison said in *Sports Illustrated.* "What he needed to be was a leader. He'd see guys hanging out on the corner, and he'd know they were followers. I told him I'd whup him rather than have the guys on the corner whup him. I told him there's no half-stepping in this life."

The family moved to San Antonio, Texas, in 1987, where Harrison was stationed at Fort Sam Houston. O'Neal attended Cole High School, was an average student, and continued to grow, reaching 6 ft. 10 in. tall and tipping the scales at 250 pounds. He led Cole High to a 32–1 win/loss record, but he was still not considered an outstanding prospect. During senior year, his father told O'Neal that if he was not going to play his hardest, then he may as well not play at all. O'Neal scored 52 points in his next game. The next week, he received recruiting letters from Georgetown and North Carolina.

Shaquille O'Neal

Joined LSU's powerhouse team

Cole High went undefeated that season and won the Texas state title. Several colleges offered O'Neal scholarships, and he chose LSU, where Brown was still coach. "I chose LSU, first, because Coach Brown was honest. Second, the players were like family. They were close. Other places, one goes this way, one goes that way. Here, they're together," O'Neal told the *Houston Post.*

LSU had a powerhouse team when O'Neal joined in 1989. It featured Stanley Roberts, a seven-foot freshman power forward; and Chris Jackson, an All-American who averaged more than 20 shots per game. O'Neal found himself the third-wheel on the team, and it was a difficult transition for him. Jackson did most of the shooting on the team, and O'Neal was delegated to rebounding. He still averaged 13.9 points and 12 rebounds, and he established a Southeastern Conference

record of 115 blocked shots. He also fouled out of nine games. The year ended when LSU lost in the first round of the NCAA Tournament.

A year later O'Neal played in the National Sports Festival, an event featuring the country's top amateur athletes. During the tournament he dominated players that were three and four years older. He finished with 24.5 points and 13.8 rebounds per game and was named the tournament's most valuable player.

When O'Neal returned to LSU that year, he found himself in a considerably different position. Jackson had left college to join the National Basketball Association and Roberts went to play in Spain, after being ruled academically ineligible. Coach Brown made O'Neal co-captain. He also developed his vertical jump to 42 inches. This new ability made O'Neal the dominant player in college basketball. During the 1990–91 season, he led the NCAA in rebounding with 15.2 a game. He was also sixth among all college players in scoring (28.5 points), fourth in blocked shots (4.8), and fourteenth in shooting (63.9 percent).

The key to O'Neal's success has been to use his size to intimidate his opponents. Tim Povtak, an *Orlando Sentinel* writer, called O'Neal "a powerful giant with a feathery touch who can control a basketball game in so many ways. He blocks shots like [New York Knicks player] Patrick Ewing, but runs the floor like [the Utah Jazz's] Karl Maline. He is strong enough to knock down anyone, but is graceful enough to dribble the length of the court and athletic enough to take an errant alley-oop pass, change his course in midflight and still slam it."

Signed $40 million contract with Orlando Magic

In 1991 LSU coach Dale Brown asked two tutors to help O'Neal with his game—Hall of Fame centers Kareem Abdul-Jabbar and Bill Walton. Abdul-Jabbar showed him his sky hook, while Walton taught him offensive moves and shot-blocking. The training picked up his already great game. Brown told the *Rocky Mountain News*: "Bill and Kareem did many things we'd been trying to teach Shaquille. But it's like raising a child. You can keep telling him something. But when somebody he respects tells him the same thing, it makes an indelible impression."

Although his parents wanted him to finish university, O'Neal decided to forego his senior year at LSU in April 1992 to be available for the upcoming draft. He was the first overall draft pick, signing with the Orlando Magic for a reported $40 million over seven years. *Sports Illustrated* revealed that he worked out a deal with a trading card company for $1 million, and he will likely receive a great deal more through future commercial endorsements.

Jesse Owens

Olympic athlete, businessman
Born September 12, 1913, Oakville,
  Alabama
Died March 31, 1980, Phoenix, Arizona

"Any black who strives to achieve in this country should think in terms of not only himself, but also how he can reach down and grab another black child and pull him to the top of the mountain where he is. This is what a gold medal does to you."

C ertain moments in Olympic history remain alive no matter how much time has passed, as with athlete Jesse Owens, who set four records and received four gold medals at the Olympic Games in Berlin, Germany, in 1936, thwarting the Nazis' desire to turn the games into a demonstration of Germany's racial and ethnic superiority.

After the Olympics, Owens held a variety of jobs before opening his own public relations firm. He lectured on clean living, fair play, and patriotism to young Americans and groups around the world and received numerous awards and citations, including a Congressional Gold Medal.

Ran track at college

Owens was born on September 12, 1913, in Oakville, Alabama, to Henry and Emma Owens. His parents were sharecroppers who headed north to Cleveland, Ohio, in 1922 to better their lives. When Owens attended his first day of school, his teacher mistook his name for Jesse instead of J.C., dubbing him with the name he was known by for the rest of his life. Though he was frail and sickly, the school's coach convinced him to try out for the track team. He quickly developed as a runner, and by junior high he set a new record for the 100–yard dash. He continued his success by winning the 100–yard dash, the 220–

Jesse Owens

yard low hurdles, and the long jump at the 1933 Interscholastic Championships in Chicago.

After graduating Owens attended Ohio State University. Even with working three jobs, Owens found time for track and earned the nickname "Buckeye Bullet" because of his speed. At the National Intercollegiate Track and Field Championships in Ann Arbor, Michigan, on May 25, 1935, Owens broke three world records in forty-five minutes, despite intense pain from a week-old back injury.

Owens experienced racism while at college. He lived in a house with other black members of the track team and took most of his meals there. Black athletes could not dine in restaurants or use rest room facilities when traveling to and from meets, and an angry cook once refused to serve Owens and his friends in their car. These incidents only served to motivate Owens even more.

Won four Olympic gold medals

In August 1936 Owens was one of ten blacks selected to the sixty-six-member Olympic team, held that year in Berlin, Germany. Germany's chancellor, Adolf Hitler called the black athletes subhuman and said they could easily be defeated by the unquestionably superior German athletes. Though some suggested that the games be boycotted because of Hitler's racist statements, the games went on as scheduled. German athletes won many of the early medals, and it began to look like they might run away with the Olympics, until Owens competed.

Owens was matched against German superstar athlete Lutz Long. Their first event was the long jump, and Long set an Olympic record with his first jump. Owens missed his first two attempts, but on his last try he not only beat Long's new record but also his own former record. His record in the long jump would stand for twenty-five years. As Hitler left the stadium, Long embraced Owens while the mostly German crowd chanted Owens's name. Owens went on to win gold medals in the 100-meter sprint, the 200-meter sprint, and the 400-meter relay, in which he substituted for another runner.

Hitler was reportedly so angry that a black athlete had defeated the Germans that he refused to congratulate Owens, although he had congratulated several other medal winners— mostly Germans—on the first day of the games. When Olympic officials asked him to stop, Hitler decided to forgo the public displays and met privately with medal-winning Germans, but the story of Hitler's apparent snub spread quickly and enhanced the symbolic importance of Owens's success as a triumph over Nazism.

Owens returned to the United States to a ticker-tape parade in New York, but he was unable to find a job to pay for the rest of his college education. Years later he told *Ebony* magazine: "I came back to my native country and I couldn't ride in the front of the bus. I had to go to the back door. I couldn't live where I wanted.... I wasn't invited to shake hands with Hitler, but I wasn't invited to the White House to shake hands with the President, either."

Called an American hero

Owens was forced to drop out of college for a short time, and he worked briefly as a playground janitor and made some money racing against cars, trucks, motorcycles, horses, and dogs. He also made several personal appearances, including tap dancing with Bill "Bojangles" Robinson, and he made speeches on behalf of Alf Landon, the Republican presidential candidate. With money from these ventures Owens finished college, but because he had accepted payment for running, his career as an amateur runner was over. He could never compete in the Olympics again.

During the late 1930s Owens had a variety of jobs. He led a swing orchestra, had a bit part in a movie, served as an official with the Works Progress Administration in Cleveland, worked as a salesman, and established a chain of dry cleaning stores. By 1939 the dry cleaning business faltered, and Owens's partners disappeared, leaving him with heavy debts that forced him into personal bankruptcy. From 1940 to 1942 he was the Office of Civilian Defense's national director of physical education for black Americans. He served as director of black personnel for the Ford Motor Company from 1942 to 1946, after which he resigned to become a salesman for a sporting goods firm.

In 1949 Owens moved to Chicago. Still selling sporting goods, he also became involved in several state and local programs designed to keep blacks out of trouble by involving them with athletics. Owens took his status as a role model very seriously, and he became an inspiration to those who faced the same obstacles and prejudices that had held him back.

Owens's skills as a speaker eventually led him to open his own public relations firm. He spoke on behalf of several charities, the Olympics, and had dozens of corporate clients. His message on the virtues of fair play, clean living, and patriotism was in such high demand that he earned an estimated $100,000 a year. He came under fire in 1968 for opposing a black American boycott of the Olympics, and some people accused him of being a toady to white people. The charges hurt Owens, and he defended himself in his 1970 biography, *Blackthink*. Two years later he became more militant and published another book, *I Have Changed*.

In 1972 Owens retired to Phoenix, Arizona, though he remained an "ambassador of sports" for the U.S. State Department, a position that called on him to make periodic goodwill tours around the world. He received a Presidential Medal of Freedom from President Gerald Ford in 1971, and the Living Legend Award from President Jimmy Carter in 1979. A longtime cigarette smoker, Owens developed lung cancer and died on March 31, 1980, after a long stay in a Phoenix hospital. He was buried in Chicago a few days later.

Owens received his highest honor ten years after his death when Congressman Louis Stokes from Cleveland lobbied to present him with a Congressional Gold Medal. The award was presented to Owens's widow, Ruth, by President George Bush in 1990. During the ceremony, Bush said Owens was "an Olympic hero and an American hero every day of his life."

Satchel Paige

Baseball player
Born July 7, 1906, Mobile, Alabama
Died 1982

"Don't look back. Something might be gaining on you."

For years baseball historians have argued over the impact Satchel Paige would have had on the major leagues if the color barrier had not existed for so many years. Paige ruled the Negro baseball leagues during the 1930s and 1940s, and many tales emerged of his pitching prowess. Clint Courtney, a former catcher, said, "You hear about pinpoint control, but Paige is the only man I've ever seen who really has it. Once he threw me six strikes out of ten pitches over a gum wrapper." When the color barrier finally crumbled in the mid-1940s, allowing Paige to enter the major leagues, he was past forty and at the end of his career. Even in decline, Paige was one of the most potent relief pitchers in the game and made the All-Star team in 1952.

Throwing stones at tin cans

Paige was born on July 7, 1906, in Mobile, Alabama, with the given name Leroy Robert Paige. As a youngster he used to spend all day throwing stones at tin cans and playing sandlot baseball. It is difficult to say when he made his professional debut since detailed rosters were not retained, but Paige is mentioned as pitching for the Chattanooga Lookouts in 1925. The Lookouts were a part of the Negro leagues that formed in 1920 in Kansas City, Missouri. Originally called the Negro National League, a year later they were joined by the Negro Eastern League. They began playing their own World Series in 1924 and continued to operate until 1932, when the Depression caused them to fold.

Paige was listed with the Birmingham Barons in 1928, and later with the Baltimore Black Sox, the Chicago American Giants, and the Pittsburgh Crawfords. He rose to prominence in 1933, when he pitched forty-two games, winning thirty-one and losing four with seven no decisions. At one time he had a winning streak of twenty-one consecutive games and sixty-two scoreless innings. The next year he played for a team in Bismarck, North Dakota, which lost only once in 105 games. "And I pitched in every game, I guess," Paige said in a *New York Times* interview. "I know there was one month when I started twenty-nine games." When the regular season finally ended, he defeated Dizzy Dean by a 1 to 0 score in a thirteen-inning exhibition game. Bill Veeck, owner of the major league Cleveland Indians, was in attendance and commented, "It's the best I've ever seen."

Rafael Trujillo, president of the Dominican Republic, organized an all-Negro team to dominate winter ball in Latin America. He signed several Negro stars, including Paige, and for several winters, Paige pitched in Venezuela, Mexico, Cuba, Puerto Rico, Colombia, and elsewhere. It is believed Paige received five hundred dollars per game, and he returned to the U.S. in the summer to make more money. He played with a variety of teams including the Homestead (Pennsylvania) Greys and the Kansas City Black Monarchs.

Wins the Negro World Series

In 1941 Paige decided against returning to Latin America. The Second World War and the revival of the Negro American and National Leagues made it more attractive for him to stay in the U.S. He rejoined the Kansas City Monarchs and helped to pitch the team to victory in the 1942 Negro World Series. Four years later he helped the team win the league pennant by allowing only two runs in ninety-three innings and running a streak of sixty-four scoreless innings.

Off the field, Paige was a loner and not held in high esteem by teammates and friends. Many Negro leaguers resented the attention and the 10 to 15 per cent of the gate receipts he received. But he always exuded humor and a flair for life. "He could laugh, and dance, and sing," Newt Allen once said. "He was a man who just loved life itself." As the major gate attraction, Paige called his own shots. Many times he arrived late to the game, and the park would be buzzing with "Where's

Satchel Paige

Satchel?" Sometimes several innings passed before Paige arrived.

By the time Jackie Robinson broke the color barrier in major league baseball in 1947, Paige's best days were behind him. His much-celebrated fastball was slowing down. Although more blacks were finding jobs in the major leagues, little interest was shown in Paige at first. That changed when Paige struck out sixteen batters and defeated Bob Feller of the Cleveland Indians, 8 to 0 in an exhibition game in Los Angeles. Veeck, the Indians' owner, renewed his interest in Paige, and with the Indians heading toward a pennant, he decided to offer Paige a contract in July 1948. Paige became the seventh black player to play in the majors. He played his first game on August 13, and scattered nine hits to defeat the Chicago White Sox, 5 to 0. A week later he shut out the White Sox again on three hits. Paige went on to win four out of five games with a respectable 2.47 earned run average. In the fourth game of the World Series against the Boston Braves, he allowed no hits in two-thirds of an inning.

In 1949 Paige suffered from a stomach disorder and was relegated to the bullpen. He won only four of eleven decisions, and when Veeck sold his interest in the Indians later that year, the new owners decided to release Paige. He rejoined the Kansas City Monarchs of the Negro League and pitched sixty-two games across the country in 1950. His stomach ailment was cured, and his fastball had found its old zip. In July 1951, Veeck purchased the St. Louis Browns of the American League and summoned Paige back to the majors. He made twenty-three appearances, winning three and losing four, but his supporting cast was weak. The team made major trades in the off-season, and in the first half of the 1952 season, Paige won six important games and lost four. He was named to play in the All-Star game against the National League at Philadelphia on July 9, but he never got a chance to play. Although manager Casey Stengel promised to play him in the eighth inning, the game was called after five innings because of rain. He finished the season with twelve wins and ten losses, and had the best earned-run average on the team.

In 1965, at the age of fifty-nine, Paige signed for a one-time appearance with the Kansas City As. He pitched three scoreless innings, allowing only 1 hit and striking out one batter.

In 1971 Paige was awarded membership in the Baseball Hall of Fame in Cooperstown, New York, for his twenty-five-year career in the Negro Leagues and the Major Leagues. Paige died in 1982 at the age of seventy-five.

In an interview with historian Stephen Banker, Paige summed up his baseball career: "You're born with speed, see, but you can get the control. We had a lot of players when I came up who could throw the ball hard, way harder than I could, as far as that's concerned, but they couldn't gain control. It's such a thing as I practiced all the time; I just practiced control. Anything you practice you begin to come good at, regardless of what it is, whether it's baseball or not."

Gordon Parks

Photographer, filmmaker, writer
Born November 30, 1912, Fort Scott, Kansas

"As I tell young black people, you can fight back, but do it in a way to help yourself and not destroy yourself."

When Gordon Parks accepted the NAACP's Spingarn Medal in 1972, he said he had tried so many different things in life because he was "a black boy who wanted to be somebody." Having started out with every disadvantage—turned out onto the street at the age of fifteen with little education and no money—he fought back and in fact became more than a "somebody." Parks has made his name in an amazing range of creative fields, as photographer, journalist, poet, musician, novelist, composer, filmmaker, and choreographer.

While pursuing this varied career, Parks led the way for other African Americans by breaking down racial barriers. He was the first black photographer to work for *Life* magazine, the first to take pictures for *Vogue,* and the first black director to work for a major Hollywood studio. During World War II, he was the first African American to work for the Office of War Information and for the Farm Security Administration. His work has brought him many awards, including an Emmy, a Photographer of the Year Award, and the National Medal of the Arts.

A tough start in life

Gordon Roger Alexander Buchanan Parks was born into a poor farming family, the youngest of fifteen children. His parents, Andrew and Sarah (Ross) Parks, were strict Methodists, and although they had no money to lavish on their children, they dispensed plenty of good advice. Parks was taught to value honesty, justice, courage, and perseverance. His mother often told him, "If a white boy can do it, so can you, so don't you ever give me your color as a cause for failing."

Parks was particularly close to his mother and was shattered when she died during his teenage years. He was sent to live with one of his sisters in St. Paul, Minnesota, but as a result of an argument, his brother-in-law threw him out of the house. This ended any hope Parks had of finishing high school. Alone, penniless, and forced to live by his wits, the fifteen-year-old took what work he could get, mopping floors in the daytime and riding the streetcars at night to keep warm.

Sometimes Parks found work as a waiter, and for a while he had a job playing the piano in a brothel. He had been able to play by ear since early childhood and liked to make up his own songs. While he was working as a busboy in a St. Paul restaurant, a visiting bandleader heard him playing on the ballroom piano and invited him to join the band. This was better than waiting tables, and Parks toured with the band until it broke up in New York in 1933. He then did a brief stint with the Civilian Conservation Corps before marrying his first wife and returning with her to St. Paul, where he took a job as a dining car waiter on the railroad.

Self-taught photographer

While he was working on the railroad, Parks became interested in photography. He bought a second-hand camera, taught himself the techniques, and began to take pictures in the cities he stayed in on his route. Most of these photos were of ordinary black people going about their daily lives, but in 1937 he established himself as a fashion photographer in St. Paul.

Moving to Chicago a few years later, Parks continued to work as a fashion photographer to support his wife and children, but his real interest was in the pictures he was taking in his spare time. These powerful and honest photographs documented conditions in Chicago's slums, and they won Parks a Julius Rosenwald Fellowship in 1941. As well as paying $200 a month, the fellowship offered Parks the choice of an employer, and in January 1942 he signed on with the photography section of the Farm Security Administration (FSA), joining some of the country's finest documentary photographers.

While with the FSA, Parks continued to take photos of the everyday life of African

Americans in order to expose it to the eyes of white America. "I had known poverty firsthand," he later explained, "but there I learned how to fight its evil—along with the evil of racism—with a camera." After the FSA disbanded in 1943, Parks worked as a war correspondent with the Office of War Information, but he left in disgust when, because of his color, he was not allowed to go overseas as a combat photographer.

Parks's color also proved a barrier to his getting a job with *Harper's Bazaar,* but *Vogue* and *Glamour* magazines were both glad to hire such an experienced photographer. So was Roy Stryker, his former boss at FSA, who offered Parks a position with Standard Oil of New Jersey. From 1945 to 1948, Parks took documentary photographs for Standard Oil, and during this time he also wrote his first book, *Flash Photography* (1947).

A man of many skills

In 1948, Parks did a freelance story on a Harlem gang, which was published in *Life* magazine, and this led to his being hired as a staff photographer. Parks stayed with *Life* for more than twenty years, turning out an impressive portfolio of photographs and photo stories. His work took to him to France and Brazil as well as throughout the United States, where he photographed everything from fashionable celebrities to condemned criminals. During the 1950s, he did a memorable series on segregation in the South, and he was a leading documentarian of the civil rights movement in the 1960s.

In 1963, Parks's first novel, *The Learning Tree,* was published—a story about a black family in Kansas. Like so many of Parks's photographs, it gave a positive view of black people while at the same time exposing the miserable conditions of daily life. In 1968, the book was made into a film, which Parks directed. He already had some experience in film, having written and directed a movie about a Brazilian boy who had been the subject of one of his photo essays. However, *The Learning Tree* was made for a major studio, Warner Brothers, which had never before had a black director.

Having made his breakthrough into Hollywood, Parks went on to direct other major films: *Shaft* (1971), *Shaft's Big Score* (1972), *The Super Cops* (1974), and *Leadbelly* (1976). During this period he also had several more books published, including his first poetry book, and he had an exhibition of his photographs in New York, for which he composed a concerto as the background music.

Gordon Parks

The 1980s saw Parks making several documentary films as well as a film of the ballet *Martin* about Martin Luther King, Jr., which was aired on the Public Broadcasting Service on the anniversary of King's birthday in 1990. Typically, Parks did far more than merely direct *Martin*. He also wrote the libretto and music and worked on the choreography.

Along with all this activity, Parks has found time to write three volumes of autobiography, *A Choice of Weapons* (1966), *To Smile in Autumn* (1979), and *Voices in the Mirror* (1991). He has also written personal sonatas for his children. In the course of three marriages, Parks has had four children, one of whom died in a plane crash. Although Parks's life has seen tragedy and adversity, he has always fought back, expressing his feelings in a burst of creative activity.

Rosa Parks

Civil rights activist
Born February 4, 1913, Tuskegee, Alabama

"I felt just resigned to give what I could to protect against the way I was being treated."

O n December 1, 1955, Rosa Parks refused to give up her seat on a bus to a white man who wanted it. By this simple act, which today would seem unremarkable, she set in motion the civil rights movement, which led to the Civil Rights Act of 1964 and ultimately ensured that today all black Americans must be given equal treatment with whites under the law.

Parks did not know that she was making history nor did she intend to do so. She simply knew that she was tired after a long day's work and did not want to move. Because of her fatigue and because she was so determined, America was changed forever. Segregation was on its way out.

Growing up in Montgomery

In the first half of this century, Montgomery, Alabama, was totally segregated, like so many other cities in the South. In this atmosphere Parks and her brother grew up. They had been brought to Montgomery by their mother, Leona (Edwards) McCauley, when she and their father separated in 1915. Their father, James McCauley, went away north and they seldom saw him, but they were made welcome by their mother's family and passed their childhood among cousins, uncles, aunts, grandparents, and great-grandparents.

Rosa Parks

Parks's mother was a schoolteacher, and Parks was taught by her until the age of eleven, when she went to Montgomery Industrial School for Girls. It was, of course, an all-black school, as was Booker T. Washington High School, which she attended briefly. Virtually everything in Montgomery was for "blacks only" or "whites only," and Parks became used to obeying the segregation laws, though she found them humiliating.

When Parks was twenty, she married Raymond Parks, a barber, and moved out of her mother's home. Parks took in sewing and worked at various jobs over the years. She also became an active member of the National Association for the Advancement of Colored People (NAACP), working as secretary of the Montgomery chapter.

The arrest of Rosa Parks

In 1955 Parks was forty-two years old, and she had taken to protesting segregation in her own quiet way—for instance, by walking up the stairs of a building rather than riding in an elevator marked "blacks only." She was well respected in the black community for her work with the Montgomery Voters League as well as the NAACP. The Voters League was a group that helped black citizens pass the various tests that had been set up to make it difficult for them to register as voters.

As well as avoiding black-only elevators, Parks often avoided traveling by bus, preferring to walk home from work when she was not too tired to do so. The buses were a constant irritation to all black passengers. The front four rows were reserved for whites (and remained empty even when there were not enough white passengers to fill them). The back section, which was always very crowded, was for black passengers. In between were some rows that were really part of the black section, but served as an overflow area for white passengers. If the white section was full, black passengers in the middle section had to vacate their seats—a whole row had to be vacated, even if only one white passenger required a seat.

This is what happened on the evening of December 1, 1955: Parks took the bus because she was feeling particularly tired after a long day in the department store where she worked as a seamstress. She was sitting in the middle section, glad to be off her feet at last, when a white man boarded the bus and demanded that her row be cleared because the white section was full. The others in the row obediently moved to the back of the bus, but Parks just didn't feel like standing for the rest of the journey, and she quietly refused to move.

At this, the white bus driver threatened to call the police unless Parks gave her up her seat, but she calmly replied, "Go ahead and call them." By the time the police arrived, the driver was very angry, and when asked whether he wanted Parks to be arrested or let off with a warning, he insisted on arrest. So this respectable, middle-aged woman was taken to the police station, where she was fingerprinted and jailed. She was allowed to make one phone call. She called an NAACP lawyer, who arranged for her to be released on bail.

The bus boycott

Word of Parks's arrest spread quickly, and the Women's Political Council decided to protest her treatment by organizing a boycott of the buses. The boycott was set for December 5, the day of Parks's trial, but Dr. Martin Luther King, Jr., and other prominent members of Montgomery's black community realized that here was a chance to take a firm stand on segregation. As a result, the Montgomery Improvement Association was formed to organize a boycott that would continue until the bus segregation laws were changed. Leaflets were distributed telling people not to ride the buses, and other forms of transport were laid on.

The boycott lasted 382 days, causing the bus company to lose a vast amount of money. Meanwhile, Parks was fined for failing to obey a city ordinance, but on the advice of her lawyers she refused to pay the fine so that they could challenge the segregation law in court. The following year, the U.S. Supreme Court ruled the Montgomery segregation law illegal, and the boycott was at last called off. Yet Parks had started far more than a bus boycott. Other cities followed Montgomery's example and were protesting their segregation laws. The civil rights movement was underway.

Mother of the civil rights movement

Parks has been hailed as "the mother of the civil rights movement," but this was not an easy role for her. Threats and constant phone calls she received during the boycott caused her husband to have a nervous breakdown, and in 1957 they moved to Detroit, where Parks's brother, Sylvester, lived. There Parks continued her work as a seamstress, but she had become a public figure and was often sought out to give talks about civil rights.

Over the years, Parks has received several honorary degrees, and in 1965 Congressman John Conyers of Detroit appointed her to his staff. Parks's husband died in 1977 and she retired in 1988, but she has continued to work for the betterment of the black community. She is particularly eager to help the young, and in 1987 she established the Rosa and Raymond Parks Institute for Self-Development, a training school for Detroit teenagers.

Each year sees more honors showered upon her. In 1990, some three thousand people attended the Kennedy Center in Washington, D.C., to celebrate the seventy-seventh birthday of the indomitable campaigner and former seamstress, Rosa Parks.

Sidney Poitier

Actor, director
Born February 20, 1927, Miami, Florida

"The few black faces passing across the silver screen were not anywhere near enough to assuage the frustrations our people felt.... However inadequate my steps appeared, it was important that we make it."

S idney Poitier was the first black actor to break through the stereotyping in Hollywood that limited African Americans to such roles as cheery servants and happy-go-lucky jazz musicians. Poitier acted with the same sophistication and sensitivity as Cary Grant and Clark Gable. He was the first African American to win an Oscar for best actor.

Poitier has starred in some forty films in the course of his career. They include such classics as *Cry the Beloved Country* (1952); *The Blackboard Jungle* (1955); *The Defiant Ones* (1958), which brought Poitier an Academy Award nomination; *Lilies of the Field* (1963), which won him an Academy Award; *Guess Who's Coming to Dinner* (1967); *In the Heat of the Night* (1967); and *To Sir, with Love* (1967). His greatest hit as a director was *Stir Crazy* (1980), which starred Richard Pryor and Gene Wilder.

Failed his first two acting auditions

Sidney Poitier was the son of Reginald and Evelyn (Outten) Poitier, who were tomato farmers in the Bahamas. Poitier weighed only three and a half pounds at birth, for he was born two months early—he came into the world unexpectedly when his parents were in Miami, Florida, selling their tomato crop.

Although Poitier's parents were very poor, he had a happy childhood at the family home on Cat Island in the Bahamas. Along with his six brothers and sisters, he spent much of his time fishing, swimming, and catching turtles. Not until he was ten years old did he know what ice cream and electricity were. In his autobiography *This Life* (1980), he recalled: "My mother dressed me in flour sacks because she couldn't afford clothing.... She taught me that the only undignified thing about wearing such clothes was if they were dirty."

Poitier stayed only four years at school before he dropped out to help his father on the farm. When he was about thirteen he joined one of his brothers in Miami, where for the

Sidney Poitier

first time he experienced segregation and other overt forms of racism. Shortly thereafter he left for New York City, where he arrived in 1940 without any money but with plenty of hope, and with the lesson drummed into him by his mother that good manners and dignified behavior would take him a long way. With her advice in mind, he approached a white policeman in New York: "I had gone downtown to look for a dishwashing job and I had no money and I said, 'I wonder if you could loan me a nickel for the subway and if you'll tell me where you're working tomorrow I'll return the nickel.' And he did."

Poitier worked for various restaurants in New York until he was sixteen, when he lied about his age in order to join the army, in which he served for about nine months toward the end of World War II. Back in New York in 1945 he came across a newspaper article saying that the American Negro Theater was looking for actors. Although Poitier knew nothing about acting, the idea appealed to him and he went for an audition. But because of his thick West Indian accent and poor reading skills, he was rejected after stumbling through only three lines.

During the next few months Poitier painstakingly altered his accent by copying radio broadcasters, and he improved his reading skills by getting a friend to help him. Although he was again rejected when he next auditioned six months later, the people at the American Negro Theater offered to take him on as a janitor while giving him acting lessons. Soon Poitier had the chance to be an understudy, and in 1946 he had his first lead role in the play *Days of Our Youth*. More stage roles followed, ranging from a butler in *Strivers Road* to a Greek character in *Lysistrata*. By 1950, when Poitier was offered his first film role, he was a polished actor with a widely varied experience.

Paved way as role model for other black actors

Poitier's debut in films, as a doctor in *No Way Out* (1950), set the pattern for the type of character he would play. While his next few roles ranged from priest to basketball player, they all represented real people, not the caricaturized blacks that Hollywood usually portrayed. Moreover, they were noble characters and usually far more talented and dedicated than their white associates.

In Poitier's first big success, *The Blackboard Jungle* (1955), he played a problem high school student who sides with authority at a crisis point in the story. He acted the part so convincingly that from then on he was the first choice whenever filmmakers wanted to portray a tense and complex young African American. In *The Defiant Ones* (1958) he was cast as an escaped convict who is chained by the wrist to a white convict—a role he played with such sensitivity that he was nominated for an Academy Award. Very few black actors had ever before been nominated for an Oscar, and none had ever won, but Poitier did five years later in *Lilies of the Field* (1963). In this movie he had a totally different role—a handyman who helps build a chapel for German-speaking nuns.

Poitier's success not only made him a major star, but it represented a breakthrough for all black actors, for he opened the door into non-stereotyped roles. Nothing emphasized this more than his casting in 1967, when he played a quietly heroic teacher taming a rebellious class (*To Sir, with Love*), a sophisticated detective solving a murder mystery (*In the Heat of the Night*), and a leading scientist engaged to a white girl (*Look Who's Coming to Dinner*).

His image as the type of unaggressive black hero who whites could feel comfortable with brought him criticism during the early 1970s when black power was gaining in popularity. Some people considered Poitier a sellout and felt he should take more aggressive roles. Others accused him of being no more than "a pretty black face that Hollywood could exploit without having to acknowledge black culture." Poitier agreed that far too many barriers still faced black actors, but he did not feel he was a sellout. "However inadequate my steps appeared, it was important that we make it," he said.

As a way of taking further steps Poitier began to direct his own films. He wanted more control over the image of African Americans that was put before the public. In *Buck and the Preacher* (1972), the first movie he directed, he chose Harry Belafonte as his co-star in a very different type of western that portrayed black cowboys with strong moral values. Poitier directed seven more films over the next fifteen years. The most successful was the comedy *Stir Crazy* (1980), which starred Richard Pryor and Gene Wilder and became one of the biggest money-making films of all time. It was also made into a television series.

In recent years Poitier has once again concentrated on acting rather than directing, starring in *Little Nikita* (1988) and other films. Whereas he was once the only black leading man, he now has many rivals, some of whom are openly hostile to the type of role he has made famous. Yet Poitier was influential in breaking through the barriers in Hollywood. Sidney Poitier led the way with calm dignity to enable today's black actors and directors to succeed in the film business.

Adam Clayton Powell, Jr.

Congressman, minister
Born November 29, 1908, New Haven,
    Connecticut
Died April 4, 1972, Miami, Florida

"Like no other Negro, except perhaps the late Malcolm X, Adam knew how to anger, to irritate and to cajole his white counterparts."—Simeon Booker

A highly controversial figure in both private and public life, Adam Clayton Powell was New York's first black city councilman and Harlem's first black congressman. He served as a Democratic member of the U.S. House of Representatives from 1945 to 1967 and again from 1969 to 1970. He was also minister of the Abyssinian Baptist Church in New York City. But he was many other things too. The *New York Times* described Powell as "a civil rights leader three decades before the Montgomery bus boycott, a wheeler-dealer, a rabble-rouser, a grandstander, a fugitive, a playboy, and the most effective chairman of the House Committee on Education and Labor."

Powell's brash approach and playboy lifestyle landed him in several lawsuits over the years, yet he always managed to bounce back. Despite such legal problems, he was the most celebrated black politician in America. The one constant throughout his life was his passionate championing of civil rights. He fought relentlessly in Congress, determined to get the laws changed so that African Americans could live without prejudice in a desegregated land.

The minister's son

Powell's father, Adam Clayton Powell, Sr., was a Baptist minister who became pastor of the Abyssinian Baptist Church in New York City when Powell was a small child. The Powells lived in a comfortable middle-class home, and the light-skinned Powell was thoroughly pampered by his mother, Mattie (Fletcher) Powell. He was so light-skinned that many people thought he was white, and he took advantage of this fact to have a very active social life.

At the City College of New York, the young Powell spent more time enjoying life than studying, though he also experienced great misery, for his sister died of a ruptured appendix during his first year in college. Because he was playing around so much in Harlem, he was sent to study at Colgate University in upstate New York, where the college president, who was a friend of Powell's father, agreed to keep an eye on the boy. At Colgate, Powell was assumed to be white until he tried to join an all-white fraternity, which checked out his background. His duplicity made him temporarily unpopular with both blacks and whites, though it did not inhibit his style. Despite his father's efforts, he continued his happy-go-lucky ways, though he did complete the course, graduating with a B.A. in 1930.

Since Powell had agreed to follow his father into the ministry, he became a part-time student at Union Theological Seminary, and in 1932 he graduated with a master's degree from Columbia University. The following year, much against his family's wishes, he married the actress Isabel Washington. They were later to divorce because of an affair he was having with the pianist Hazel Scott, who became his second wife in 1945. That marriage, too, ended in divorce, as did his third marriage, to the secretary Yvette Diago. Each marriage brought Powell a son.

Political activist

In 1930, Powell joined his father at the Abyssinian Baptist Church, and he took over as pastor when his father retired in 1937. As assistant pastor, he had turned his talents to helping the many families who were hard hit by the Depression. He found that he was good at making things happen, and as the Depression deepened he tackled the task energetically, laying on a range of social and welfare programs at the church. His soup kitchen and other relief operations provided food, fuel, and clothing for thousands of Harlem families during the 1930s.

Powell was a natural leader and a persistent one, and he soon emerged as a champion of the black community—never backing out of a scrap and always persevering until he achieved his aims. Time and again, he led demonstrations against businesses and bus companies, forcing them to hire black workers, and he helped form the Coordinating Committee on Employment, an organization that strove to get more jobs for blacks. In 1939–40 Powell gained hundreds of jobs for

Adam Clayton Powell, Jr.

black workers at the New York World's Fair as a result of the picketing he organized.

All this activity gained Powell the nickname "Fighting Adam," and when he ran for New York city council in 1941, he had strong support. At the age of thirty-three he became the city's first black councilman. The following year, Powell added another string to his bow when he co-founded the newspaper *People's Voice*. For ten years previous to that, he had written a column called "Soap Box" for the Harlem *Amsterdam*, and he continued it in his own paper. As before, he used the column to express his views and to attack discrimination wherever he saw it. During this period, he was also at work on his first book, *Marching Blacks: An Interpretive History of the Rise of the Black Common Man* (1945).

Congressman Powell

In the early 1940s, Powell decided to run for national office in the newly established twenty-second congressional district in Harlem. He received the Democratic nomination in the 1944 primary and was unopposed in the November election.

Powell began his time in Congress the way he was to continue—by confronting racism head on and by irritating many of his fellow politicians. The first person he annoyed was President Harry Truman, who had attended a function given by the Daughters of the American Revolution (DAR). Since the DAR banned black performers (including Powell's current wife), Powell told the president he should not have attended. As a result, Powell was never invited to the White House during Truman's presidency.

In the 1940s there was one other black congressman, William Dawson, but he was not the same type of aggressive fighter as Powell. For the first time, Congress had a loud, angry black voice in its midst, calling for an end to segregation and for passage of the Powell Amendment, which would deny federal funds to schools that did not admit black students. Powell never did get his amendment passed, but he went on fighting for it year after year. Meanwhile, he pressed for desegregation on all fronts and succeeded in getting a number of measures passed.

In 1960, Powell was appointed chairman of the House Committee on Education and Labor. This position made him one of the most powerful African Americans in the country. During his chairmanship, the committee passed forty-eight laws of major importance, including the Minimum Wage Bill and the Anti-Poverty Bill. But the more successful Powell became, the more domineering he grew, clashing with influential politicians (including more than one president) and gathering a mounting number of opponents. He even fell out with black civil rights workers, for he found that his position in the limelight had been upstaged by Martin Luther King, Jr.

Over the years, Powell's opponents accused him of various offenses, ranging from loose living to tax fraud. He spent several years being investigated for tax evasion, though he survived the trial without being convicted. He was less successful over an accusation that he had misused the funds of the Education and Labor committee. At the same time this charge was being considered, Powell was engaged in a much-publicized libel suit with a woman he had insulted. As a result of both affairs, the House voted to expel him from Congress in 1967. This brought an end to his chairmanship of the committee, but it did not end his service as a congressman, because he was voted back in by his electors. Moreover, six months after his return to Congress in 1969, the Supreme Court ruled that his expulsion had been illegal.

Powell finally left Congress in 1970, when for the first time in twenty-five years he failed to get re-elected. The following year he retired as pastor of the Abyssinian Baptist Church and went to live in the Bahamas. Undoubtedly, he had been an abrasive character, easily quarrelling with colleagues, both black and white. Undoubtedly he had enjoyed a flamboyant lifestyle that ill suited a minister and reformer. Undoubtedly he was brashly ambitious, hating to share the limelight with anyone. Yet Adam Clayton Powell, Jr. could not have achieved all he did if he had been a humbler, quieter person. Because of his larger-than-life character, great strides were made in the field of civil rights.

Colin Powell

Career army officer, Chairman of the Joint Chiefs of Staff
Born April 5, 1937, Harlem, New York

"You go in to win, and you go in to win decisively."

The first black American to hold the country's top military office, Chairman of the Joint Chiefs of Staff, U.S. Army general Colin Powell was an instrumental figure in Operations Desert Storm and Desert Shield, and he served as President Bush's key adviser during the Gulf War. He was credited with skillfully balancing the political objectives of President Bush and the strategy needs of General Norman Schwarzkopf. A career military man, Powell served two tours of duty in Vietnam and with forces in Europe, and he helped plan a variety of military actions, including the bombing raid on Libya and the invasion of Grenada.

Wounded twice while on duty in Vietnam

Powell was born on April 5, 1937, in Harlem, New York, to Luther and Maud Ariel Powell. His parents were Jamaican immigrants, and his worked as a shipping clerk and his mother as a seamstress. Powell grew up in South Bronx and attended Morris High School. He earned a bachelor's degree in geology from City College of the City University of New York in 1958. Though his academic career was average, he excelled in the college's Reserve Officer's Training Corps (ROTC). He led the precision drill team and attained the top rank, cadet colonel. His achievements won him a commission as a second lieutenant in the U.S. Army.

His first assignment was at the Fulda Gap in West Germany, where American and Allied troops stood as an obstacle to the Soviet bloc's probable invasion route of Western Europe. In the 1960s he served two tours of duty in South Vietnam, and in 1963, while acting as an adviser to South Vietnamese troops, he was wounded by an enemy booby trap, earning him his first Purple Heart medal. During his second tour, from 1968 to 1969, he was injured again in a helicopter crash. Wounded himself, he managed to rescue two of his comrades, for which he received a Purple Heart, a Bronze Star, a Soldier's Medal, and the Legion of Merit.

Back in the states he attended George Washington University and earned his M.B.A. Then he received a White House fellowship, giving him his first taste of politics. From 1972 to 1973 Powell worked for Frank Carlucci, then deputy director of the Office of Management and Budget. Powell began to understand how Washington's bureaucracy worked, and over the next fifteen years he has returned to the political arena from time to time.

From 1979 to 1981 Powell served as executive assistant to Charles Duncan, Jr., the Secretary of Energy, and was then named senior military assistant to the Deputy Secretary of Defense. When Ronald Reagan became president, Powell was a member of the Defense Department's transition team. From 1983 to 1986 he was the military assistant to the Defense Secretary and helped plan the invasion of Grenada and the bombing of Libya.

Appointed to ever more visible positions

Powell's military career has also been distinguished. He commanded a battalion in South Korea in 1973, and a year later he returned to Washington as a staff officer at the Pentagon. He finished his military education at the National War College in 1976 and took command of the Second Brigade of the 101st Airborne Division at Fort Campbell, Kentucky. During the early 1980s he was the assistant commander of the 4th Infantry Division at Fort Carson, Colorado, and the deputy director at Fort Leavenworth, Kansas. In 1987 he was the commanding general of the 5th Corps in Frankfurt, West Germany, before being called back to Washington to work with the new National Security Adviser.

Powell helped reorganize the National Security Council to reduce the possibility of freelance foreign policy. When Frank Carlucci was appointed Secretary of Defense, Powell became NSC leader. The move was greatly approved of in Washington because, as the *New Republic* once stated, Powell is "a national security adviser strong enough to settle policy disputes, but without a personal agenda."

While at the NSC, Powell addressed a wide range of issues, including economic strength, control of technology exchanges, protection of the environment, a stable defense budget, free trade and foreign investment, research and development, and education. He also voiced his opposition to overthrowing Panamanian dictator Manuel Noriega and to the huge amount of spending on the Strategic Defense Initiative (nicknamed Star Wars).

Powell became Chairman of the Joint Chiefs of Staff in 1989. He was the youngest man and first black ever to hold that position. When announcing Powell's appointment, President Bush stated: "As we face the challenges of the '90s, it is most important that the Chairman of the Joint Chiefs of Staff be a

Colin Powell

person of breadth, judgement, experience and total integrity. Colin Powell has all those qualities and more." Powell's peacetime duties entailed overseeing the prioritization of Pentagon spending and keeping the channels of communication open between the military and the White House. They also involved drawing up plans for military action, first in Panama and then the Middle East.

Made key decisions as Chairman of the Joint Chiefs during Desert Storm

President Bush redefined Powell's position in 1986, giving him more influence than any other Chairman of the Joint Chiefs of Staff since World War II. The Iraqi invasion of Kuwait on August 2, 1990, forced Powell to use his new power. The day after the invasion he advised the president of a number of options available, including economic and dip-

lomatic sanctions, as well as military force. The Bush administration decided the use of force was necessary. Operation Desert Shield, which required the massive movement of troops and supplies to Saudi Arabia, was soon initiated both as a show of force and to serve as a deterrent to further Iraqi aggression. Powell toured the Middle East and recommended increasing the number of troops to ensure that a divide-and-conquer strategy would work. He was quoted in *U.S. News and World Report* as saying, "You go in to win, and you go in to win decisively."

Despite the complexity of organizing an international coalition, Powell was instrumental in directing the quick integration of communications, operations, and authority into a command network under the direction of General Schwarzkopf. During the campaign Powell informed the president of military plans and aided him in making political decisions. He also convinced the Washington generals to let the commanders in Saudia Arabia make their own decisions.

Powell avoided day-to-day involvement in the desert operations and only exerted his authority when needed on major issues. He oversaw bombing missions on Baghdad only after the destruction of a suburban bunker killed 400 civilians. He rejected Marine requests to launch a true amphibious assault on Kuwait instead of the feint scheduled to aid Schwarzkopf's encirclement of Kuwait by an end run through Iraq. He also counseled the president to respond to the February 21 Iraqi peace proposal with an ultimatum: the Iraqis must pull out of Kuwait by noon Washington time on February 23. When the deadline passed, the coalition began its land attack, Operation Desert Storm, as scheduled.

In May 1991, Powell was reappointed for a second two-year term as chairman. Shortly after Bill Clinton assumed the presidency in 1993, Powell ran into odds against the new administration. Powell voiced his concerns with President Clinton's intentions to reduce the Pentagon's budget by $50 billion over four years. The two have also openly clashed over Clinton's decision to include homosexuals in the military. Despite their differences, Clinton has relied on Powell's advice in such areas as the Yugoslavian civil war and the Somalia peace initiatives.

Powell's key role in the successful liberation of Kuwait has thrown him into the country's spotlight. Some black leaders have criticized him for being a servant of the white establishment and by peace activists for being a war monger. Others have praised him as a positive role model for young blacks and a defender of liberty.

Powell has demonstrated his commitment to helping young black men and women succeed in the armed forces. He said the military should not be criticized for putting a disproportionate number of black men and women in danger, but rather praised and imitated for its history of providing opportunities to minorities.

Powell retired from the military in September of 1993, at the age of fifty-six. Many friends and observers speculated on the possibility of a political career in his future, and Powell did not rule this out.

Leontyne Price

Opera singer
Born February 10, 1927, Laurel, Mississippi

"The voice is so special. You have to guard it with care, to let nothing disturb it, so you don't lose the bloom, don't let it fade, don't let the petals drop."

L eontyne Price's warm rich voice, with its velvety tones and wide range, has made her one of the world's great opera singers. Known especially for her performances in the title role of Guiseppe Verdi's *Aïda,* she was the first African American to be hailed as a superstar in opera.

Although there had been black opera singers before her—most notably Marian Anderson—they were basically concert singers who were given the occasional chance to appear in opera. In their day, white audiences were still uneasy seeing black performers in "white" roles. By the time Price began to make her mark, much of this prejudice had been dropped, and people were more likely to notice the quality of the singing than the color of the singer. Audiences across the world raved over Price's glorious soprano voice, which one reviewer described as "unfurling like a bright banner from the stage and through the opera house."

A musical family

Mary Violet Leontyne Price was surrounded by music throughout her childhood. Both her parents were keen musicians, though neither made it a career. Her father, James Price, worked in a sawmill, and her mother, Kate (Baker) Price, worked as a midwife to help support Price and her brother, George.

Both parents sang in the choir and played in the band of St. Paul's Methodist Church in their hometown of Laurel, Mississippi. Their daughter became a member of the choir too, singing lustily and enjoying every minute of it. She also learned the piano, and from an early age she was taken to concerts, including one given by Marian Anderson. Though Price was only nine years old at the time, that concert was to have a lasting effect. "It was one of the most enthralling, marvelous experiences I've ever had," she later said, explaining how it made her want to become a singer like Anderson. "I can't tell you how inspired I was to do something even similar to what she was doing."

Leontyne Price

When Price graduated from Oak Park High School in 1944, she enrolled at the College of Education and Industrial Arts (now Central State College) in Wilberforce, Ohio. There she studied music education, with the idea that she would become a music teacher if she couldn't make it as a performer. But the faculty realized that she had an exceptional voice and encouraged her to get special training. As a result, Price applied to the prestigious Juilliard School of Music in New York City, hoping to study there after graduating from Wilberforce. She won a four-year scholarship and, with great excitement, set off for New York in 1949.

Price's four years at Juilliard were among the best years of her life. She not only studied singing, but she learned about stage presence, acting, makeup—all the things an opera singer needs to know. Coached by Florence Page Kimball, she learned how to use her voice to its fullest ability. Meanwhile, her money worries were taken care of by a family friend, Elizabeth Chisholm, which meant that she did not have to get part-time jobs to pay for her support.

The rising star

Immediately after graduating from the Juilliard in 1952, Price made her first appearance as a professional singer in the opera *Four Saints in Three Acts,* by Virgil Thomson. This led to her being offered the role of Bess in George Gershwin's *Porgy and Bess,* which brought her to a wide audience. For the next two years, Price toured the United States and Europe, playing to packed houses and receiving glowing reviews. Meanwhile, she married her co-star, William Warfield, but the marriage was not a success. The couple later separated and eventually divorced.

Back in New York in the fall of 1954, Price made her concert debut at Town Hall, and early the following year she appeared on NBC-TV, playing the title role in *Tosca*. As the first African American artist ever to appear in an opera on television, Price was a tremendous success, and over the next few years she starred in other televised operas. Even more important in terms of her future career, was the impression that her television performance as Tosca made on the conductor Kurt Herbert Adler. It was he who launched Price on her operatic stage career by inviting her to sing in *Dialogues of the Carmelites* at the San Francisco Opera in 1957.

That same year, Price first played the role of Aïda, though it happened by accident. The opera singer who had been chosen for the part was rushed to hospital with appendicitis, and a replacement was urgently needed. As Price recounted it, "Adler walked into the room and asked if I knew *Aïda*. I told him yes, and I was on." So began Price's association with the role that became her speciality.

The international star

Price made her European opera debut in 1958 under the baton of conductor Herbert von Karajan, a great admirer of her singing. The tour began in Vienna with performances of Mozart's *Die Zauberflöte* (The Magic Flute) and *Aïda* at the Vienna State Opera. Price went on to sing in all the major European opera houses, including La Scala in Milan, where an Italian reviewer paid the ultimate compliment

on her performance as Aïda, saying, "Our great Verdi would have found her the ideal Aïda."

Back in New York in January 1961, Price at last achieved her ambition to sing at the Metropolitan Opera. Not only that, but her performance in Verdi's *Il Trovatore* brought the audience to their feet in a standing ovation that lasted forty-two minutes. This was the first of many successes that Price was to have in her long association with the Met. Between 1961 and 1969 she appeared in 118 Metropolitan Opera productions, continually adding to her reputation as a superlative singer and impressive performer.

In 1970, Price began to cut down on her operatic appearances in order to give her voice and herself a rest. From then on, she concentrated more on concert recitals and recording sessions—her records have won her twenty Grammy Awards during her career. Her official retirement from opera came in 1985 with a spectacular and memorable performance of *Aïda* at Lincoln Center. People who were present that day will never forget the occasion. Although Price was fifty-seven years old, her voice was as clear and strong as when she first sang the same demanding role a quarter of a century earlier.

Since her retirement, Price has written *Aïda: A Picture Book for All Ages* (1990), which captures the thrill of the opera. Although she no longer appears on the opera stage, she continues to give recitals and to take part in special functions. Over the years she has performed at presidential inaugurations and state visits and has sung before the Pope, and in May 1991 she was among the select group of world-famous opera stars who sang at the celebrations marking the hundredth anniversary of Carnegie Hall in New York.

Charley Pride

Country and western singer
Born March 18, 1938, Sledge, Mississippi

"I'm not a black man singing white man's music. I'm an American singing American music. I worked out those problems years ago—and everybody else will have to work their way out of it too."

F amed for such hits as "Is Anybody Goin' to San Antone," "I Don't Think She's in Love Anymore," and "Kiss an Angel Good Morning," Charley Pride is one of country and western music's greatest superstars. He has won many of the highest awards in the business and was named top male country artist of the decade by *Cash Box* magazine in 1980.

When Pride first launched his career it was almost unheard of for an African American to sing country music, yet he quickly gained a huge audience. Within ten years of cutting his first record for RCA Victor, he sold more records for the company than any singer since Elvis Presley.

As a black artist with so many white fans, Pride has shown that music can break down barriers. He was the first black artist to perform at that shrine of country and western, the Grand Ole Opry in Nashville, Tennessee. To those who find his choice of music odd, Pride has a simple reply: "I'm not a black man singing white man's music. I'm an American singing American music."

Celebrated as the singing baseball player

Charley Frank Pride spent his early years on the cotton plantation where his father, Mack Pride, was a sharecropper. For as far back as he can remember, he loved country music and sang it lustily, even though his brothers and sisters sometimes teased him for it. In the small cotton town of Sledge, Mississippi, country music was considered white music. Members of the black community sang blues and gospel songs.

Pride had seven brothers and three sisters, and like them he started working in the cotton fields when he was five. As he picked the cotton he sang the songs he had heard on the radio during the Grand Ole Opry's weekly broadcasts. By listening carefully, he taught himself all the verses of the songs by his favorite stars, and when he bought a guitar he taught himself the same way—by listening to the weekly broadcasts and then imitating the picking styles he heard. Pride was fourteen when he bought his first guitar, and by the time he graduated from Sledge Junior High School he was a competent guitarist.

Nevertheless, Pride did not concentrate on music when he left school. He was an exceptionally good baseball player and had long dreamed of starring in the major leagues. This was a far greater ambition than becoming a musician, so at the age of seventeen he headed for Memphis, where he joined the Negro American League, an organization for black players.

During the next ten years Pride played for Detroit and then for the Birmingham Black Barons and the Memphis Red Sox. In 1956 he had to break off to do his two years' military service, but he returned to the Red Sox in 1958. The following year he left the Negro American League to play for a class C team in Great Falls, Montana. Here Pride also took a job in the tin-smelting plant, for he had married a few years earlier and needed the extra income to support his wife, Rozene, and their three children.

Still hoping to make the major leagues, Pride won a trial with the Los Angeles Angels in 1961. But after a few weeks he was told he did not have a major-league pitching arm. Despite this disappointment, he continued to play baseball in Montana. Meanwhile, he carried on with his job at the smelting plant—and also took his first steps as a performer.

A country music group practiced in an apartment near Pride's, and after Pride came to know them they invited him to play with them and occasionally to perform with them at local clubs. As Pride gained confidence, he took to singing between innings at the baseball games. When a newspaper wrote a story about the singing baseball player, he became a local celebrity. This led to further engagements, so that as well as playing baseball and working at the smelter, Pride sang most weekends at local nightclubs.

First black country & western star to sing at the Opry

In 1963 country star Red Sovine was in Great Falls and heard Pride sing at one of the clubs. He was so impressed that he gave the young singer the name of a contact in Nashville and urged him to go for an audition. But Pride was still hoping to make the big time in baseball, so he did not take up Sovine's offer until the following year, when an unsuccessful tryout with the New York Mets finally shattered his dream of becoming a baseball star. Stopping off at Nashville on his way home from New York, Pride sang for Jack D. Johnson, a music manager. Johnson was tremendously impressed. He could not believe that a black singer could sound so like a white one. "Sing in your natural voice," he told Pride—to which Pride replied that he had just done so.

That same week Johnson became Pride's manager, and in 1965 he got Pride a recording contract with RCA Victor. But both RCA and Johnson were worried about Pride's impact on a white Southern audience. Sure, Pride was a great singer, but how would the Country and Western crowd react to having their music

Charley Pride

sung by a black artist? Johnson decided not to find out. When Pride's first single, "Snakes Crawl at Night," was released in 1966, there were no photographs of the performer.

Pride released two more singles and gathered a large number of fans before he gave his first large concert. It was held in Detroit later in the year. When Pride's name was announced there was a roar of applause, but as he strode onto the stage the applause faltered. People stared in surprise. Not for long, though. By the end of the first song everyone was clapping and cheering. As Pride had been telling Johnson all along, his color was not going to be a drawback to his career.

This was proved time and again within the next few months as Pride gained thousands of fans, won Most Promising Male Artist awards from several music magazines, and was nominated for a Grammy Award. When in January 1967 he appeared at the Grand Ole Opry in Nashville, he was given a tumultuous welcome and hailed as the Opry's first black singing star. Meanwhile, his first album, *Country Charley Pride* (1966), had become a best seller. It eventually went gold, as did his next album, *The Best of Charley Pride* (1967). Since then at least seven more of Pride's albums have gone gold.

Having established himself as top country singer, Pride went from success to success. In 1970 he was named the Country Music Association's Entertainer of the Year and Male Vocalist of the Year. In 1971 he won his first two Grammy Awards. In 1972 he won another. In 1973 he had the hit single "Amazing Love." In 1974 his hit was "We Could"… and so it went on.

Pride has achieved a hit single or album virtually every year, including such recent hits as "Shouldn't It Be Easier Than This" (1988) and "Amy's Eyes" (1989). Although some black critics object to Pride singing "white" music, he regards that as their problem, not his. "Sooner or later black people are going to start coming out of the closet and admitting they like country music," he says.

Barbara Gardner Proctor

Entrepreneur, advertising executive
Born November 30, 1933, Black Mountain, North Carolina

"My grandmother always thought I would do something. She taught me what is important isn't on the outside, but inside. She said it was important to put something inside you, some courage, knowledge and a skill, things that no one can take from you."

After refusing to work on a commercial that she deemed was in poor taste, Barbara Gardner Proctor found herself without a job. She viewed the situation as an opportunity to establish her own advertising agency. She began Proctor & Gardner at the right time for a minority agency. Her company was able to tap into a virtually untouched market, totalling millions of dollars annually, and at the same time improve the public's perception of blacks by creatively casting them in a positive and constructive manner. Proctor's career has been marked by clear direction, strong leadership skills, and a willingness to reach beyond barriers.

The only child
of a single mother

Proctor was the only child of a single mother and was raised by her grandmother and an uncle. She was an excellent student and received a scholarship at Talladega College in Alabama. She attended college during the 1950s and received a B.A. in English and a B.A. in psychology and social science. In 1954 she received the Armstrong Creative Writing Award.

After graduating Proctor took her writing skills to *Downbeat* magazine in 1958, where she became jazz music critic and contributing editor. In 1961 she went to Vee-Jay Records International in Chicago to write descriptive comments for jazz record album covers and eventually became international director. She worked at several advertising agencies until the early 1970s, when she was fired for refusing to work on a project she felt was discriminatory toward blacks. Proctor said in a *Forbes* interview that the agency came up with the concept of a television commercial that parodied civil rights marches and sit-ins. It contained "a mass demonstration of housewives running down the street waving a can demanding that their hairdressers foam their hair." She thought the commercial was tasteless and offensive and refused to work on it.

Proctor decided it was time to go into business for herself. She felt the time was right for a minority agency, since commercial awareness of the black consumer market was rising. Believing that the advertising world wasn't ready for a black woman owner, she called her firm Proctor & Gardner. Most men assumed there was a "Mr. Gardner" running the company; no such person existed.

Proctor created her agency with the assistance of a loan from the Small Business Administration (SBA). She received her first client after being in business for six months, but she still needed operating capital at the end of her first year. She went back to SBA, which sent an accountant to review the books. He told her she would be out of business in three years. She proved him and her other detractors wrong.

Proctor relied on her energy and impeccable instincts to build her agency. She worked hard to create a relaxing atmosphere for clients and staff and thrived on countering problems through timely innovations and strategic planning. Proctor refused to accepted "ethnically dubious advertising pitches" aimed at women and minorities. She has frequently criticized advertising by drug, tobacco, and alcohol companies that target these markets. She says many of these companies have been responsible for the increased use of drugs, sleep-inducing medications, and nicotine. Her firm refuses to handle liquor and cigarette accounts in favor of supporting accounts that reflect family values.

In constant demand

As her agency's high standards became known, Proctor was in constant demand in the business arena. She had served on the boards of directors of the Illinois Telephone Company, Northwestern Hospital, the 1988 Illinois Olympic Committee, the council of the Chicago Better Business Bureau, the *Louisville Courier-Journal,* the Girl Scouts of Chicago, and the Economic Club. She is also a governing council member of the Illinois State Bar Association's Institute for Public Affairs.

Proctor's professional and community affiliations are amazingly diverse, ranging from president of the League of Black Women (1978–82) to delegate to the White House Conference on Small Business, and from honorary board member for Handicapped Organized Women to council member for the American Advertising Federation. Her success in the business world is reflected in numerous awards and honors she has received. Just a few of these are: Frederick Douglass Humanitarian Award (1975), Small Business Woman of the Year (1978), Black Media Award for Outstanding Professional (1980), and "Hero

Barbara Gardner Proctor

of the 80s" awarded by President Ronald Reagan (1987). She has also received more than twenty advertising industry awards for excellence, including Clio Awards, which are equivalent to Oscars in the advertising world.

As a business leader, Proctor encourages women to seek their own opportunities. She says many women have been afraid to fail and are too quick to blame others for their own lack of business success. Proctor was quoted in *Working Woman* as saying, "one of the things women fear is risk. They don't want to risk anything; they want guarantees. If you are able to risk, able to lose, then you will gain. When women get to the point where they take the risk, fail and try again, without any loss of self-esteem, they will be free."

Proctor says that women are not trained to use teamwork. If they realize the importance of this skill, she believes there is no limit to the amount of success they can achieve. She adds that while women have made significant gains in the workplace over the past twenty years, many have not reached the pinnacle of success because they have been taught that power is unfeminine. She urges women to abandon the attitudes of self-effacement and self-sacrifice.

The power of positive thinking

Proctor has been described as a lithe and fashionable woman who maintains a chic appearance and a business-like, though relaxed demeanor. She lives in a twenty-two room condominium that includes exercise facilities (however, she confesses that working—often as much as fifteen hours a day—is her truest form of relaxation).

Proctor has always believed in the power of positive thinking. She falls back on her earlier successes as her ace in the hole for handling setbacks and conflicts. She told the *New Orleans Times-Picayune* that "in every case where something would have been an obstacle, I've found a way to turn it to an advantage.... I cannot buy the concept that anyone outside is responsible."

Rather than being a hindrance to her success, Proctor believes being a black female helped her get her first loan. "I think blacks have a different acceptance of reality than white people," she told *Working Woman*. "We're more realistic. There is less fear. Being poor was good for me. Once you've been poor and black and you survive, there's nothing left to be afraid of. Most people are afraid of taking risks."

Richard Pryor

Comedian, actor, writer
Born December 1, 1940, Peoria, Illinois

"I'll never forget going up to Harlem and seeing all those black people. Jesus, just knowing there were that many of us made me feel better."

During the 1970s and 1980s, Richard Pryor was a top celebrity in the entertainment industry. He sold a half-dozen million-selling albums, produced two now-classic concert videos, and made several credible dramatic performances. But it is for his live routines with their uncensored social and psychological commentary that Pryor may be best remembered. Following in the footsteps of other groundbreaking black comedians like Bill Cosby and Dick Gregory, Pryor created a bold new type of comedy. He turned black American life into humorous performance art without softening either the message or its delivery.

Raised in grandmother's brothel

Pryor's parents were LeRoy and Gertrude Pryor. He claims he was raised in his grandmother's brothel, where his mother worked as a prostitute. He often ran into trouble with school authorities. One of his best experiences occurred when he was eleven, when his teacher, Juliette Whittaker, cast him in a drama and then let him entertain his classmates with his antics. When Pryor won an Emmy Award for writing a comedy special for Lily Tomlin years later, he presented the award to Whittaker.

Pryor was expelled from high school after striking a teacher and never returned. He found work in a packing house and joined the army in 1958. He spent two years in West Germany, but often clashed with his superior officers. He returned to Peoria and married the first of his five wives. He fathered his second child shortly afterward (his first child, daughter Renee, was born three years earlier).

Since he had always enjoyed entertaining, he sought work as a comedian. The owner of a popular black nightclub in the city gave him his first big break. He soon found himself performing on a circuit that included East St. Louis, Youngstown, and Pittsburgh. In 1963, Pryor decided to move to New York City and performed an act that was similar to Bill Cosby's.

In 1964 Pryor got his first television break by appearing on a show called *On Broadway Tonight*. Other television shows followed including *The Ed Sullivan Show* and *The Merv Griffin Show*. He moved to Los Angeles, where he received bit parts in movies such as *The Green Berets* and *Wild in the Streets*. He also played to live audiences, especially in Las Vegas.

As his success climbed, so did Pryor's cocaine use, up to one hundred dollars worth a day. While his new, more personal act was becoming popular, it also alienated Las Vegas management. Pryor argued with landlords and hotel clerks, was audited by the Internal Revenue Service, and was sued for battery by one of his wives. He faded from the limelight and did not work for several years. In 1972 he resurfaced with a new act and a supporting

Richard Pryor

role in the film *Lady Sings the Blues*, for which he earned an Academy Award nomination.

It was also at this time that Pryor became known for his writing talents. He wrote for *The Flip Wilson Show* and *Sanford and Son*, and helped comedian-director Mel Brooks write the classic western comedy, *Blazing Saddles*. In 1973 he earned an Emmy Award for the special *Lily,* starring comedienne Lily Tomlin.

Pryor wrote and starred in *Bingo Long and the Travelling All Stars* and *Motor Kings* in 1976. That year he also co-starred with Gene Wilder in the film *Silver Streak*. The movie grossed $30 million and Pryor received solid reviews.

Comedy albums sell well

Pryor also did well selling his comedy albums. He earned Grammy Awards for *That Nigger's Crazy* (1974) and *Bicentennial Nigger* (1976), and both albums went platinum. He went on to win a total of five Grammy Awards for best comedy album.

In 1978 Pryor had a serious heart attack and underwent another divorce after he riddled his wife's car with bullets on New Year's Eve. The next year he starred in *Richard Pryor Live in Concert,* in which he treated these two episodes in a lighthearted fashion. This show received rave reviews because Pryor imitated winos, junkies, whores, street fighters, and pool hustlers.

By 1980 Pryor was freebasing cocaine—using ether to help light the drug for smoking. On June 9, 1980, Pryor nearly burned himself to death, suffering severe injuries to half his body. At first he said the fire was an accident while he was freebasing. He later stated he poured rum on himself and set himself on fire. The rehabilitation process was long and anguishing. When he was finally released from the hospital he returned to freebasing.

In his final concert movie, *Live on Sunset Strip,* Pryor received excellent reviews for his description of the accident, his drug use, and his hospital stay. Shortly afterward he joined a rehabilitation program and worked with other addicts to overcome his problems. He also began work on *Jo Jo Dancer, Your Life is Calling,* a movie loosely based on his autobiography. The film was released in 1985 and Pryor wrote, directed, and starred in it. He played a comedian who relives his life immediately after a nearly fatal accident. Critics praised the movie—especially Pryor's decision to use black workers for every aspect of the production—but the film was not a hit.

Over the next few years Pryor made several movies that did well at the box office, but were poorly received by the critics. The *Los Angeles Times* considered his movies *The Toy, Brewster's Millions, Stir Crazy,* and *Bustin' Loose* "resignedly bland.... Anything malign or threatening has been bleached out." Others, like Eddie Murphy, held greater respect for Pryor. In 1989 Murphy asked Pryor to co-star in the movie *Harlem Nights.*

Diagnosed with multiple sclerosis

Part of Pryor's later failures can be attributed to being diagnosed with multiple sclerosis in 1986. His last movies showed him to be thin, frail, and weak. His health problems were further complicated by heart surgery—he had triple bypass surgery and is often confined to a wheelchair. His most frequent visitors are his four children, his ex-wife Lee, and Jan Gaye, widow of singer Marvin Gaye.

Although Pryor's current ill health has placed him off the stage, there is no doubting the impact he has had on the entertainment industry. Lily Tomlin summed up his career in *Premiere:* "Richard lost jobs, was blackballed and everything else, because people thought he was too hard to deal with or incorrigible or out of control. Now people's careers are built on drug use or rehab. And I can't imagine anything happening to Eddie Murphy like what's happened to Richard. Richard paid the price for using language on the stage ... and Eddie has been celebrated for it. And I don't think Eddie would ever be conflicted the way Richard was about playing [Las] Vegas, playing white clubs with white managers and taking white money. It was a different consciousness."

Public Enemy

Rap group
Formed as Spectrum in the early 1980s

"The black community is in crisis. Our mission as musicians is to address these problems.... We are not anti-Jewish. We are pro-black, pro-black culture, and pro-human race."—lead singer Chuckie D.

Before rap became part of mainstream music, it was being plugged by deejay Chuckie D at a college radio station on Long Island. Sometimes he would have to play a record twice to finish the show since there was so little material available. The music slowly caught fire with the audience, and Chuckie D and several other deejays were hosting the music at parties across Long Island, New York. Eventually they started putting their own raps together and were signed to a major record contract as Public Enemy.

The band has been at the cutting edge of rap music. Their raps exhort young blacks to be proud of their race and to fight against oppression. Always controversial and often in the media spotlight, the band's albums have consistently climbed to the top of the record charts.

Life at Adelphi University

The band started at Adelphi University on Long Island, where most of the members lived. Lead rapper Chuckie D (Carlton Ridenhour) attended the university as a graphics arts major. He was a big fan of rap music and became a disc jockey at the campus radio station. Adopting the name Chuckie D, he played only rap and hip hop music long before they were part of the mainstream music scene. Sometimes there was so little material available that Chuckie D would have to play songs twice in the same show. To increase the amount of material, he contributed his own raps over pre-recorded rhythm tracks.

One day a deejay friend, Hank Shocklee, asked him to emcee a few parties. The duo were an instant hit, and they formed a deejay collective known as Spectrum. They played at many parties around Long Island and publicized their events with posters designed by

Chuckie D. In 1983 Spectrum took over the campus radio station's Saturday night airwaves with the Super Spectrum Mixx Show, and they also hosted a local video show, WORD (World of Rock and Dance).

Bill Stephney, a sometimes-member of Spectrum, became a record company executive after graduating from Adelphi. He thought the group could be turned into a successful rap band and discussed the idea with Rick Rubin, an entrepreneur who had launched the careers of Run DMC and LL Cool J. Rubin listened to a Spectrum song, "Public Enemy Number One," and was convinced the group had enormous potential. Chuckie D and the others avoided Rubin because they felt many record companies victimized rap artists. Rubin's persistence and Stephney's reassurances eventually convinced them to sign a contract. In 1986 Flavor Flav (William Drayton), Terminator X (Norman Rogers), and Chuckie D signed a contract with Def Jam, Columbia Records' newly created rap division.

Public Enemy's first album, *Yo! Bum Rush the Show,* was aimed at disenchanted young blacks. It attacked the materialism of the mid-1980s. In an interview with *Rolling Stone,* Hank Shocklee said, "Everybody was into 'Let's get dumb, let's get crazy, let's get stupid.' That was the thing of 1985, '86. So we decided, 'Let's put something together that will give people something to think about as well as listen to.'"

In 1987 the band released *It Takes a Nation of Millions to Hold Us Back.* The album was designed to make people understand the corruption that exists in society. They released *Fear of a Black Planet* in 1990, which was about white people's problems, and the next year they released *Apocalypse '91: The Enemy Strikes Back,* which focussed on black problems. In 1992, Public Enemy's song and video, "By the Time I Get to Arizona," caused another public outcry. The song fueled anger over Arizona's failure to make Martin Luther King, Jr.'s birthday a state holiday. The video was criticized for depicting the burning of an Arizona state trooper's car.

Shocklee told *Spin:* "We wanted to put certain hooks in the sound so that when you heard it coming out of a car, you knew what record was on. It was Noise [with a] capital N.... We wanted to submerge you in sound, a thunderstorm of sound. And Chuck's voice would come out of it like the voice of God." Most critics found their sound interesting. Gary Graff, a *Detroit Free Press* writer, described Public Enemy's sound as "an aural assault of buzzes, sirens, knife-edged guitar riffs, turntable scratches and a bass-drum attack that pummels like uppercuts to the chin."

Ideas spring from black revolutionaries

Although Public Enemy's sound may be unique, many of the ideas expressed in the lyrics are not. They come from black revolutionaries like Nat Turner, Marcus Garvey, Malcolm X, Huey Newton, and Louis Farrakhan. Their lyrics bring to mind the 1960s Black Power movement. They consider their backup group, S1W (Security of the First World), as paralleling the Black Panther party. The S1W began as Public Enemy's security force. As a backup group, they wear military uniforms and carry plastic Uzi machine guns.

Public Enemy

They stand at attention throughout most of the performance, except when they take occasional breaks and perform martial-arts moves.

Many consider the band to be at the vanguard of the rap movement. Since the sound they create and the message they deliver are uniquely intense, they've referred to themselves as "prophets of rage." They constantly exhort young black men and women in their audience to be proud, to be aware of their culture, to fight oppression, and to take responsibility for themselves and their race.

Public Enemy's controversial style and music have brought them criticism. Many are threatened by their violent imagery and opposition to the existing power structure. Criticism in 1989 almost them to disband. Richard Griffin (Professor Griff), leader of S1W and Public Enemy's minister of information, made anti-Semitic comments in a *Washington Times* interview. He said many black problems could be traced to Jews who financed the slave trade and are "wicked ... (and responsible for) the majority of the wickedness that goes on around the globe." The article also included praise for deposed Ugandan dictator Idi Amin. These comments were widely reported in the media, and Public Enemy came under attack from many quarters. Even the Jewish Defense Organization sent a group armed with clubs and chains to Public Enemy's offices.

Public Enemy seemed unsure of how to handle the situation. Chuckie D originally stated that they were going to disband, then said the group would continue, but would refuse to sign a deal with a record company. The controversy finally seemed to die down after Chuckie D announced that Griffin was no longer with the group because his remarks were not in line with Public Enemy's beliefs.

Raps continue to climb the charts

Despite the controversy, Public Enemy's music continued to sell well. "Fight the Power," a song that served as the theme for Spike Lee's movie, *Do The Right Thing*, climbed the record charts. Griff eventually returned to the band, but Public Enemy stirred up more trouble with the lyrics in their song, "Welcome to the Terrordome." The rap brought new charges of anti-Semitism because of the lines: "Crucifixion ain't no fiction/so-called chosen frozen/Apology made to whomever pleases/Still they got me like Jesus."

Chuckie D maintains the group is not well liked because they are a bunch of black men who speak their opinion on many issues. Gene Santoro in the *Los Angeles Times* wrote that Chuckie D is probably right in this

belief. "There's no denying that blacks, especially young black males, are stuck at the bottom of the socioeconomic heap. That remains Public Enemy's main point, and it's been validated over recent months by the barely submerged racism in print and television discussions about hip-hop in the wake of the [Public Enemy] controversy."

Although Public Enemy doesn't show the world in a pretty light, many reviewers have praised their portrayal of tough issues. Graff wrote that "Public Enemy has walked as dangerous an edge as any rap group has traversed.... As [the group] confronts racism, oppression, cultural genocide and self-destruction in the black community—touching on drugs, gangs, education and interracial relationships—Chuckie D charges through each topic without apology or diplomacy.... (Public Enemy has) brought the Big Picture to modern rap."

Lloyd Albert Quarterman

Chemist, researcher
Born May 31, 1918, Philadelphia, Pennsylvania
Died 1982, Chicago, Illinois

"We are in an age of discovery.... We live in the world of the unknown. That's the only place to live."

In hidden laboratories across the United States during World War II, scientists engaged in a race against enemy forces to build the first atomic bomb. Lloyd Albert Quarterman was in the forefront of this race. A chemist by training, Quarterman helped split the first atom and create the first atomic reactor. He later developed peaceful uses for nuclear energy and experimented with new chemical compounds. A great believer in the opportunities science offered, Quarterman often lectured students on rewarding and interesting careers in science.

Hired for the Manhattan Project

Lloyd Quarterman discovered science at a early age. He used to spend hours experimenting with a chemistry set, and his love for science took him to St. Augustine's College in Raleigh, North Carolina. He earned a bachelor's degree in 1943 and was immediately hired by the U.S. War Department to work on the highly secretive Manhattan Project, which was aimed at developing an atomic bomb. He was one of only six African Americans to work on the project.

Quarterman became an assistant to an associate research scientist and chemist. He was hired to work with a huge network of scientists spread across the country at different laboratories, each team pursuing a separate portion of the work necessary to develop an atomic bomb. Quarterman was sworn to secrecy at that time, and he was unable to speak on even the smallest tasks. It is for this reason that little was written about him prior to his death.

Although his specific duties were kept quiet, it is known that Quarterman worked with two of the laboratories in the overall network, at Columbia University in New York City and at the hidden University of Chicago

Lloyd Albert Quarterman

facility in Chicago, Illinois. The Columbia team was assigned the task of splitting an atom, which would provide the energy necessary to fuel the atom bomb. To complete this task, the scientists had to create a uranium isotope. Quarterman played a key role in developing this isotope.

The Chicago team was responsible for developing and building the first nuclear reactor or pile. This structure allows for the massive conversion of plutonium into nuclear energy. The scientists worked under Enrico Fermi, an Italian physicist who was responsible for many of the major developments in the field of nuclear physics. The empty locker rooms and racquet courts beneath the unused university football stadium, Stagg Field, were converted into a system of laboratories.

In December 1944, the Manhattan Project created two atomic bombs, which were dropped on the Japanese cities of Hiroshima and Nagasaki in August 1945. A short time

603

later the Japanese unconditionally surrendered. On August 6, 1945, Quarterman received a certificate of recognition from the U.S. War Department for his work "essential to the production of the Atomic Bomb, thereby contributing to the successful conclusion of World War II."

Joins Argonne National Laboratories

The Manhattan Project officially closed in 1946. The government converted what remained of the Chicago research team into the Argonne National Laboratories and brought it above ground to a Chicago suburb. Most of the work was now geared toward the peaceful uses of nuclear energy. *Ebony* profiled ten black scientists working at Argonne, including Quarterman, and stated, "most of the experiments at Argonne are involved in such projects as disease prevention, prolonging human life and producing new sources of power."

Quarterman stayed at Argonne for about thirty years. He worked on some of the most important scientific projects of the time. Working with Fermi's scientific team, Quarterman contributed to the first nuclear power plant. Although nuclear energy has always been a controversial subject, the scientists believed that they were creating a revolutionary peacetime application from their military research. Quarterman studied quantum mechanics under some of the best scientists in the world. He supplemented and refined his skills as a chemist and physicist, earning a master's degree in science from Northwestern University in 1952.

Most of Quarterman's work dealt with creating new chemical compounds and, as a result, created new molecules from fluoride solutions. Ivan Van Sertima, who interviewed Quarterman in 1979 for *Blacks in Science: Ancient and Modern,* stated, "When Quarterman was going to school there were no 'compounds' of zeon or argon or krypton. These were ... thought to stand sovereign and alone, reacting with nothing. But Quarterman and his team made them react with fluoride atoms. They made zeon tetrafluoride—zeon difluoride—zeon hexafluoride .... Quarterman took zeon difluoride and incorporated it in other experiments, making a whole series of new compounds." Van Sertima stated that "for a period of time they were the greatest fluoride chemists on earth."

Besides chemistry, Quarterman was also interested in spectrometry, which focuses on the interaction between matter and radiation. In order to "look at" a highly corrosive solution, hydrogen fluoride, Quarterman developed a unique, corrosion-resistant "window" made of diamonds, later known as the diamond window. After years of experimentation, Quarterman made his first discovery trial of the diamond window in 1967. Four years later he was awarded an honorary doctorate of science in chemistry from St. Augustine's College.

Quarterman was also interested in producing synthetic blood. This substance had the potential to save thousands of lives. Although he initiated a research project, his funding was cut before he could complete the work. The reasons behind this cut are not clear, but it is said to have greatly disappointed Quarterman. He would only tell Van Sertima that he "ran into socio-political problems."

Despite working with complicated problems, Quarterman was adept at simplifying the complex into something that was easy and exciting to understand. He used to tell black students in Chicago public schools that science could be both rewarding and interesting. Quarterman was also committed to the African American community in other ways through his membership in the National Association for the Advancement of Colored People (NAACP).

Toward the end of his life, Quarterman suffered from a paralyzing illness. In the late summer of 1982, he died from this disease at Billings Hospital in Chicago. He donated his body to science.

Queen Latifah

Rap singer
Born around 1970, New Jersey

"Being Afrocentric and proud of my heritage, that's something I grew up with. My mother always taught me that. When I started rapping, I wanted to make it part of my image."

Since 1988, when Queen Latifah released her first single, she has become one of the most popular performers of rap music. Clothed in eye-catching African outfits, she stands out from most other rappers, not only because she is a woman in a male-dominated genre, but also because of her proud self-confidence.

In her lyrics as in her life, Latifah promotes pride in the African American culture and pride in being a woman, with a strong emphasis on self-respect. Yet she rejects any suggestion that she is a feminist. "I'm just a proud black woman," she says. She is also extremely musical. It is this mixture of intelligent lyrics and musical ability that makes her so successful, enabling her to bring rap music to a wide audience that includes all cultures and all ages. "It's a great feeling to know that people listen to you," she says, "that what you say makes a difference to them."

A mother's influence

Latifah inherited her musical talents from her parents, especially from her father, who used to hold jam sessions at home. She gained many of her values from her mother, Rita Owens, including pride in her African American heritage. Latifah's parents separated when she and her brother were quite young, so her mother was the main influence during her childhood.

Latifah's birth name was Dana Owens. "Latifah" is a nickname given her by a Muslim cousin when she was eight. In Arabic it means "delicate and sensitive." When Latifah landed her first recording contract, she added the word "Queen"—not to make herself sound important, but to remind African Americans that they were descended from African kings and queens. It was a foretaste of the type of message prominent in her lyrics.

Latifah's mother had a tough time after she and her husband separated. She was so strapped for money that she moved her family to a housing project in East Newark, New Jersey. To support the children, she took a part-time weekend job as well as working full-time during the week— and in the evenings she studied for a degree in education. Although this was an exhausting regimen, she believed it was worth it. At the end of two years, she had saved enough to be able to leave the housing project and to send Latifah to a Roman Catholic parochial school called St. Anne's. She was also well on her way to becoming a qualified teacher.

By 1980, Latifah's mother was teaching at Irvington High School and Latifah was a student there. Like her mother, she was a hard worker, but she also found time to have fun. She and her girlfriends often did rap music in the school washrooms, and she became expert at the human beat box (making rhythm noises by blowing into her cupped palm). At a school talent show, Latifah and two other girls, Tangy B and Landy D, tried out as a rap group called Ladies Fresh, performing songs written by her brother Lance. They were such a success that

Queen Latifah

they gave performances whenever possible, even at school basketball games.

For one of the school dances, Latifah's mother engaged rapper Mark James, known as D. J. Mark the 45 King. From then on, Latifah and her friends were often to be found rapping with James in his parents' basement. James made some demos of their music, and soon after Latifah graduated from high school, he took a demo of her music to Fred Brathwaite, the host of "Yo! MTV Raps." Braithwaite liked it and played it for the people at Tommy Boy Records. They liked it too—so much so that they signed a contract with Latifah. Instead of studying for a career in broadcasting as she had intended, she began her career as a rap singer.

All Hail the Queen

Latifah's first single, "Wrath of Madness," was released in 1988, when she was little more than eighteen. It sold 40,000 copies, an encouraging amount for a beginner. She followed up with "Ladies First," an anti-apartheid video, and then went on a European tour. The following year she brought out her first album, *All Hail the Queen,* which was an instant hit. Eventually, it reached the number 6 spot on *Billboard's* rhythm and blues charts. The album was popular partly because it broke with rap tradition by concentrating on the woman's point of view—it called for chivalry from men and encouraged women to take a stand. Another novel feature was that it mixed rap with straight singing. And, of course, many of the songs emphasized African American pride.

With the release of this album, Latifah was recognized as an intelligent and talented musician who had something important to say. She also became known as a generous person who avoided the infighting so common in rap music. Rather than trying to cut out her rivals, she has often gone out of her way to include them (as when she invited other female rappers to feature in her "Ladies First" video). "There's room for everybody," she said. "I don't feel threatened when other girls put out good records—I feel motivated to make a good record as well." She went on to do so with *Nature of a Sista* (1991) which, like her first album, combined intelligent lyrics and musical ability. After it was launched, she gained further publicity by doing a concert tour of the United States with reggae star Ziggy Marley.

As well as making records and touring as a performer, Queen Latifah has appeared on such television programs as "Fresh Prince of Bel Air," "In Living Color," and "The Arsenio Hall Show." She has also appeared in the movies *Jungle Fever* (1991), *Juice* (1992), and *House Party 2* (1992). Regarded as a role model by many young women, she was named "Best Female Rapper" in the 1990 *Rolling Stone* readers' poll.

Although Latifah clearly loves being in the spotlight, she is a little uneasy about acting as a role model. "Some people put you on a pedestal and don't let you be human," she says. "You're forced to feeling you should be perfect. That's not a comfortable thing." Despite this, she has become a spokesperson for women, especially for young black women. But she tries not to preach. Her aim is to "speak common sense" both in her rap music and in her public statements.

Dudley Randall

Poet, publisher
Born January 14, 1914, Washington, D.C.

"A poet can change the way people look and feel about things. And that's what I want to do in Detroit."

In 1981 the mayor of Detroit appointed Dudley Randall first poet laureate of the city of Detroit in honor of his invaluable contribution to poetry. Both as a poet and as a publisher, Randall has given immense impetus to black poetry, not only in Detroit but throughout the United States.

Writing in the magazine supplement of the *Detroit Free Press,* journalist Suzanne Dolezal summed up Randall's achievements: "As publisher of Detroit's Broadside Press between 1965 and 1977, Randall provided a forum for just about every major black poet to come along during those years. And dozens of anthologies include his own rapid, emotional lyrics about Detroit's bag ladies, lonely old drunks, strapping foundry workers and young women with glistening, corn-rowed hair."

Won $1 First Prize in poetry contest

From his earliest childhood, Dudley Felker Randall was encouraged to read widely and to express his ideas on paper. Both his parents were intellectuals. His mother, Ada (Bradley) Randall, was a teacher; his father, Arthur Randall, a Congregational minister.

Dudley Randall

Randall was only four when he wrote his first poem—a lyric for the tune "Maryland, My Maryland," which was played at a band concert in the suburb of Baltimore where his family was staying at the time. The family moved to Detroit when Randall was nine. As he grew older, his father took him to lectures by such distinguished African American visitors as author W. E. B. Du Bois. By the time Randall was a teenager he not only had a deep appreciation of poetry but had developed his own style, which instinctively reflected that of the black writers he most admired.

At the age of thirteen Randall won first prize for a sonnet he submitted to the *Detroit Free Press*. The prize was only a dollar—poems did not bring in much money. When Randall graduated from high school in 1932, he therefore looked around for a practical way of earning a living and took a job as a foundry worker with Ford Motor Company in River Rouge, Michigan. Meanwhile, he continued

to express his feelings in beautifully crafted verse.

With the security of a steady income, Randall embarked on the first of his three marriages in 1935. During the war he joined the U.S. Army Signal Corps and served in the Pacific. After his release from the army in 1946, he was at last able to raise the money for a college education, and in 1949 he graduated with a bachelor's degree from Wayne State University. During the next two years, while studying for his master's degree, Randall worked as a clerk and letter carrier for the U. S. Post Office. Then, in 1951, he graduated with a master's degree in library science from the University of Michigan.

Admired publisher of Broadside Press

For the next three years Randall was a librarian at Lincoln University in Jefferson City, Missouri. In 1954 he moved to the library at Morgan State College in Baltimore, Maryland, where he worked for two years before accepting a position with the Wayne County Federated Library System in Michigan. Randall remained with the Wayne County library from 1956 until 1969, rising from assistant branch librarian to head of the reference-interloan department.

It was during these years that Randall founded his publishing company, Broadside Press. The press was so named because it developed from two broadsides Randall printed in 1963. He had composed a poem called "The Ballad of Birmingham," about four children who had been killed in a bombed church, and he was worried he might lose the copyright, since the poem had been set to music by folksinger Jerry Moore and was becoming popular. On checking out the copyright laws Randall discovered he could retain the rights to the poem if he printed it as a broadside—a one-page leaflet—so this is what he did. Later the same year he printed his second broadside, the poem "Dressed All in Pink," about President John F. Kennedy's assassination. The broadsides sold for a few cents each.

Broadside Press formally came into existence in 1965, when a group of black poets attending a conference at Fisk University asked Randall to compile a book of poems about black nationalist Malcolm X. The book took some time to organize for it contained the work of a number of African American poets, some of whom had not yet written their contributions. When published in 1967 under the title *For Malcolm: Poems on the Life and Death of Malcolm X,* it contained poems by such well-known writers as Gwendolyn Brooks and Robert Hayden, as well as up-and-coming young writers like Sonia Sanchez and Amiri Baraka.

During the next ten years, Broadside Press published almost sixty voumes of poetry by African American writers. Many were young writers who received tremendous encouragement by having their verses published by Randall. Others, like Pulitzer Prize-winning Gwendolyn Brooks, chose to have their works published by Broadside rather than by major publishing houses such as Harper & Row, because they admired what Randall was doing for black literature and wanted to support his efforts.

Broadside Press needed all the support it could get, because Randall's aim was to promote African American literature, not to make money. "I am not well qualified to operate in a capitalistic society," he once said. "I came of age during the Great Depression, and my attitude toward business is one of dislike and suspicion. Writers who send me manuscripts and speak of 'making a buck' turn me off."

Although Randall was meticulous in paying royalties to his writers, the sums were never very big; he made a point of keeping the price of Broadside books extremely low so that they would be available to the largest number of readers. Because of this policy Broadside Press sank deeply into debt, and in 1977 it was bought by Alexander Crummell Memorial Center, a church in Highland Park, Michigan.

The church retained Randall as consultant, and though he was no longer editor and publisher of Broadside, he had never relied on the press for his income. From 1969 to 1975 he was reference librarian and poet-in-residence at the University of Detroit, and he has since been a visiting lecturer at several universities as well as a speaker at seminars and festivals. Since 1970 Randall has been a member of the Advisory Panel on Literature for the Michigan Council for the Arts, and he has also been a member of delegations visiting the Soviet Union, Ghana, and other countries.

Believed in high writing standards

Not least of Randall's contributions to black literature is his own poetry, which has appeared in numerous anthologies as well as in books published by Broadside Press. The first of of his Broadside volumes was *Poem Counterpoem* (1966), a collection of twenty poems, ten of which were by Randall and ten by poet Margaret Danner.

Randall has published several collections that are entirely his own poetry, including *Cities Burning* (1968), *Love You* (1970), and *After the Killing* (1973). He is also the author of *Broadside Memories: Poets I Have Known* (1975). In his prose as in his poetry, Randall is a meticulous writer, setting great store on the craft of wordplay. "Precision and accuracy are necessary for both white and black writers," he says. "'A black aesthetic' should not be an excuse for sloppy writing."

Randall also believes that black writers should make sure that they reject only the false part of white culture. They should not reject elements that are universal to all cultures. "What we tend to overlook," he says, "is that our common humanity makes it possible to write a love poem, for instance, without a word of race, or to write a nationalistic poem that will be valid for all humanity."

His clear thinking has made Dudley Randall an invaluable influence on a whole generation of black poets. Many a young poet has derived continuing inspiration from Randall's perceptive criticism and rock-hard encouragement.

A. Philip Randolph

Labor and civil rights leader
Born April 15, 1889, Crescent City, Florida
Died 1979

"The idea of separation is harkening to the past and it is undesirable even if it could be realized, because the progress of mankind has been based upon contact and association, upon social, intellectual and cultural contact."

Before young and dynamic leaders like Malcolm X and Dr. Martin Luther King appeared in the civil rights movement, A. Philip Randolph was quietly rocking the foundations of racial segregation. Using a nonviolent, consensus-building approach, Randolph pressured large corporations and American presidents to recognize and remedy the injustices faced by the country's blacks. His methods drew praise from some and criticism from others for being too conservative. Despite any criticism, there is no doubting his commitment to the movement and his determined effort in helping to end segregation.

Son of former slaves

Randolph was the son of former slaves, James and Elizabeth Randolph. His father, a tailor and itinerant minister, wanted him to enter the clergy, but Randolph wanted to become a congressman or lawyer. While other children were reading *Alice in Wonderland,* Randolph was reading works by the German political philosopher, Karl Marx. After graduating from high school, he went to New York City, attracted by the ideas of W.E.B. Du Bois, an educator and social theorist who wrote about the need for talented blacks to succeed.

Randolph attended City College of New York and worked at odd jobs before meeting Chandler Owen, a young Columbia University law student. Owen shared a lot of

Randolph's ideological interests, and the two started a small employment bureau for unskilled blacks arriving in the city from the South. They also started *The Hotel Messenger,* a publication that represented the interests of a new union for black headwaiters. Owen and Randolph used the paper to discuss a wide range of issues, including black suffrage, that were deemed too radical by the union and their relationship ended. The duo renamed the paper, *The Messenger;* it became one of the best magazines in the history of black journalism. They continued to write about causes they believed in. They argued that the U.S. should not get involved in World War I and advised blacks across the country to arm themselves against white mob violence. The U.S. Attorney reportedly called Randolph "the most dangerous Negro in America."

Despite their best efforts, Owen and Randolph couldn't get the black labor forces in the city organized. In 1925, after the two had parted company, Randolph was asked to unionize the sleeping car porters of the Pullman Railroad Company. This company was the largest employer of blacks in the country, and it had successfully stopped any attempts of its porters to organize since 1909. The company always fired the porters who tried to rally their co-workers to seek higher pay and better working conditions. The porters believed Randolph was a brilliant leader who would not succumb to pressure.

Organizes first black union

Randolph had to cope with the general impression that porters had a good life—traveling around the country and meeting the rich—although they were mainly waiters and shoe-shiners. During his ten years of negotiations with the Pullman Company, Randolph refused to let words like *nigger* and *darkie* rattle him. He maintained his composure and used his quiet dignity to overcome his adversaries. At one time they offered him a $10,000 bribe, but he rejected it. Eventually the Pullman Company gave in. It sanctioned the Brotherhood of Sleeping Car Porters, the first black union in the country, and gave its members $2 million in wage increases. Randolph's long association with the porters eventually garnered him the nickname "Saint Philip of the Pullman Porters."

Randolph continued to rise through the ranks of organized labor. He founded the Negro American Labor Council and became the first black vice-president of the American Federation of Labor and Congress of Industrial Organizations (AFL-CIO), the largest federation of unions in the country. His interest in organized labor was fueled by his belief that if blacks continued taking menial and low-paying jobs, they would remain second-class citizens.

Many black militants were angered at Randolph's slow, consensus-building style; they believed he should be less conciliatory. He disagreed with several other black leaders, especially Marcus Garvey, who said blacks should give up their hardship in the United States and return to Africa.

With the Pullman victory behind him, Randolph began looking at other areas where he could lend his special skills. In 1940 he fought against the discrimination practiced in private defense plants and the segregation of the U.S. armed forces. Randolph asked President Franklin Delano Roosevelt to end this discrimination, but Roosevelt refused. To pressure the government, Randolph decided to organize ten thousand blacks to stage a protest march on Washington, D.C., a city still caught in segregation. Most newspapers and civic leaders doubted Randolph could organize that many people, but the idea seemed to catch fire. Randolph raised the pressure on Roosevelt by saying fifty thousand blacks would march, and then a hundred thousand. As the march was being planned, Randolph came under criticism for excluding whites from the march. Some said he was supporting the divisiveness he was trying to eliminate. In an interview with *The New York Review of Books,* Randolph said, "You take ten thousand dollars from a white man; you have his ten thousand dollars, but he's got your movement. You take ten cents from a Negro; you've got his ten cents, and you also have the Negro."

Executive Order 8802

Since the criticism of Randolph was minor compared to the excitement building toward the march, Roosevelt sent his best negotiators—including his wife, Eleanor—to convince Randolph to stop the march. The negotiators warned that so many blacks in a hostile city could lead to violence. Randolph refused to back down. On July 25, 1941, less than a week before the scheduled march, Roosevelt issued his historic Executive Order 8802, which banned discrimination in the defense industry and led to the establishment of the Fair Employment Practice Committee.

Although Randolph was praised for his

A. Philip Randolph

tough stance against the president, many called him a sell-out when he agreed to cancel the march in exchange for the order. Many blacks, including some from within Randolph's committee, said the president did not provide adequate means of enforcing the order. They also claimed that there were many other injustices that the march would have helped expose and perhaps remedy. Discrimination continued in spite of the Fair Employment Practice Committee, since it became entangled in bureaucratic inefficiency and politics, and faced opposition in the South.

On March 31, 1948, Randolph told a congressional committee that he would advise black and white youths to boycott any draft until the U.S. armed forces were integrated. One senator suggested that such advice could be considered treason, but Randolph said he was prepared to go to jail for his beliefs. In June he formed the League for Non-Violent Civil Disobedience Against Military Segregation. Randolph said it was hypocritical for the government to condone segregation in its own forces—including the armed forces—even though Roosevelt's order had forced private industry to integrate. President Harry Truman was reluctant to give in to Randolph's demands, but since he was in the middle of a heated reelection campaign, he wanted to use civil rights to appease northern urban voters.

It wasn't until fifteen years later that Randolph actually organized a march. Like his predecessors, President John F. Kennedy worried that bringing thousands of blacks to Washington could lead to violence. Using his slow, consensus-building style, Randolph was able to convince Kennedy that his concerns were unfounded and eventually received his endorsement. The march on Washington took place on August 28, 1963, with revered civil rights leader Dr. Martin Luther King Jr. delivering his historic "I Have a Dream" speech. The march helped to unify and electrify the civil rights movement. Randolph wrote in *The New York Times*: "The full march was a challenge to the conscience of the country; it was a creative dialogue between Negroes and their white allies, on the one hand, and the President, the Congress and our American democratic society, on the other. Its aim was to achieve a national consensus not only for civil rights legislation, but for its implementation."

Fades from limelight

Randolph's influence on the civil rights movement faded for the remainder of the 1960s. Younger and more dynamic leaders began to appear on the horizon. Despite Randolph's diminishing status, Martin Luther King, who was recruited into the movement by a Randolph protégé, referred to him as "the Chief." Even Malcolm X, a member of the Black Muslims who advocated violence against racism, gave Randolph a back-handed compliment by saying he was the least confused among black leaders. Randolph was quoted by *Ebony* in 1969 as saying, "I love the young black militants. I don't agree with all their methodology, and yet I can understand why they are in this mood of revolt, of resort to violence, for I was a young black militant myself, the angry young man of my day."

Randolph died in 1979. Bayard Rustin, a close friend, wrote in *The Yale Review* in 1987 that Randolph was "a self-made gentleman and a prudent tactician with the grit and toughness of a boxer. Mr. Randolph was a man of quiet courage, of resoluteness without flashiness, of perseverance without pretension."

William Raspberry

Journalist
Born October 12, 1935, Okolona,
  Mississippi

"Like all human beings, my interest is attracted to certain things out of a range of possibilities. I'm not quite sure why the interest develops. It has to do with who I am and how I grew up. Having children tends to get you interested in schools. Just living in society gets you interested in aspects of society—some more than others—especially if people aren't writing about things you find interesting, you find yourself looking at those areas more closely."

Although he may have been reluctant to become the *Washington Post*'s "Potomac Watch" columnist, William Raspberry has gone on to become of the country's most notable writers. His column delves into areas that most columnists have avoided, such as drug abuse, criminal justice, and minority issues. He has appeared as a television panelist, written for several magazines, and was nominated for the prestigious Pulitzer Prize. He has received numerous awards for his writing including the Capital Press Club's Journalist of the Year award in 1965 for his coverage of the Los Angeles Watts riot.

Learns journalism at *Indianapolis Recorder*

Raspberry was born on October 12, 1935, in Okolona, Mississippi, to two teachers, James Lee and Willie Mae. While attending Indiana Central College in Indianapolis, Raspberry worked for the black weekly newspaper, the *Indianapolis Recorder*. From 1956 to 1960 he worked as a reporter, photographer, proofreader, and editorial writer, and eventually became associate managing editor. He studied math, history, English, and was a preseminarian before receiving his B.S. degree in 1958. Two years later he was drafted into the U.S. Army. During his two-year stay he became an army public information officer in Washington, D.C.

After his discharge, Raspberry wanted to work at the *Washington Post*. Although he had never seen a teletype machine before, he was hired as the teletype operator. He hoped that one of the editors would notice him and hire him as a reporter. He became friendly with the assistant managing editor, who would give him a few assignments during dead time on the teletype machine. After a couple of months, he was promoted to writing obituaries. Eventually Raspberry was hired as a general assignment reporter, and since he wanted to stand out from the other reporters, he began covering civil rights.

In 1965 Raspberry was named assistant city editor before taking over a year later as columnist of "Potomac Watch," which deals with local issues. When he was first approached with the column he turned it down. He thought he would quickly run out of ideas, but the other editors said they would help him. In time he shaped the column to fit his own interests. Since the thrice-weekly column is syndicated nationally twice a week, Raspberry focuses on local topics in one column and broader themes in the syndicated columns. He gained notoriety for delving into areas that other columnists avoided.

In an interview with *Contemporary Authors*, Raspberry explained his interest in these areas. "Like all human beings, my interest is attracted to certain things out of a huge range of possibilities. I'm not quite sure why the interest develops. It has to do with who I am and how I grew up. Having children tends to get you interested in schools. Just living in the society gets you interested in aspects of society—some more than others—and especially if people aren't writing about things you find interesting, you find yourself looking at those areas more closely."

Raspberry has developed a reputation as the unofficial ombudsman for local underdogs, occasionally serving as a troubleshooter for

William Raspberry

individuals grappling with government bureaucracy. People phone him with their problems hoping that he can write something that will help. Raspberry will often make a phone call to the appropriate official, get the issue resolved, and not even write a story on it.

Commonsense writing

Raspberry says that while he is an African American columnist, he does not take into account what a black columnist or black man would say about an issue. He writes what makes sense to him. He has also come into conflict with black activists who criticized him for airing views in opposition to his own. "One of the interesting things that has happened—and I'm not sure why it happened— is that most often if I write something that goes against the orthodoxies, the people who hold the orthodox view will try to educate me," he told *Contemporary Authors*. "They'll argue with me, they'll talk to me, they'll try to

persuade me, they'll point out the aspects of things that I might have overlooked, and it's almost always done on a friendly basis of mutual respect. I like that a lot."

Of course Raspberry has received his share of scathing letters. The editors usually show them to him and ask for any comments. If somebody misread the column and got the wrong message, or if Raspberry considers it an unfair attack, they want him to say that.

In addition to writing his weekly columns, Raspberry has taught journalism at Howard University and has served as commentator and discussion panelist for television stations in Washington, D.C. Raspberry has been a member of the Pulitzer Prize board for many years and was nominated for a Pulitzer Prize in 1982.

In recent years Raspberry has stopped appearing on television. He prefers his column because it allows him to think things through rather than delivering hard opinions as a television commentator. He feels his readers want to know how he reached his conclusion, and if they disagree with it, then they know why.

Although he has written for several magazines, time constraints have limited his activities in this area. He still prefers writing his column because he is able to address an issue while it is still on the public mind. Magazine pieces usually have a six-week lead time and by the time it has appeared, it is no longer a current news item. "Writing today for tomorrow or writing today for the day after tomorrow gives you a chance to play off the news, which is to say, to engage people on subjects while they're interested in those subjects. You can write about the death penalty, for instance, while there's a capital case in the news. That gives it much more immediacy than writing it in a sort of philosophical vacuum," he told *Contemporary Authors*.

Raspberry has thought about writing books, but he has stated he is not sure enough about a single topic to devote to a book. With his column, he is able to modify it as events and his opinions change. In a book, he must have solid conclusions before starting.

Another rumor that has followed him is that his columns will one day be made into a book. Raspberry has mentioned in the past that he might do that, but to date it remains an uncompleted project. "One of the reasons is that whenever I look back at something I wrote two years ago, whatever I wrote seems to be kind of naive," he told *Contemporary Authors*. "Stuff that I wrote two weeks ago always looks good; but stuff that I wrote two years ago, that's not so profound."

Ishmael Reed

Writer
Born February 22, 1938, Chattanooga,
 Tennessee

"I try to do what has never been done before."

One of America's most renowned black writers, Ishmael Reed has been called "the brightest contributor to American satire since Mark Twain." Reed directs his satire at racism, sexism, feminism, elitism, and any other "ism" that arouses his fury. Reed's work is both highly original and boldly revolutionary in that it aims to present an alternative to Western culture. The bizarre plots of his experimental novels draw on sources that range from Egyptian mythology to West Indian voodoo.

Reed has written more than twenty books, which include volumes of poetry, plays, and essays as well as his novels. He has been nominated for a Pulitzer Prize and was a finalist for the National Book Award. A fierce champion of African American creativity, he founded the Before Columbus Foundation, which promotes and encourages multicultural American writing.

His radio show was canceled after hosting Malcolm X

Ishmael Scott Reed says that the name Ishmael was chosen for him by his mother, Thelma Coleman, "the clairvoyant of the family." She was not married to Reed's father, Henry Lenoir, but in the 1930s she married Bennie Reed, an auto worker, who became Reed's stepfather. Reed has four brothers in his father's family and two brothers and a sister in his stepfather's family.

When Reed was four, he and his mother moved to Buffalo, New York, where Reed received his education. He was not an outstanding student at Buffalo's East High School—"I served time," he said—but at the age of fourteen he started writing a jazz column for a black Buffalo newspaper, the *Empire Star Weekly*.

On graduating from high school in 1956, Reed worked as a clerk at the public library while attending night school at State University of New York at Buffalo. The first short story he wrote there so impressed his teachers that they arranged for him to become a regular daytime student. However, in 1960 Reed dropped out of the university. This was partly because he was short of money and partly because he disliked the upper-class atmosphere of the university.

Moving into a a lower-class black housing project, Reed supported himself by working as a staff corresondent for the *Empire Star Weekly*. He also became co-host on WVFO radio for a program called "Buffalo Community Roundtable"—though not for long. The show was canceled after Reed interviewed Malcolm X, the famous black nationalist leader. It was during this period that Reed married his first wife, Priscilla Rose. After their divorce in 1970 he married Carla Blank, a modern dancer.

Earned two National Book Award nominations

In 1962 Reed moved to New York City, where he worked as a journalist, joined a poetry collective, wrote a considerable amount of poetry, and began work on his first novel. Published in 1967, *The Free-Lance Pallbearerers* was a biting satire of both black and white liberals, while at the same parodying the works of such esteemed black novelists as Richard Wright and Ralph Ellison. The book received mixed reviews, as did Reed's second novel, *Yellow Back Radio Broke-Down* (1969), a spoof involving cowboys and Indians. But already some people recognized Reed's genius. Author John A. Williams predicted, "It is very likely that Ishmael Reed will become the foremost satirist of American life and times in this century."

Ishmael Reed

Reed's third novel, *Mumbo Jumbo* (1972), seemed to bear out this prediction. A clever satire about words and writing, the novel includes footnotes, a bibliography, and other ingredients of scholarly works. The story concerns an ancient Afro-Egyptian culture that suddenly blossoms in North America. It appears as an epidemic called "Jes Grew," which makes people incapable of functioning in American society. A major character in the story is Papa LaBas, a voodoo detective, whose adversary is a white critic who wants to assimilate blacks into white society and destroy Jes Grew. *Mumbo Jumbo* was nominated for the National Book Award in fiction in 1973, the same year that Reed's second book of poetry, *Conjure* (1972), was nominated for both the Pulitzer Prize and the National Book Award in poetry.

By this time Reed was recognized not only as a major writer but as an important influence in West Coast cultural groups. Since

1968 he had been living in California, where he taught at the University of California at Berkeley. He was also involved in various publishing and video ventures, including the Yardbird Publishing Company, which he co-founded in 1971. In 1976 he was a major force in the founding of the Before Columbus Foundation, a Berkeley-based organization formed to promote and distribute the work of little-known ethnic writers.

Lambasted Anita Hill in his latest novel

Reed further increased his reputation with *The Last Days of Louisiana Red* (1974), which won a Rosenthal Foundation Award and was picked as a Book-of-the-Month Club alternate selection. The book again features Papa LaBas, the detective from *Mumbo Jumbo*. This time his mission is to stamp out Louisiana Red, which is literally a hot sauce but is also an experience of extreme stress which causes people who are poor or black to destroy themselves. Strongly symbolic, the story draws on Greek mythology as well as Afro-American traditions, and it includes biting attacks on two of Reed's favorite targets: feminists and the affluent middle class.

Reed's next novel, *Flight to Canada* (1976), was less controversial; but he launched a withering parody of Ronald Reagan's presidency with *The Terrible Twos* (1982) and then stirred up a storm with his attacks on black feminists in *Reckless Eyeballing* (1986). This novel was followed by *The Terrible Threes* (1989) and *Japanese Spring* (1993). The latter, which is set in an American university, draws on many of Reed's own experiences,

including his efforts to gain tenure at the University of California at Berkeley. In the book liberal professors come under attack, as do most of the women on campus. Strongly antifeminist like so much of Reed's fiction, the novel includes a diatribe against law professor Anita Hill.

Some critics have called Reed a misogynist. Others consider his books too bizarre or too angry. He is just as irascible in his nonfiction works such as his two collections of essays, *Shrovetide in Old New Orleans* (1978) and *God Made Alaska for the Indians* (1982).

Whether critics praise or condemn Ishmael Reed, all agree that he is an extremely powerful writer and a major figure in contemporary American literature. Moreover, his influence is felt in an increasing number of areas because of his aggressive championing of Afro-American writing and his vigorous promotion of Afro-American culture. As the *Washington Post* commented, "Ishmael Reed's mind must be one of the great creations of this era."

Eslanda Goode Robeson

Chemist, anthropologist, activist
Born December 15, 1896, Washington, D.C.
Died December 13, 1965, New York, N.Y.

"Before any committee starts yelling for first class loyalty and cooperation from me, they'd better get busy and put me and my Negro people in the first class department by making us first class citizens."

Perhaps best known as the fiery and determined wife of the famous actor and singer Paul Robeson, Eslanda Robeson was an outstanding woman in her own right. As well as having a career as both a chemist and an anthropologist, she was a talented writer, expressing her opinions in numerous articles and in two fascinating books: *Paul Robeson, Negro* (1930) and *African Journey* (1945).

The Robesons' life together was not smooth and easy. Like her husband, Eslanda Robeson had the courage to speak out against the oppression of black people. With her husband, she was persecuted for holding left-wing political views. As a result, the rich and famous Robesons suddenly became poor outcasts from society. This did not stop either of them from continuing to criticize injustice or to condemn inequality both at home and abroad. Eslanda Robeson was a true political activist, dedicated to improving the quality of life for black people throughout the world.

The young career woman

Eslanda Cardoza Goode Robeson once said that she was of very mixed ancestry, "some Spanish, English, Scottish, Jewish, American Indian, with a large majority of Negro blood." She grew up in a prosperous, intellectual environment. Her father, John Goode, was a clerk in the War Department. Her mother, Eslanda Cardoza Goode, who was descended from South Carolina's free black community, studied osteopathy and beauty culture, and then established her own business in New York.

Eslanda's mother moved to New York when her husband died, because she did not

Eslanda Goode Robeson

want Eslanda and her two brothers to attend segregated schools. They arrived in Harlem in the early 1900s and were still living there at the beginning of the exciting artistic development known as the Harlem Renaissance.

In the early 1920s, after studying at the State University of Illinois, Eslanda enrolled at the Teachers College of Columbia University in New York, majoring in chemistry. During this period, she met Paul Robeson, who was a student at Columbia Law School, and the two were married in 1921. Meanwhile, Eslanda continued to train as a chemist, studying partly at Columbia Presbyterian Medical Center, which offered her a permanent position when she gained her bachelor's degree in 1923. She was placed in charge of the laboratory in the surgery and pathology department and was the first black analytical chemist ever employed by the medical center.

As Paul Robeson turned from a career in law to one as a singer and actor, Eslanda continued with her laboratory work and was engaged in several research projects. She did not at first accompany Paul when he went on tour, but this was an unsatisfactory arrangement, and in 1925 she resigned her position so that she could accompany him to London, where he was to star in *The Emperor Jones.*

Writer and anthropologist

The Robesons enjoyed the atmosphere in England. It was far less racist than North America, and there were not the daily acts of discrimination. Moreover, Paul was treated as a celebrity—he was even honored with a luncheon at the House of Commons. In 1928, the year after their son Pauli was born, the Robesons decided to settle in London, and it remained their home for the next ten years.

During these year, Eslanda was extremely busy, not only writing her biography of Paul but also acting as his manager, booking his shows, and arranging his tours. Their marriage went through a rocky period because of Paul's romances with white women, but the couple came together again and in 1934 paid a long visit to the Soviet Union. During the previous few years, both the Robesons had become strongly left wing in their search for reforms that would bring equality to black people. Their visit to Russia made them even more leftist, for they saw more racial tolerance there than in capitalist countries.

Eslanda's deep interest in racial matters led her to take up the study of anthropology, and she spent the years 1935–37 as a student at London University and then, in 1938, attended the London School of Economics. As part of her studies she visited Africa, taking eight-year-old Pauli with her so that he could experience a black world and see a black continent.

The visit to Africa had a great influence on Eslanda, and she determined to do whatever she could to help Africans gain independence from the European countries that ruled them. Back home in the United States in 1939, she strove to educate the public about Africa, and in 1941 she helped found the Council on African Affairs.

Paralleling these efforts was her campaign to help the black population of the United States. She pointed out that racial inequality throughout the world was one and the same problem—the result of black people being denied the economic and educational opportunities that white people enjoyed. Calling for better education for African Americans and true equality, she was a civil rights activist long before the civil rights movement swung into action.

In 1945, Eslanda gained her Ph.D. in anthropology, published her book *African Journey,* and was a delegate to the San Francisco conference that led to the formation of the United Nations. The following year, when she made a return visit to Africa, her future looked most promising. But in fact her career was almost over. Both she and her husband had been far too openly left wing, and they were about to suffer for it.

Last years

In 1949, both Paul and Eslanda Robeson were called before Senator Joseph McCarthy's Committee on Un-American Activities and were accused of being involved in communist subversion. When Eslanda was interrogated, she boldly threw the questions back at the committee, asking about civil rights for black Americans.

Although nothing was proved against either of the Robesons, their passports were taken away and it was made impossible for them to get work. Nine years passed before the pleas of their many supporters were met, and the ban was lifted. During these difficult years, Eslanda continued to speak out on behalf of African Americans and the people of Africa.

In 1958, when their passports were at last restored, they went to England and the Soviet Union before returning home in 1963. But the strain had taken its toll, and Eslanda was not at all well. She died two years later.

Paul Robeson

Actor, activist
Born April 9, 1898, Princeton, New Jersey
Died January 23, 1976, Philadelphia,
   Pennsylvania

"My father was a slave, and my people died to build this country, and I am going to stay right here and have a part of it just like you. And no fascist-minded people will drive me from it."

During his lifetime Paul Robeson thrilled thousands with his athletic prowess on the football field, entertained thousands with his artistic presence on the stage and screen, and inspired thousands with his voice raised in speech and song. During the 1930s and 1940s, he may have been the most respected black in the United States.

He was also a firm believer in the communist system. Even when the crimes of Soviet leader Joseph Stalin became public, Robeson refused to change his beliefs. Robeson's reputation suffered and he lived his last two decades as a broken man. The *New Leader* described him as "an artist of unassailable gifts and achievement who was brought low through his own political obtuseness."

Receives Rutgers scholarship

Robeson was born on April 9, 1898, in Princeton, New Jersey, to William and Maria Robeson. His father was a clergyman and his mother a schoolteacher, so the family was more affluent than most black families. His father, a runaway slave who put himself through Lincoln University, instilled in Robeson the importance of dignity and courage in the face of racism. Robeson was an excellent student and athlete and was rewarded for his efforts by receiving a scholarship to Rutgers College. He was elected to Phi Beta Kappa in his junior year and chosen valedictorian in his senior year. Robeson continued his athletic endeavors and won a total of twelve letters in track, football, baseball, and basketball. He was also named Rutgers' first All-American in football. Football legend Walter Camp called Robeson "the greatest defensive end that ever trod the gridiron." After graduating in 1919, he earned a law degree from Columbia University, supporting himself by playing professional football on the weekends. While at law school he met and married Eslanda Cardoza Goode. She encour-

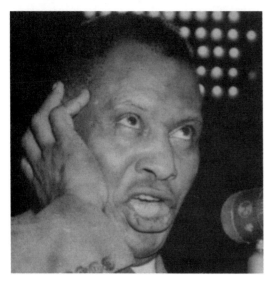

Paul Robeson

aged him to act in a few amateur theatrical productions.

After graduating from Columbia, he worked with a New York law firm, but quit soon after a secretary refused to take down a memorandum, saying "I never take dictation from a nigger." Since the upper positions were denied him in law, his wife encouraged him to try acting again. He joined the Provincetown Players, a group associated with playwright Eugene O'Neill. Robeson made his professional debut in 1922 with the play *Taboo.* He received critical acclaim after starring in *The Emperor Jones* and *All God's Chillun Got Wings. Newsweek* called him "thoroughly eloquent, impressive, and convincing." *Nation* asked, "What if Paul Robeson had wanted to use his proven mental abilities to become a great lawyer instead of employing his magnificent voice and physical presence to become a brilliant performer? A comparable career would have been unlikely."

These reviews convinced him to continue with the theater, and he won an international reputation for his performances on the London stage. He also appeared in several films, some of which were adaptations of plays in which he starred. During *Emperor Jones,* Robeson was called upon to whistle, and critics felt he had a natural inclination towards music. In 1925 he made his concert debut with a highly successful program of all-Negro music. Robeson's reputation grew even larger after appearing in the musical *Show Boat,* in which he sang the immensely popular song "Ol' Man River." His performance in Shakespeare's *Othello* was applauded by many critics. While performing *Othello* in 1943 in New York, his ovation was called "one of the most prolonged and wildest ... in the history of the New York theater." But he also had his critics. Joseph Sobran wrote in the *National Review* that, "as Othello, [Robeson] completely failed to convey the Moor's smashed self-esteem at Desdemona's supposed infidelity. Where [British actor Laurence] Olivier displayed shocking, writhing rage beyond all shame or dignity, Robeson could only work up disapproval."

Switches to music

Over time Robeson realized that his acting abilities and being a black performer would limit the number of roles he could receive. He turned to singing full time as an alternative outlet for his creativity and growing social convictions. In 1925, while performing in Britain, he decided to begin singing spirituals and work songs to audiences of common people. In his autobiography, *Here I Stand,* he stated that he turned to this music because he "learned that the essential character of a nation is determined not by the upper classes, but by the common people, and that the common people of all nations are truly brothers in the great family of mankind."

It's easy to understand this transformation in Robeson's life. John Patrick Diggins, a *New York Times Book Review* writer, said it was the result of Robeson having to take the freight elevator, being denied entry to hotels and restaurants, once having a white woman companion spat upon, and reading about the hundreds of black youths killed in racial violence.

Robeson and his wife and son settled in London in 1928. They continued to travel throughout Europe in the 1930s and came in contact with members of left-wing organizations, including socialists and African nationalists. He sang to and moved among the disadvantaged, the underprivileged, and the working class. He sought racial justice for nonwhites and economic justice for the working class.

The pivotal point in his life occurred when he and his wife visited the Soviet Union in 1934. He spent nights at the theater and opera, took long walks with film director Sergei Eisenstein, attended gala banquets and private screenings, and took trips to hospitals, children's centers, and factories. Robeson felt the country was free of racial prejudice and saw connections between Afro-American spiritual music and Russian folk music traditions. John Patrick Diggins wrote in the *New York Times Book Review* that Robeson's "attraction to communism seemed at first more anthropological than ideological, more of a desire to

discover old, lost cultures than to impose new political systems.... Robeson convinced himself that American blacks as descendants of slaves had a common culture with Russian workers as descendants of serfs."

Returns to the United States

Robeson returned to the United States in the late 1930s with a firm belief in communism. He began picketing the White House, refused to sing before segregated audiences, started a crusade against lynching, and urged Congress to outlaw racial bars in baseball.

After World War II, cold war hysteria began to break out in the United States and the Soviet Union. Many former advocates of communism started backing away. When the crimes of Soviet leader Joseph Stalin became public—forced famine, genocide, political purges—more advocates left the ranks. Robeson held firm in his beliefs. He still believed in communism, even if it was being abused by its leaders. He thought the cause of communism went beyond the Soviet Union, and he would do his upmost to support its original ideals. Robeson's continued communist rhetoric only served to alienate people. He urged black youths not to fight if the United States went to war against the Soviet Union. Soon after these comments, a violent riot broke out in Peekskill, New York, where he was to appear in concert.

During the infamous McCarthy hearings of the 1950s, Robeson was asked why he didn't stay in the Soviet Union. He replied, "Because my father was a slave, and my people died to build this country, and I am going to stay right here and have a part of it just like you. And no fascist-minded people will drive me from it. Is that clear?"

The State Department revoked his passport in 1950, after Robeson refused to sign an affidavit as to whether or not he had ever belonged to the Communist Party. This action insured that he would stay in the United States. He was blacklisted by concert managers, which meant he could get no concert bookings, and his income, which had been $104,000 in 1947, fell to $2,000 a short time later. He was also removed from the list of sports All-Americans. His career was over.

Robeson's passport was restored in 1958 after a Supreme Court ruling on a similar case, but it was of little consequence. When he published his autobiography that year, the leading literary journals refused to review it. He traveled to the Soviet Union, but his health was beginning to fail. He tried twice to commit suicide. "Pariah status was utterly alien to the gregarious Robeson. He became depressed at the loss of contact with audiences and friends, and suffered a series of breakdowns that left him withdrawn and dependent on psychotropic drugs," Dennis Drabble wrote in *Smithsonian*.

During the 1960s Robeson began to deteriorate slowly and was virtually unheard from. He settled in London, making several trips to the continent before returning to the United States in 1963. His wife died in 1965. He suffered a stroke and died on January 23, 1976, in Philadelphia, Pennsylvania. The *Nation* stated his life was "the story of a man who did so much to break down the barriers of a racist society, only to be brought down by the controversies sparked by his own radical politics.

Jackie Robinson

Baseball player
Born January 31, 1919, in rural Cairo, Georgia
Died October 24, 1974, Connecticut

"The Hall of Fame is tremendously important to me, but if it meant I had to give up anything I did or said, the Hall of Fame would have to go its own way. I did what I thought was right and, to me, right is more important than honor."

F or years only white athletes could play baseball in the major leagues, while black ball players, considered to be inferior athletes by the white establishment, were relegated to the Negro League, where they played in obscurity. Jackie Robinson changed the status quo.

The first black to play in the big leagues, he encountered racism from fans, other teams, and even his own teammates, but Robinson rose above it and was named the National League's Rookie of the Year. Other black ball players soon followed him into the majors.

Displayed great prowess in sports

Robinson was born on January 31, 1919, in rural Cairo, Georgia. Abandoned by his father when he was one year old, his mother moved the family to Pasadena, California, in search of a better life. Yet racism was a daily experience. Robinson recounted: "Pasadena treated us as intruders. My brother and I were in many a fight that started with a racial slur on the very street we lived on.... In certain respects Pasadenans were less understanding than Southerners and even more openly hostile."

Robinson became an athlete. At Muir Technical High School he excelled in basketball, football, and track. He was so successful that other students used to bring him sandwiches and dimes so they could play on his team. After graduating he attended Pasadena Junior College and UCLA, where he played four sports. He was a phenomenal athlete—in one football season he led the nation in overall yardage gained; in basketball he led the Pacific Coast League in scoring for two years; and he was an outstanding tennis player.

After college Robinson played a season of professional football with the Los Angeles Bulldogs, then joined the U.S. Army. He served for thirty-one months, spending time at Fort Riley, Kansas, and Camp Hood, Texas, where he became a lieutenant in the cavalry. At that time he met a pitcher for the Kansas City Monarchs in the Negro League of baseball, and he suggested Robinson try out for the team. He was not very interested at first, but the $400 a month salary was enough incentive to give it a try. He also hoped to use the exposure to get a job in the East or Midwest as a social worker to help underprivileged boys.

Recruited by the Dodgers

Robinson's skill soon caught the attention of the Brooklyn Dodger organization. While in Chicago, Dodger scout Clyde Sukeforth told Robinson that Branch Rickey, the Dodger's general manager, wanted to see him. For several years Rickey wanted to bring the first black

Jackie Robinson

man into major league baseball, but he knew such a player would have to be tough and talented. Rickey told Robinson that if he broke baseball's colored barrier, he would face bigoted fans, insulting hotel clerks, and anything else he could think of that people would say to him. When Robinson asked him if he was looking for a player that was afraid to fight back, Riley declared he was looking for someone who had the strength to not fight back.

The two reached an agreement, and Robinson signed with the Dodger farm club in Montreal for a $3,500 signing bonus and $600 per month. Robinson joined Montreal of the International League in 1946. Fans greeted him with a strange mix of enthusiasm, curiosity, and bigotry. Attendance tripled on the road because of Robinson, but they once had to cancel an exhibition road trip through the southern United States, because laws in the South made it illegal for blacks and whites to play on the same field. Robinson led the league a .349 batting average and in fielding with a sparkling .985 average. Montreal won the league pennant, and after one game, the fans carried Robinson on their shoulders.

Helped Dodgers to World Series win in 1955

Robinson attended Dodger spring training the next year. He made the team, although some predicted he would not last the season because he was black. A New York reporter said: "Robinson may be going good now, but colored boys have no endurance. He won't last the season out." Star catcher Dixie Walker said he would rather be traded than play on the same team as Robinson. The St. Louis Cardinals and Philadelphia Phillies threatened to boycott games with the Dodgers. To end the controversy, National League president Ford Frick said that if the players went on strike, they would be kicked out of the league. He added that if even half the league went on strike, he would kick them all out. After his comments, most of the controversy faded.

Rickey decided to help Robinson deal with the bigotry in baseball by organizing committees of leading black citizens in every National League City to advise him and Robinson. They told him to keep quiet and not show anger at racial slurs, which, as Ricky told Robinson in their first meeting, took a lot more courage than fighting back.

Despite the bigotry, Robinson did have his share of support among major leaguers. Teammate Pee Wee Reese was a close friend and helped him through his first season. Whenever opposing players would start yelling things at Robinson, Reese would go over to Robinson, put his arm around him, and talk to him in a friendly matter, smiling and laughing. That usually quieted the opposition.

The national media considered Robinson's entrance into baseball to be a social "experiment." Not only did he receive attention from baseball fans, but also from educators and civic leaders. Despite the pressure, Robinson's first year was a success. He was forced to move from his regular shortstop position to first base, but he gradually learned the position. He led the team with a .297 batting average and was named the National League's Rookie of the Year. He also helped the Dodgers win the National League pennant.

Things began to get easier for Robinson in his second year. Other black players entered the league, including several with the Dodgers. Robinson went on to become one of the best hitters and base stealers in the game. In 1949 he led the National League in batting with a .342 average and was named the league's Most Valuable Player. He helped the Dodgers win the pennant in 1947, 1949, 1952, 1953, 1955, and 1956. In the first four World Series they lost to their cross-town rivals, the New York Yankees. In 1955 they defeated the Yankees to bring the first-ever championship to Brooklyn.

Elected to Hall of Fame in his first year of eligibility

By the mid-1950s, with his skills beginning to decline, Robinson retired in 1956 at the age of thirty-eight, and he was elected on his first year of eligibility to the Baseball Hall of Fame in January 1962. Few players are elected to the hall on their first attempt, and it is the ultimate honor in baseball. He was named vice-president for personnel at the Chock Full O' Nuts restaurant chain, but he later resigned as he became more active in civil rights issues, and he worked for Harlem's Freedom National Bank (a black-owned bank), a Brooklyn-based construction company, and a life insurance company. He was also a special assistant for community affairs for New York Governor Nelson Rockefeller, and he wrote a column for the *New York Post* on sports, politics, and civil rights.

During his later years Robinson suffered the loss of his eldest son, Jackie, Jr., who was arrested for possession of drugs in 1968 and was killed in an automobile accident three years later. Robinson experienced various physical problems, including a heart ailment, arthritis, and diabetes, which caused blindness in one eye. On October 24, 1974, at the age of fifty-three, he suffered a heart attack at his home in Connecticut and died. The world mourned his loss, and thousands of people, including athletes, civil rights leaders, and politicians, attended his funeral.

Charlemae Hill Rollins

Librarian, author
Born June 20, 1897, Yazoo City, Mississippi
Died February 3, 1979, Chicago, Illinois

"Storytelling is a wonderful way of breaking down barriers, or getting acquainted with new people, and drawing groups and individuals together."

For thirty-one years Charlemae Hill Rollins was head of the children's department at the George C. Hall Branch Library in Chicago. When she took up the position in 1932 she was known chiefly as a warm and friendly librarian who told wonderful stories. When she retired in 1963 she was still known as the children's friend and storyteller, but she was also famed as an author, lecturer, consultant, specialist in children's literature, and especially as an authority on African American literature.

It was Rollins's lifelong concern to see that children's storybooks and textbooks gave an accurate picture of African American life—not the stereotyped picture so often given in books written early in this century. After she published a lists of books she considered suitable, she was consulted by publishers and school boards and asked to write articles and give lectures. She was an instructor in chil-

Charlemae Hill Rollins

dren's literature at Roosevelt University, Chicago (1949–60), and in the 1950s she also gave lectures at Fisk University and Morgan State College.

Surrounded by books during her happy childhood

The oldest child of Allen and Birdie Hill, Charlemae Hill Rollins was raised on her parents' farm in Oklahoma, which was then Indian Territory. She inherited her interest in books from her grandmother, who had been a slave. "I've always loved books because of her," Rollins recalled. "She gave us all the books that belonged to her master who was the father of her children, one of whom was my father." Rollins also gained her love of storytelling from her grandmother.

Rollins had a happy childhood, growing up among an extended family group that included uncles, aunts, and cousins as well as her immediate family. Until she was thirteen she studied at an elementary school for black children that had been started by her family in Beggs, the local town. For her secondary education she attended schools in St. Louis, Missouri, and Holly Springs, Mississippi. She then taught at the school in Beggs before studying for a year at Howard University in Washington, D.C. On her return to Oklahoma in 1918 she married Joseph Rollins, thus beginning what was to be a long and happy partnership. Two years later their son Joseph, Jr., was born.

The young couple settled in Chicago, where in 1927 Rollins applied for a job as a children's librarian. "The best thing I ever did," she later said. She started as a junior assistant in the Harding Square Branch Library, and from the first she loved the work. During the next few years she took courses in library science at Columbia University and the University of Chicago, and in 1932 she was appointed head of the children's department at the George C. Hall Branch Library, which had just been opened in the heart of Chicago's black community.

Believed storytelling could break down barriers

Rollins took up new duties with enthusiasm. The job combined two of her favorite pursuits—handling books and inspiring children to read. She soon became well liked for her easy manner with the children, and especially for her storytelling sessions. Rollins regarded these sessions as particularly valuable. "Storytelling is a wonderful way of breaking down barriers," she said, "or getting acquainted with new people, and drawing groups and individuals together. Hearing a wonderful story well told can bring escape from hunger, from drab surroundings, from hate and rejection, and escape from injustices of all kinds."

Rollins gave talks in the local schools to attract more children to the library, and she also arranged for class visits to the library. She set up a Reading Guidance Clinic for parents and started a number of clubs, including the Negro History Club. This was part of her campaign to inform black children about their heritage by providing them with books that gave an accurate picture of African American culture. The library had very few books of this type when Rollins took over as head of the children's department, but she gradually built up a large collection.

To help other librarians and school boards, Rollins compiled a bibliography of recommended books, which was published in 1941 as *We Build Together: A Reader's Guide to Negro Life and Literature for Elementary and High School Use.* The book was so popular that Rollins updated it with revised editions in 1948 and 1967.

National specialist on children's literature

After *We Build Together* was published, Charlemae Hill Rollins was the person educators sought out when they wanted to be sure their textbooks were not biased. As a result, her life became extremely busy. As well as running her children's library, she reviewed manuscripts from publishers and authors; she taught at Roosevelt University and other colleges and gave countless lectures and workshops on children's literature and storytelling; and she was chairperson of several local library associations, serving for four years on the council of the American Library Association and as president of the Children's Services Division from 1957 to 1958.

Rollins was often asked to contribute articles about children's literature, and in 1962 she edited a collection called *Call of Adventure.* When she retired in 1963 she felt the urge to do more writing. "I got hooked on books and children while working at the library," she said. "I attended lots of lectures on writing by many famous authors. I just had to try to do a book of my own." Later that year she published a collection for young people, *Christmas Gif': An Anthology of Christmas Poems, Songs, and Stories, Written by and about Negroes.*

In the next few years Rollins produced four more books for young people: *They Showed the Way: Forty American Negro Leaders* (1964), *Famous American Negro Poets* (1965), *Great Negro Poets for Children* (1965), and *Famous Negro Entertainers of Stage, Screen, and TV* (1967). Rollins's final book was *Black Troubadour: Langston Hughes* (1970), which won the Coretta Scott King Award the following year.

Rollins had known Langston Hughes personally, for the writer had often visited Rollins's library to give lectures. Another black writer connected with Rollins was the Pulitzer Prize-winning poet Gwendolyn Brooks, who had been a regular library visitor during her childhood. When Rollins died at the age of eighty-one, Brooks paid tribute to her with a poem that included these lines:

> Nothing is enough
> For one who gave us clarity—
> Who gave us sentience—
> Who gave us definitions—
> Who gave us her vision.

Diana Ross

Singer, actress
Born March 26, 1944, Detroit, Michigan

"I think I know what's right for me. There isn't anything anyone can tell me about my career that I haven't already considered.... If I haven't done something it's because it was not the way I wanted to do it or because I made another choice."

D iana Ross's career has been called a shining example of the American dream. She started out with talent and ambition but not much else, and within a few years she was a household name as lead singer of the Supremes, one of the most popular groups in musical history. She went on to star as a soloist, a nightclub and television entertainer, and a movie actress. She also has become a successful entrepreneur, setting up her own multimillion-dollar corporation, Diana Ross Enterprises.

One of the most glamorous stars in show business, Ross has won a sheaf of honors and awards, including a Grammy, a Tony, and an Academy Award nomination. In 1988, she was inducted into the Rock and Roll Hall of Fame.

The Detroit teenager

A crowded apartment in a low-income housing project in Detroit, Michigan, was the home Diana Ross knew as a child. Eight people lived in these cramped quarters, for there were six children in the family. Ross shared a bed with her two sisters, and if they wanted to play, they went outdoors because there was no space in the apartment. Yet Ross's memories of those times are of "fun, fun, fun." There was rollerskating in the streets, baseball with her brothers and sisters, and street-corner dancing with the neighbors. Although Ross's parents, Fred Ross, a factory worker, and Ernestine (Earle) Ross, had to scrimp and save, the children did not really feel poor.

The Rosses were a musical family. Both parents and all the children sang in the choir at Olivet Baptist Church, and Diana Ross also sang in the performances at her elementary school. After attending Dwyer Junior High School, where again she excelled in singing, she was accepted at Cass Technical High School, one of the best schools in Detroit.

While studying dress design and cosmetology at Cass—and making her own clothes—Ross teamed up with some girl-friends to form a singing group called the Primettes. There were four in the group originally, but the number was later reduced to three: Diana Ross, Mary Wilson, and Florence Ballard.

The Primettes made about fifteen dollars a week singing at local parties and dances, but they were aiming for higher things. While Ross was still at high school, she approached Berry Gordy, Jr., a Detroit businessman who had founded the Motown Record Corporation a few years earlier. In her effort to get him to hire the Primettes, she took a secretarial job in his office, though it lasted only a couple of weeks. Her persistence paid off. In 1960, when the three teenagers were in their final year in high school, Gordy hired them to do background singing for Motown recording stars. This turned out to be just a first step, for he soon realized he had found some good talent. Renaming the group the Supremes, he had them groomed for a starring role.

The Supremes

Gordy put Ross and her two colleagues in the hands of Motown's artist development department, a type of charm school that trained promising youngsters to become sleek and confident professionals. The Supremes then recorded their first few singles, which attracted very little notice. Blaming their failure on the

Diana Ross

songs rather than the singers, Gordy assigned the group a new writing team—Eddie Holland, Lamont Dozier, and Brian Holland—and in 1964 these writers came up with the catchy "Where Did Our Love Go?" With Ross singing the lead and Wilson and Ballard purring "baby, baby" in the background, the song was an instant hit, soaring to first place on the pop record charts and selling more than 2 million copies. The Supremes had arrived.

The group's light, velvety harmonizing ensured the success of five more singles they released that year: "Baby Love," "Come See About Me," "Stop in the Name of Love," "Back in My Arms Again," and "I Hear a Symphony." The Supremes were the first group ever to have six gold records in one year, and two years later did even better, going gold with seven records. They continued to produce hits throughout the 1960s, adapting their style to fit the changing fashions. Their albums ranged from their Beatles selec-

tion, *A Bit of Liverpool* (1965), to *The Supremes Sing Rodgers and Hart* (1967).

In 1969, the group was renamed Diana Ross and the Supremes, to recognize Ross's role as the lead singer. This was the first step in her move toward a solo career, and in 1970 she left the group. She was replaced as lead singer by Jean Terrell.

Solo performer and actress

Ross began her solo career with a number of nightclub appearances and concert tours. Wherever she went, she was hailed as a superstar, attracting huge audiences. In 1971, she had her first television special, and in 1972 she starred as jazz singer Billie Holiday in the movie *Lady Sings the Blues*. Although Ross had appeared in movies with the Supremes, she had never before had a major part, and there was some doubt about whether she would be able to handle such a challenging role. She captured Holiday's singing style superbly, and her portrayal of the tragic singer brought her an Academy Award nomination as best actress.

Despite Ross's performance, the film itself was not considered very good. She went on to appear in *Mahogany* (1975) and *The Wiz* (1978), both of which were box-office successes. She also became known for her spectacular stage and television shows—dramatic extravaganzas of sight and sound, with special effects of lighting and costumes. Meanwhile, she turned out more hits, including "Last Time I Saw Him" and "Believe in Yourself."

In recent years, Ross has cut down on her long concert tours in order to spend more time with her family. In the 1970s, she was married for six years to Robert Silberstein, by whom she had three daughters, and from her 1985 marriage to the shipping magnet Arne Naess, she has a son. Ross has become such a superstar that at least six biographies have been written about her, and more are bound to follow. Meanwhile, her many fans eagerly await the next development in her career.

Carl T. Rowan

Journalist
Born August 11, 1925, Ravenscroft,
  Tennessee

"When you are plucked out of a totally Jim Crow environment at age seventeen and thrown into a totally white environment where more is at stake than your personal life, you mature rapidly."

When history was being made in the United States during this century, Carl Rowan was usually there to cover it. During his journalism career Rowan has documented some of the biggest political and social stories of the last fifty years. He wrote about the cold war, the U.S. civil rights movement, the Vietnam War, and the economic policies of the Ronald Reagan administration. In addition to his journalism career, Rowan has written six books and held top-level government positions.

Education breaks poverty cycle

Rowan's parents, Thomas and Johnnie Rowan, were extremely poor, and Rowan had to per-

form various menial jobs for people in the local white community in McMinnville, Tennessee. Many of his teachers stressed the values of education and persistence. One white teacher, "Miss Bessie," was especially important in his development since she used to smuggle books out of the all-white library in McMinnville and give them to him.

Rowan was an excellent student at the all-black Bernard High School and graduated as class valedictorian. He then moved in with his grandparents in Nashville, Tennessee, and worked as a hospital attendant to earn money for his university tuition. He enrolled at the all-black Tennessee State University in 1942, and the next year was recommended by a professor to take an examination for a U.S. Navy commission. He passed the exam and was assigned to Washburn University in Topeka, Kansas. Rowan was one of the first fifteen blacks in Navy history to be admitted to the V-12 officer training program. He later attended Oberlin College in Ohio and then the Naval Reserve Midshipmen School in Fort Schuyler, the Bronx. After his training was completed, he was commissioned an officer and assigned to sea duty, where he was worked as deputy commander of the communications division.

In 1946 Rowan's naval career ended, and he returned to Oberlin to complete his college degree. He majored in mathematics and worked as a freelance writer for the Negro newspaper chain, the *Baltimore Afro-American*. While attending graduate school in journalism at the University of Minnesota, he became the northern correspondent for the *Afro-American* and also wrote for the Twin Cities' two black newspapers, the *Minneapolis Spokesman* and the *St. Paul Recorder.*

Big break at *Minneapolis Tribune*

After graduating from the university, Rowan got a big break when he was hired at the copy desk of the all-white *Minneapolis Tribune*. He became the paper's first black reporter two years later and was one of the first black journalists in the country. Rowan started as a general assignment reporter, but he received permission from the *Tribune* to take a trip through the South and discover the effect of discriminatory laws on Negroes. In 1951 he embarked on a six-thousand-mile journey through thirteen states, writing a series of eighteen articles entitled, "How Far From Slavery?" The articles were an instant sensation. Rowan won the Sidney Hillman Award for best newspaper reporting of 1952 and used the articles as a basis for his first book, *South of Freedom,* published in 1952.

Two years later he returned to the South for a series of articles that focussed on the historic case *Brown vs. Board of Education,* the landmark Supreme Court decision that outlawed racial segregation in public schools. In 1954 Rowan received the prestigious Sigma Delta Chi Journalism Award for the best general reporting of 1953 and was named by the U.S. Junior Chamber of Commerce as one of America's ten most outstanding men of 1953. Later in 1954, Rowan was invited by the U.S. State Department to travel to India and lecture on the role of a free press in a free society. After writing a series of articles for the *Minneapolis Tribune* on India, he received his second Sigma Delta Chi Award, this time for

Carl T. Rowan

foreign reporting. His third straight Sigma Delta Chi Award was for a series of articles he wrote on the tense political climate in India and for his coverage of the 1955 Bandung Conference, a gathering of twenty-three underdeveloped countries. In 1956 he wrote *The Pitiful and the Proud,* which documented his Indian experiences. It was named one of the best books of the year by the American Library Association.

During the 1950s Rowan also covered the growing civil rights movement in the South, including the historic Montgomery, Alabama, bus boycott in 1955, which resulted from Rosa Parks's refusal to relinquish her bus seat to a white passenger.

Besides his journalism career, Rowan was also a member of the Committee of 100, a group of citizens who raised money across the country for the legal defense fund of the National Association for the Advancement of Colored People (NAACP). Since he was one of the country's few black reporters, Rowan was increasingly called upon to speak on the impact of the civil rights movement, and his articles appeared in numerous magazines and newspapers. In 1957 he wrote *Go South to Sorrow,* which lashed out at those he believed were preventing the freedom of black people.

In 1956 Rowan covered the United Nations. The international events of that year included the Suez Canal crisis and the Hungarian uprising against the Soviet Union.

Joins the State Department

Rowan interviewed presidential candidates Richard M. Nixon and John F. Kennedy during the 1960 campaign for the *Tribune.* After Kennedy was elected, he asked Rowan to become the deputy assistant secretary of state for public affairs, responsible for press relations for the State Department. In 1963 he was named U.S. ambassador to Finland, making him the youngest ambassador in diplomatic service and only the fifth black to ever serve as an envoy. Following President Kennedy's assassination, President Lyndon Johnson named Rowan head of the United States Information Agency (USIA), which made him the highest-ranking black in the federal government and the first to ever attend National Security Council meetings. Rowan headed a staff of thirteen thousand and was responsible for overseeing a vast government communications network, which included the International Voice of America radio system and the daily communiques to U.S. embassy personnel. In 1965, he resigned to take a lucrative offer to write a national column for the Field Newspaper Syndicate and to prepare three weekly radio commentaries for the Westinghouse Broadcasting Corporation.

As a columnist and commentator on the national scene, Rowan became known as an independent and often controversial voice on national political and social issues. He has been a spokesman for civil and economic rights for blacks and has been critical of blacks whom he feels should address more aggressively the serious issues that affect them.

In 1991 he published *Breaking Barriers: A Memoir,* which the *New York Times* termed an "anecdotally rich memoir" that appealed to the "interests of a whole spectrum of readers." Rowan currently lives in Washington, D.C.

Wilma Rudolph

Athlete, Olympic gold medalist
Born June 23, 1940, Bethlehem, Tennessee

"From that day on, people were going to start separating me from that brace, start thinking about me differently, start saying Wilma is a healthy kid, just like the rest of them."

O lympic gold medalist Wilma Rudolph was born with polio. She could barely use her left leg and suffered pneumonia and scarlet fever before the age of four, but hard work and determination changed Rudolph's life. With vigorous therapy she regained the use of her leg, began participating in track meets, and went on to win three Olympic gold medals as well as many more races.

Daily therapy strengthened her crippled leg

Rudolph was born on June 23, 1940, to Ed and Blanche Rudolph in Bethlehem, Tennessee. Diagnosed with polio at birth, she also weighed only four-and-a-half pounds. Her first few years were difficult as she suffered from double pneumonia twice and scarlet fever. The polio made it difficult to use her left leg, but doctors at Meharry Medical College in Nashville, Tennessee, said Rudolph might regain the use of her leg if she underwent daily therapeutic massages. Her mother took Rudolph to Meharry for heat and water therapy once a week for two years. The rest of the week her mother and three of her older siblings massaged her crippled leg at least four times a day. This treatment had an immediate, beneficial effect.

At five Rudolph was fitted with a steel brace, which she wore for the next six years. The first time she ever attended school was at the age of seven, when she started second grade at Cobb Elementary. Her life took an important turn in the seventh grade when a new high school was constructed for blacks. While attending Burt High School, Rudolph was introduced to organized sports, especially basketball. A year later her basketball coach resurrected the track team and asked her to join. She immediately excelled and ran in the 50 meter, 75 meter, 100 meter, and the relay events. When she was thirteen years old, she ran in twenty different races and won them all. Rudolph's first track coach, Clinton Gray, is credited with nicknaming her "Skeeter," because she was always buzzing around.

Wilma Rudolph

Her light complexion and red, sandy hair, often caused her to be mistaken for white, but racism had a deep psychological effect on Rudolph. Her belief that "all white people were mean and evil" was eventually tempered by her religious commitment at the age of fifteen.

Qualified for the Olympic team

During her sophomore year, Rudolph entered her first major track meet at Alabama's Tuskegee Institute. The competition attracted girls from across the South, and Rudolph lost every race. The losses convinced her that if she wanted to be successful in track, she would need proper coaching. Edward Temple, the track coach at Tennessee State University, invited Rudolph to training camp at the university. She ran twenty miles a day at the camp and used cross-country training to build endurance. At the end of the summer Temple took his team to the National Amateur Athletic Union (AAU) contest in Philadelphia, where Rudolph won all nine races she entered, and demonstrated potential as a possible Olympic athlete.

As a high school junior Rudolph participated in the Olympic trials held in Seattle, and she made the team as its youngest member. In 1956 she attended the Olympic Games in Melbourne, Australia, but was eliminated from the 200 meter. She ran the third leg in the relay, and the team won a bronze medal. At the end of the games, she vowed to return to win more medals.

Took three gold medals in Rome

Rudolph entered Tennessee State University in September 1958, and she and other members of the track team became known as "Tigerbelles." To stay in school Rudolph worked two hours a day, five days a week, at various jobs around campus. In 1960 she attended Olympic trials at Texas Christian University and set a world record in the 200 meter that would stand for eight years. She qualified for the Olympic team in the 100 meter, 200 meter, and relay events. At the Olympic Games in Rome, she became the first American woman to win three gold medals, and afterwards she and the rest of the American team were invited to meet Pope John XXIII.

Rudolph participated in several other meets, including the British Empire Games in London, where she won all the events she entered. She also attended meets in West Germany, Holland, and elsewhere in Europe. Wherever she went, she was met by hundreds of admirers. When she returned to the States, her hometown greeted her with a parade in her honor. The parade was the first integrated event in that city's history. Rudolph also received the key to the city of Chicago, and she met with President John F. Kennedy and Vice-President Lyndon Johnson. She spoke at numerous banquets, appeared on television, signed autographs, and made countless speeches.

In 1961 Rudolph received the Sullivan Award, which is given to the country's top amateur athlete, and the Female of the Year Award. She was the first woman to be invited to run in such meets as the New York Athletic Club Meet, the Melrose Games, the Los Angeles Times Games, the Penn Relays, and the Drake Relays. She also ran against the Russians and made two goodwill trips—one to French West Africa and another with evangelist Billy Graham and the Baptist Christian Athletes to Japan.

Rudolph graduated from Tennessee State University on May 27, 1963, and accepted a job as girls' track coach and second grade teacher at the elementary school she attended as a child. She married her high school sweetheart, Robert Eldridge, and later moved to Evansville, Indiana, where she became the director of a community center. Afterwards she moved to Boston and became involved with the Job Corps program in Poland Springs, Maine.

Her autobiography became a TV movie

Vice-President Hubert Humphrey invited her to work with him on Operation Champion in 1967. The program was designed to take star athletes from sixteen of the largest city ghettoes in the country and give them professional training. Rudolph became one of the track specialists. When this project ended, the Job Corps transferred her to St. Louis. She later moved to Detroit and took a teaching position at Palham Junior High School. Eventually she worked with the Watts Community Action Committee.

Rudolph published her autobiography in 1977, and NBC television made it into a movie starring Cicely Tyson. The book and movie provided special inspiration to handicapped youths who otherwise might never work to overcome their physical problems. Rudolph also moved to Clarksville in 1977, and then to Detroit, where she resides today. She is currently president of the Indianapolis-based Wilma Rudolph Foundation.

Bill Russell

Basketball player, coach
Born February 12, 1934, Monroe, Louisiana

"All I have finally asked is for everybody to succeed or fail on their own merits.... I have never worked to be well-liked or well-loved, but only to be respected.... I have my own ideas for the future.... I believe that I can contribute something far more important than mere basketball."

During the 1950s and 1960s, professional basketball was dominated by such stars as Oscar Robertson, Jerry West, and Wilt Chamberlain. But for many basketball fans,

that time is known as the "Bill Russell Era." Although he was not noted for his scoring prowess, Russell's defensive ability revolutionized the game. He was a superb rebounder, shot blocker, and passer. Russell was a firm believer in team play, and his team won eleven championships in thirteen years, including eight in a row.

When he began his career with the Boston Celtics, Russell was the only black player on the team. He became an outspoken critic of racial prejudice and was often surrounded by controversy. His actions helped open the door for many younger black basketball players. Russell later became the first black head coach of any team in major professional sports.

Added to the team

Russell was born on February 12, 1934, in the small town of Monroe, Louisiana. His father worked in a factory before moving the family

Bill Russell

to Oakland, California. The Russells lived in a house that contained nine families, including one in the garage. Russell's mother died when he was nine, forcing his father to give up a successful truck career to be near his sons.

When Russell entered McClymonds High School in Oakland, he didn't set the basketball court on fire. He was the sixteenth man on a fifteen-man team, but the coach thought he had some potential and expanded the roster by one. Russell and the fifteenth player had to share the same jersey. He credits coach George Powles's decision for keeping him out of trouble. "I believe that man saved me from becoming a juvenile delinquent. If I hadn't had basketball, all my energies and frustrations would surely have been carried in some other direction."

Russell worked hard and by his senior year he was a starter. His six-and-one-half foot height did not hurt either. A basketball scout from the University of San Francisco (USF) was sent to watch Russell's team take on another team from the city. The scout initially was interested in a player from the rival team, but he was so impressed with Russell that Russell was eventually offered a scholarship. It was the only offer he received, and he did not turn it down.

Although Russell was a poor shooter, he compensated by blocking shots, rebounding, and playing stellar defense. At USF, he roomed with K.C. Jones, a quiet young man who would later star on the same professional team as Russell. During his junior and senior years, Russell led USF to two straight NCAA national basketball championships and was twice named an All-American. The team won fifty-

six consecutive games. The NCAA decided to institute two rule changes, mainly because of Russell. The free-throw line was widened to keep centers from guarding the basket, and shots could no longer be blocked if they had started down toward the basket.

Russell's play caught the attention of the National Basketball Association's Boston Celtics. They wheeled and dealed to make sure he could be drafted by them. Before he began playing professionally, he was selected to play for the 1956 U.S. Olympic basketball team in Melbourne, Australia, and helped the team to a gold medal.

A star-studded lineup

When Russell joined the Celtics, the team was loaded with stars such as Bob Cousy, Bill Sharman, Frank Ramsey, and Tom Heinsohn. They were coached by the legendary Red Auerbach. Russell fit in nicely with his new teammates. He finished second in the Rookie of the Year balloting, averaging 14.7 points per game and 19.6 rebounds. He was also an important component of the Celtics' first NBA championship.

The Celtics lost the championship the next year when Russell was injured in the playoffs. During his third year, the Celtics began a string of eight straight NBA championships (1959–66). In fact, the Celtics won eleven titles during Russell's thirteen-year career. Although many players came and went during that time, Russell remained the one constant. He was named Most Valuable Player five times (1958, 1961–63, 1965), and became famous for his defense and rebounding. He inspired a new generation of young people to become team players. His on-court activities caused Los Angeles Laker great Jerry West to say, "They can talk about individual players in any sport, but I tell you that when it comes to winning, there is no one like Bill Russell. The guy is the greatest of them all."

Russell's biggest task may have been off the court. He was the only black player on the team, and there was considerable prejudice around the league, especially by bigoted fans. Russell did not have a problem with the Celtics because the team owner, Walter Brown, was unconcerned with skin color, and the other Celtic players were only interested in winning. The league, however, seemed to have an unwritten rule that no team would have more than one or two black players. In 1958 Russell publicly stated that he believed many teams had quotas on blacks. Although his comments were widely criticized, his actions helped pave the way for more blacks to enter the league.

Russell is well noted for his confrontations with Wilt Chamberlain, arguably the best individual player in basketball history. Chamberlain's statistics were usually better than Russell's, but when it came to winning the NBA title, it was usually Russell's team that came out on top. Only once did Chamberlain's team, the Philadelphia '76ers, win a title. The two met time and time again in the championship series, and Russell won every head-to-head competition.

First black coach

In 1966 Russell became the Celtics coach after Red Auerbach retired. He was the first black head coach in the NBA and in American professional sports history. During his first year as player-coach, the Celtics missed the playoffs, but they came back to win the title the following two years (1968–1969). It was a remarkable achievement considering Russell and the Celtics were in decline and had to battle past younger and more physically talented teams. Eventually players like K.C. Jones, Bob Cousy, and Bill Sharman were replaced by Sam Jones, Bailey Howell, Larry Siegfried, Don Nelson, and John Havlicek.

Russell coached the Celtics until his retirement as a player in 1969. He ended his career as the NBA leader in career minutes (40,726) and second in career rebounds (21,721). Russell became a color commentator on NBC-TV's Game of the Week, before accepting a lucrative contract in 1974 to be coach and general manager of the Seattle Supersonics. That same year he was inducted into the Basketball Hall of Fame. Russell left active basketball for a while, before becoming coach of the Sacramento Kings in 1987 and 1988. He then moved to a new position as team vice-president.

Bayard Rustin

Civil rights leader
Born March 17, 1910, West Chester, Pennsylvania
Died August 24, 1987

"We are in a society where young people—particularly young Negroes—are being systematically taught that unless they resort to violence there is no future for them."

W hen violent race riots broke out in Harlem in the mid-1960s, Bayard Rustin, a noted pacifist and civil rights organizer, was sent to quell the unrest. He avoid bottles, jeers, and insults as he made a desperate attempt to explain the hopelessness of violence and to restore order. It was an act that typified Rustin's career. A firm believer in non-violence, Rustin clashed with other African Americans who wanted more violent means to end racial injustice. He was a chief organizer of the 1963 March on Washington and the 1964 New York school boycott. Rustin later headed the A. Philip Randolph Institute, a New York-based educational, civil rights, and labor organization, which served as a platform for his economic ideas. Roy Innis, national chairman of the Congress of Racial Equality, told the *New York Times*, "Bayard Rustin was a planner, a coordinator, a thinker. He influenced all of the young leaders in the civil rights movement, even those of us who did not agree with him ideologically."

Lived on leftover food

Rustin was born in West Chester, Pennsylvania, on March 17, 1910. His parents were Janifer and Julia Rustin, but he was raised by his grandparents. "My father was from the West Indies. My grandfather was a caterer and extremely poor, but there was always enough to eat because of leftovers from the banquets. Sometimes there would be no real food in the house, but there was plenty of pate de foie gras and Roquefort cheese," he told the *Saturday Evening Post*.

Rustin was an honor student at West Chester High School and was a member of the glee club, the debating society, the tennis team, and state-championship track and football teams. After graduating in 1928, he drifted across the country doing odd jobs. He occasionally returned to Pennsylvania to study literature and history at Cheney State Teachers College and Wilberforce University. Rustin joined the Young Communist League since he was opposed to war and racial discrimination. He went to New York City as an organizer for the league in 1938, moving into his aunt's home in Harlem and studying at City College of New York.

By 1941, Rustin left the Young Communist League and joined the Fellowship of Reconciliation, a nondenominational religious organization devoted to solving problems through peaceful methods. He worked for twelve years with the fellowship as field secretary and race relations secretary. He also organized the New York branch of the Congress of Racial Equality, a non-religious spinoff from the fellowship. Later that year Rustin was the youth organizer for a planned march on Washington by the Sleeping Car Porters Union. The march was called off when President Franklin D. Roosevelt issued an executive order banning racial discrimination in all industries with defense contracts and established the Committee on Fair Employment Practice.

Pacifist and freedom rider

In 1942 Rustin went to California to help protect the property of Japanese-Americans, who had been placed in work camps. The next year he began a two-and-a-half year sentence in Ashland Correction Institute and Lewisburg

Penitentiary as a conscientious objector to military service. After his release he became chairman of the Free India Committee and was often arrested for sitting in at the British Embassy in Washington. Three years later he was invited by the Indian Congress party to study Gandhi's non-violence movement for six months.

Rustin was a member of the first "freedom ride" in the South in 1947. The "journey of reconciliation" was to test a court ruling against discrimination in interstate travel. Rustin was arrested in North Carolina and sentenced to twenty-two days on a chain gang. He wrote an article about his chain-gang experiences that was published by the Baltimore *Afro-American* in 1949. It was picked up by other newspapers and led to an investigation of chain gangs, which eventually were abolished in North Carolina. At around the same time, Rustin became director of A. Philip Randolph's Committee Against Discrimination in the Armed Forces. In the early 1950s, he and George Houser formed the Committee to Support South African Resistance, which became the American Committee on Africa.

In 1953 Rustin resigned from the Fellowship of Reconciliation to become executive secretary of the War Resisters League. Five years later he went to England to help the Campaign for Nuclear Disarmament mobilize the first of its annual protest marches from Aldermaston to London. He also journeyed to the Sahara Desert in 1960 to participate in a protest against the first French nuclear test explosion, and shortly afterwards to Europe to lay the groundwork for the San Francisco-to-Moscow Peace Walk.

Besides his involvement with the peace movement, Rustin was also busy with civil rights activities. In 1955 he went to Montgomery, Alabama, at the invitation of Martin Luther King to help organize the bus boycott. He organized the initial plans for King's Southern Christian Leadership Conference and acted as King's special assistante for seven years. In 1960 Rustin organized civil rights demonstrations to coincide with the Democratic and Republican party conventions. As deputy to A. Philip Randolph (the director of the March on Washington for Jobs and Freedom on August 28, 1963), Rustin was the chief behind-the-scenes organizer. Rustin was also invited to help Rev. Milton A. Galamison in his fight against racial injustice in the New York City school system in 1964. Rustin helped lead a boycott in which 44.8 percent of the city's schoolchildren co-operated. It was the largest civil rights demonstration of any kind up to that point.

Bringing calm to Harlem

Rustin helped calm a potentially explosive situation during the Harlem riots of 1964. He walked down 125th Street, braving physical dangers and taunts of "Uncle Tom," to use his influence in quieting the riots. "I'm prepared to be a Tom if it's the only way I can save women and children from being shot down in the streets," he told the *New York Herald Tribune*.

Rustin was a strong believer in non-violence even though many of his demands fell on deaf ears. He was appalled after authorities gave into demands following a series of violent riots in Watts and Chicago in 1965. "We are in a society," he once said, "where young people—particularly young Negroes—are being systematically taught that unless they resort to violence there is no future for them." Rustin set his sights on discussing a broad platform of economic proposals to assist the poor and underprivileged of all races. The general solution was for groups dedicated to these causes to bind together and seek political power.

Rustin's beliefs were often criticized by other black leaders, who wanted to use more violent means to bring about change. "Bayard has no credibility in the black community," James Farmer, a senior official with the Congress of Racial Equality, once said. "Bayard's commitment is to labor, not to the black man. His belief that the black man's problem is economic, not racist, runs counter to black community thinking."

Rustin ignored this criticism and in late 1964, he became executive director of the A. Philip Randolph Institute. This post allowed him to develop and promote radical programs that would cure the country's basic economic and social problems. He was able to combine his intellectual abilities with his organizing skills to create a clearinghouse of information on alternatives to violence and communist rhetoric. In 1972 Rustin was still committed to consensus rather than racial solutions to the problems faced by blacks. "Black power was born in bitterness and frustration—has left us with a legacy of polarization, division and political nonsense.—Black power was [al-

Bayard Rustin

ways]—likely to produce basically conservative answers.—The challenge we face is to rebuild a broad-based coalition which embraces intellectuals, organized labor, young people, minorities and liberals," he wrote in *Newsweek*.

In his later years Rustin advocated black-Jewish harmony and supported Israeli endeavors. The American Jewish Congress gave him one of its annual Stephen Wise Awards for "illustrious leadership in the cause of racial justice, world peace and human understanding." His close relationship with the Jewish community often brought him into conflict with other blacks.

Rustin continued to be active in the civil rights movement until his death on August 24, 1987.

Index

Volume number appears in **bold**.